# RHYTHM OF THE WILD

ALSO BY KIM HEACOX

Memoir:
*The Only Kayak*

Biography:
*John Muir and the Ice That Started a Fire*
*Shackleton: The Antarctic Challenge*

Essays & Photography:
*Alaska Light*
*Alaska's Inside Passage*
*In Denali*
*Iditarod Spirit*

Natural History & Conservation:
*Visions of a Wild America*
*Antarctica: The Last Continent*

History & Conservation:
*An American Idea: The Making of the National Parks*

Fiction:
*Jimmy Bluefeather*
*Caribou Crossing*

# RHYTHM OF THE WILD

## *A Life Inspired by Alaska's Denali National Park*

## KIM HEACOX

Guilford, Connecticut

An imprint of Rowman & Littlefield

Distributed by NATIONAL BOOK NETWORK

Small portions of this book appeared previously in National Service literature about Denali National Park.

British Library Cataloguing in Publication Information Available

Library of Congress Cataloging-in-Publication Data Available

ISBN 978-1-4930-0389-1 (hardcover)
ISBN 978-1-4930-1665-5 (ebook)

∞™ The paper used in this publication meets the minimum requirements of American National Standard for Information Sciences—Permanence of Paper for Printed Library Materials, ANSI/NISO Z39.48-1992.

*For my brothers, Mick and Bill, the colonel and professor,*
*who, when I graduated from high school, gave me a hardcover*
American Heritage Dictionary of the English Language

*Wilderness, the word itself is music.*
—EDWARD ABBEY

# CONTENTS

## Author's Note

As the arc of this story covers nearly thirty-five years, and some memories remain clearer than others, I've taken a novelist's license to reconstruct the spirit of certain events and conversations as best I could.

# The River Has Been Here for Ten Thousand Years

I AWAKEN, and for an instant, socked deep in my sleeping bag, I have no idea where I am. Then it comes to me . . . and I smile.

Melanie sits up and zips open the tent.

"Kimmy, Kimmy, Kimmy," she says, "it's here. Look. It's out."

I rise onto my elbow and there it is, blushed pink above the clouds, floating, as if it arrived only minutes ago, late for its own show. The summit of Denali, eighteen thousand feet above our campsite, the highest mountain in North America.

I pull out my journal and write . . . nothing.

"There it is," Melanie says again, trying to convince herself of its improbable size and beauty and height. Always higher than expected. Right there. Right *here*.

All morning we stand outside our tent and sip tea and watch the great mountain undress, cloud by cloud, playful one moment, shy the next. I shiver against the September chill. Camping is not as easy at age sixty as it was at age six, back in Spokane. But I'm not complaining. It's good to be here; it's great to be here.

Melanie and I have a site at Wonder Lake Campground, in the middle of Denali National Park, near the end of the park road. Other campers stand in admiration, their tents sprinkled across the autumn-burnished tundra. They speak in English, German, French, Spanish, Korean, Japanese,

Chinese; their voices animated, sweetened with laughter, old people and young, grateful in this place we call Nature. Not a bad deal, this Denali. Wild country in every direction, a university of the far north, a holy place, of sorts, a cathedral without walls, made of the earth itself, no improvements needed. Sky blue and black; spokes of silver light. Who needs stained glass when you have a clearing storm? Who needs flying buttresses when you have sandhill cranes?

After a week of hard rain, this is our reward.

I hear a guitar, somebody fingerpicking. A Beatles tune? Bob Dylan? Fleetwood Mac? I can't tell. What I can tell is this: the guitar fits. The notes float like leaves on water, as if Denali National Park were a work in progress, an unfinished symphony waiting for our most delicate gestures of accompaniment.

Later, when sandhill cranes fly overhead once more, fluting their ancient music, the guitar stops. Everybody stops. And once the cranes are gone, the guitar resumes, softly. This time I recognize it. A John Lennon song: "Across the Universe."

YEARS AGO in a cowboy cafe in Moab, Utah, I met a nine-fingered guitarist who poured Tabasco on his scrambled eggs and told me matter-of-factly that Utah was nice, Montana too. And of course, Colorado. But any serious student of spirituality and the American landscape must one day address his relationship with Alaska, and once in Alaska, he must confront Denali, the heart of the state, the state of the heart.

Spirituality and landscape, I thought. What kind of double major is that?

By Denali he meant both the mountain and the national park. Each complements the other. One is the highest mountain in North America; more massif than solitary peak, a granitic seductress white with snow and ice, so high and imposing that it veils itself in weather of its own making, and by slow degrees or sudden boldness, it appears. And when it does, people fall silent, lost in deep regard.

The other Denali is a six-million-acre national park and preserve, the world's most accessible subarctic sanctuary, nearly three times the size of Yellowstone, more than twice as close to the North Pole as it is to the Equator, a vast ice age stage of glaciers, rivers, tundra, and taiga. From its mountain centerpiece the park runs in every direction as an ocean of land, storm-tossed yet still, silent yet *alive*. It is fetching in all seasons, in every dress, where winter sets down cold as iron, spring is a brittle wind, summer a short, exuberant breath, and autumn a splash of crimson and gold.

Add to that the wildlife. Gyrfalcons and grizzly bears, Lapland longspurs and lynx. Marmots, merlins, and moose. Great braided rivers, blizzards of blueberries, and constellations of wildflowers, Dall sheep and wolves, things near and far, seen and unseen, as if we had witnessed—or dreamed of witnessing—the making of something wondrous, wild, and profound, a reinvention of the beginning, and ourselves in that beginning.

Nine Fingers was right. I see that now as I consider the chiseled mountains and rounded hills, the tendrils of willow among dwarf birch, the glacial-fed rivers shining in the sun, the clouds dashing about the ever-changing sky, the trees solemn and serene, keeping their opinions to themselves yet offering wise counsel whenever we listen.

Denali is what America was; it's the old and new, the real and ideal, the wild earth working itself into us on days stormy and calm, brutal and beautiful, unforgiving and blessed. It's where we came from, long before television and designer coffee, even agriculture itself. Before we lost our way and granted ourselves dominion over all living things, before our modern, paradoxical definitions of progress and prosperity, and too much stuff; it's the lean, mean, primal place buried in our bones no matter how much we might deny it, no matter how fancy our homes, how busy our routines, how cherished our myths. Denali resides in each of us as the deep quiet, the profound moment, the essence of discovery. It offers a chance to find our proper size in this world.

Anything can happen. During a 2005 field trip in the park, a geology professor rested his hand on an outcropping of the Cantwell Formation along Igloo Creek and said this kind of Cretaceous sedimentary rock has all the characteristics to preserve dinosaur tracks. Be on alert. A student pointed beyond his gesturing hand and said, "Like this one?" And there was the track of a three-toed meat-eater called a theropod, a small cousin of Tyrannosaurus Rex, roughly seventy million years old, the first evidence of dinosaurs found in Denali and Interior Alaska.

—◆—

OTHER IMAGES don't come so easily.

I know a painter from Fairbanks, a gracious man named Kes Woodward, who says this of the mountain, "It took me fifteen years of visiting the park to work up the courage to take on the image of Denali itself, as it is the most daunting icon in Alaska art." Another artist, Steve Gordon, describes it as the *Mona Lisa*. "Unless you can approach it in a fresh way, it's been done." And another artist, Diane Canfield Bywaters, admits, "The landscape continues to delight, challenge and amaze me. It could be a lifetime goal to paint this successfully."

When Garrison Keillor, host of the popular radio program *A Prairie Home Companion*, visited Anchorage and accepted a bush pilot's offer to fly him into the heart of the Alaska Range, Keillor said he "ran out of adjectives in the foothills."

Many generous people have given their lives to this place; they've settled here, and reset their clocks, reset their conscience. They stand *for* what they stand *upon*. In so doing they make their lives extraordinary. They get visitors to slow down and shake the city tinsel from their eyes.

"The train's late by an hour."

*Relax. The river has been here for ten thousand years.*

"The bus is full; the dust is bad."

*It's okay. The river has been here for ten thousand years.*

"I've come all the way from Mexico. Where's the sun?"

*Tranquilo. The American golden plover flies here from Argentina, the Wilson's warbler from Costa Rica, the wandering tattler from Hawaii, or as far away as Australia, the wheatear from sub-Sahara Africa. This is the place to be. You're fine.*

"It's cold."

*Imagine January at fifty below, and dark. The Dall sheep do not complain. The ptarmigan do not complain. The ravens do not complain; they somersault as they fly.*

"When will the mountain come out?"

*Any day now. Any week. Next month maybe, or the month after that. Breathe deep the northern air. The river has been here for ten thousand years.*

BUT LET ME BEGIN with my first summer, as good a beginning as any. How this affair got started is not reasonable, painless, or altogether wise. Love never is. But it's honest.

It's May 1981. Ronald Reagan has just completed his first one hundred days in the White House. He means business; he loves business. Soon he'll deregulate Wall Street, beef up the Pentagon, triple our national debt, and make us believe we can grow our economy forever.

On a Saturday afternoon, thousands of miles west-northwest of Reagan's sunny fantasy in Washington, DC, I and twenty other new ranger recruits board a bus in Anchorage, Alaska. Dour clouds roll in from Cook Inlet and spill rain against the Chugach Mountains. A sharp wind blows. We don't care. We're guys with beards and gals with bandanas, northbound to Denali, dimly aware that outside of Reagan's nation, another America awaits.

Of course we're naive. We're university graduates with liberal arts degrees, versed in critical thinking and deep time, but not venture capitalism. Most of us fall between the ages of twenty-five and thirty-five, making a nice bell curve, with me in the middle, one month shy of thirty. I have fifty dollars in the bank and no health insurance, home, mortgage, wife, kids, debt, or pets, and no plans to acquire them. I've traveled around the world on tramp steamers and the Trans-Siberian Railway, sung in Arabic with Turks on the Bosporus, walked across London's Abbey Road, hitchhiked through Utah in search of a different Abbey (a writer, not a road); ridden my bike off the Sand Cliffs of Spokane's Hangman Creek, been arrested in Spain for setting caged birds free, and been seduced by an Italian girl in Venice who drank more wine than me, never got drunk, complimented my guitar playing, and disappeared with my money belt. I've never been to Interior Alaska, or heard of Adolph Murie, Joe and Fannie Quigley, the Sourdough Party, or the Honorable Judge James Wickersham, Charles Sheldon, or Belmore Browne.

Jackson Browne and the Cleveland Browns, yes, but not Belmore Browne. That will change. Everything's about to change. All my possessions fit in my VW hatchback. But I've left my rusty, trusty car down south for the summer, maybe forever.

Wasilla flashes by. Big signs announce: "Guns," "Ammo," "Tobacco," "Liquor," "Fireworks," "Freedom," and "Reagan for President."

John Muir was one month shy of thirty when he hiked across California's Central Valley (then filled with knee-high wildflowers) to the Sierra Nevada, his "Range of Light," to find the writer and activist within. It does not occur to me.

Lesser thoughts fill my head. Does it occur to me that Keats was dead at twenty-five, Hendrix at twenty-seven, Percy Shelley and Hank Williams at twenty-nine? No. I watch south-central Alaska roll by, waves of forested land. Melville comes to mind, his feeling, like mine, of a profound "unfolding within myself." I listen to the Beatles, Stones, Doors, and the Who, and speak with false authority on the writings of Garrett Hardin, Paul Ehrlich, Barry Commoner, and Roderick Nash. All to impress the gals with bandanas.

They fall asleep.

LOOKING BACK, I see now that Denali did more than charm me that first summer; it saved me. The whole damn place beguiled me and believed in me when I didn't believe in myself. Call me crazy or blessed or crazy blessed. But I swear that again and again Denali has done this—made me buckle down and find inspiration and become the free man I am today.

Yes, I think about life and death and all that; I think about impermanence, but not for long. As for tomorrow, I'm not enthused about our hypertechnological, genetically engineered future, unless I can be programmed to think otherwise.

As I sit now in the historic East Fork Cabin on the Toklat River, on my final night as the park's writer-in-residence, thirty-one years after that first summer, my career is stalled. Two beloved book manuscripts—my unborn children, one ten years in the making, the other five—earn me only publishers' rejections, little missives that say, "No thanks." Yet it's a small travail compared to the September crescent moon sliding over Polychrome Mountain, or the bear on the porch, or the river with its own story to tell.

Do rivers ever despair in not getting published?

Just keep writing.

If at first you don't succeed, find another definition of success. Money, like the sun, offers great warmth and light. It also burns and blinds.

What you hold, dear reader, is a story of love and hope, equal parts natural history, human history, personal narrative, and conservation polemic. I make no attempt to be a neutral journalist, a rare bird in today's corporate culture. I'm a storyteller. And I'm not alone. The same strength, clarity, and inspiration given to me by this place I've seen given to others. Many others. Many times.

That's not to say Denali is what it used to be. It is not. Visitation grows. Traffic increases. There will always be a good economic argument to overcrowd an experience until we redefine what a good economy is. Law enforcement rangers wear Kevlar vests and big guns that would, I think, dismay Olaus and Adolph Murie, the pioneering wildlife biologists who first came here in the early 1920s. The park is warmer, brushier, and more forested than it used to be. And sadly, for the first time in the park's history, a bear killed a visitor; the National Park Service responded by killing the bear. The visitor had a camera, and perhaps got too close. I find myself wondering if an innocence has been lost.

But let us remember that the land rolls, the rivers run. Denali can make the world a better place. It already has. All we have to do is slow down and listen, look, and love, and every so often sing like angels, howl like wolves.

Patient persistence.

The river has been here for ten thousand years.

---

IT'S 1981. The bus rumbles north, past the Chulitna River, over Broad Pass, into the Nenana River Canyon. Everything is so big, so Alaska. I stare like a starving man. Up ahead is a national park that belongs to everyone and no one, a place to practice freedom but also restraint, a world to explore deeply but also lightly. Up ahead is the heart of the state, the state of the heart, an oracle of some kind, the promise of a wilder, wiser life.

Up ahead is Denali.

# THE FIRST SUMMER

# CHAPTER ONE

# The Midnight Ride of Kimmy the Kid

SUNDAY, a day of rest. I find an old ten-speed bicycle—did I borrow it? Steal it? I can't remember. I begin riding west into the park, the direction of dreams. I follow the paved road and leave behind seasonal ranger housing and park head-quarters in Hines Creek drainage and climb slowly uphill toward tree line and beyond. I have a daypack with food and water, nothing else. No first-aid kit, no radio.

A cell phone is science fiction in 1981.

The country beckons me.

I'm pumping hard, as alive as I'll ever be. I've made no decision to do this. I'm not sensible. I just go, storm-tossed, a spore on the wind. I have no idea how far I'll get, or when I'll turn around. Somewhere out there a wolf stalks a cari-bou, a grizzly circles a moose, a lynx tracks a snowshoe hare, a pasque flower rises through late spring snow. Somewhere out there a drama plays out, older and more elemental than anything cooked up by the Romans or the Greeks. Some-where out there—everywhere out there—is a corrective lens.

I'm riding hard with a freewheeling ferocity, my head down, lactic acid burning, when a pickup pulls alongside and a voice says, "Where you going?"

"Huh?" I'm rasping for breath.

"Where you going?"

"West."

"I can see that. West to where?"

"Far as I can get."

"I can take you to Toklat."

The Toklat River, big, braided, rambunctious, north-bound off the Alaska Range. I'd never seen it. I stop and throw the bike in the bed of the truck; a little voice tells me that for every mile I ride west with this guy, I'll have to peddle back in the predawn hours, as I'm scheduled to report for duty on my first day at 8 a.m. No problem. I'll ride all night if necessary; bivouac in a wolf den.

I say "duty" because the National Park Service (NPS) is a paramilitary organization. We rangers don't have a main office or departments. We have a headquarters, and divisions. We're not the private sector or free enterprise. We're the federal government, US Department of the Interior. We wear uniforms and shiny gold badges and read *Mother Jones* and *The Far Side*. Maintenance division employees take care of the roads and trails, buildings, and utilities. Administrators administrate. Resource managers manage the resource. Law enforcement rangers follow the Code of Federal Regulations and protect the park from terrorists, litterbugs, and other wrongdoers.

I'm an interpretive ranger, an education guy—a teacher of sorts—a seasonal naturalist in the interpretive division, here to interpret for summertime visitors the park's natural and human histories. I carry no briefcase, Day-Timer, or gun. Should somebody make trouble, I'll fight him with words, an adjective here, an adverb there. I might even assail him with a story. Take him down with haiku.

The pickup driver is Brad Ebel, a road grader operator based at the Toklat Work Camp, at mile 53, on the Toklat River. We shake hands and introduce ourselves. He has a firm grip, an easy smile.

"You know what they say," he says, as if I know what they say.

"No. What do they say?"

"Happiness is headquarters in the rearview mirror."

I'm thinking about this when he adds, "Funny name for a guy . . . Kim."

"I'm a funny guy." Some of the time.

The road climbs. The country opens up. The forest drops below and behind. Out ahead, tundra runs in every direction, a vast quilt of willow and dwarf birch, dry, gray branches with pale green leaves—the meager hints of spring. Stands of spruce huddle in low areas, protected from the wind, where a degree or two of added warmth spells survival. Somber clouds rake the top of Healy Ridge to the north, the Alaska Range to the south. It's not the kind of day you see in travel brochures, courtesy of the chamber of commerce. It's edgy, raw, the real deal.

We cross the Savage River Bridge, at mile 14, where the ninety-two-mile-long park road—the only road in the park—goes from pavement to hard gravel, and makes a fetching hemline as it skirts the lower slopes of Primrose Ridge. Brad knows it well, and speaks about the road as if it were a living thing, a lovely thing, every curve and dip, every culvert and bridge. "It was built by the Alaska Road Commission [ARC] over sixteen summers," he says, "from 1922 to 1938. Guys graded the road with horses, tractor-crawlers and motor-graders, and made five dollars a day, and lived in canvas-walled tents with wood-burning stoves, and worked late into the fall when the temperature would drop to twenty degrees below zero. They had no scheduled days off, and they were thankful for the work."

"During the Great Depression."

"Yep."

"How many guys?"

"Some summers as many as one hundred, other years only a dozen or so." Brad adds that the original Mount McKinley National Park, established in 1917, didn't get its first funding and first employee until 1921. The ARC spent

five hundred dollars that summer doing preliminary recon-
naissance. The next summer, 1922, the ARC spent two
thousand dollars brushing the road route and erecting sur-
veying tripods. "You know how many visitors the park had
that summer?"

"A million?"

"Seven."

"Seven million?"

"No. Seven. Just seven."

———

TODAY it has hundreds of thousands.

The original Mount McKinley National Park was the
vision of a few dedicated people who encountered resis-
tance at every turn, and never gave up. Consider Charles
Sheldon. A Yale graduate who made his fortune in the
railroad industry, he retired in 1903 at age thirty-five to
pursue his fascination with—and studies of—the mysterious lives of wild animals, especially wild mountain sheep.
Teddy Roosevelt said of him, "Charles Sheldon is not only a
first-class hunter and naturalist but passionately devoted
to all that is beautiful in nature." A member of the influential Boone and Crockett Club, Sheldon spent a month
in the Denali area in the summer of 1906. Entrusted by
the US Biological Survey to study and collect Dall sheep,
he returned for ten months in 1907–1908 and hunkered
down for the long cold winter. He rode it out and loved it,
thanks in no small part to his capable twenty-nine-year-
old guide, Harry Karstens, who'd come to Alaska during
the Klondike Gold Rush. Everything intrigued Sheldon: the
silence of the snow, the voices of rivers, the family dynamics of wolves, the power and beauty of grizzly bears, the
hibernations of marmots and arctic ground squirrels, the
feeding and breeding strategies of ptarmigan, the migrations of golden eagles and arctic terns.

On a cold January day in 1908, Sheldon stood on a rise in the Kantishna Hills and pulled out his field glasses—more important to him than his hunting rifle—and looked around. Everything his eyes feasted on could one day be a premier national park, he told himself, the Yellowstone of Alaska, preserved and protected for one reason above all others: to celebrate restraint as an expression of our freedom, our rare ability to leave a place as we found it. Sheldon studied the ocean of land, the waves of rolling tundra, vast, intact, winter white, the blue-green earth holding its breath, so still yet dynamic, epic and epoch in its dimensions. Such an ambition. More than a dream, it was a spark of idealism. Could he do it? Could one man—with help from a few committed colleagues and friends—successfully campaign for the creation of a national park?

I'm thinking about this when Brad tells me, "Watch for bears."

"Bears? Where?"

"Everywhere. Riding your bike on this road at night, in low light. Be careful, that's all I'm saying."

"I thought it stayed light all night, this far north, in summertime."

"You thought wrong. It doesn't get pitch dark, but it gets pretty damn dusky. We're still a month shy of summer solstice, the longest day of the year, and we're two hundred miles south of the Arctic Circle."

"And bears use the road?"

"Sometimes, late at night. You don't want to come upon them suddenly and frighten them, especially a mother with her cubs. She'll charge you."

I feel my voice constrict. "Right," I say. "A charging mother bear. Not good." But my fear makes it come out as, "Rigghh, a charring mudda beh, na goo."

⌐∙⌐

7

THOMAS JEFFERSON, mastermind of the Lewis and Clark Expedition, said it would take one thousand years for enterprising Americans to civilize their emerging continental nation and build cities on the Pacific as they had on the Atlantic. It took fifty. Throughout the nineteenth century, the so-called myth of superabundance—that we would never run out of fish, bison, and bears—was rapidly becoming just that: a myth. One hundred years after Jefferson, Charles Sheldon headed west, as hungry for discovery as Lewis and Clark had been. But he had another vision, and a different president. Cut from the same cloth as Teddy Roosevelt, Sheldon was a keen student of zoology and natural history, a hunter/conservationist who was already rich. Gold didn't interest him. He arrived in Alaska when the young US territory had no roads and only eighty thousand people (fewer than twelve percent of what it has today), and found his way to the mountains.

Let us imagine him in the Kantishna Hills on that January day, the sun demure below the horizon, the air brittle, the night falling, the stars cold and watchful, beginning to take their places in the winter sky. To the south rises the icy granite massif gold miners in Fairbanks called Mount McKinley, but Sheldon called "the mountain," or "Denali," the Athabascan name meaning "the high one." (Both names are used today.) Certainly a mountain like that could take care of itself, being the highest in North America. But what of the magnificent wild animals that embroidered it, the grizzly bears, caribou, wolves, moose, Dall sheep, and others that moved about with ancient mystery and grace? Market hunters were coming into the country to kill wild game to feed gold miners and railroad workers. It had to stop. Sheldon made detailed notes of everything and headed back east with one purpose: to make a national park. No easy task.

"This is fine," I tell Brad as we cross the Teklanika River Bridge. "I'll get out here."

"You sure?"

"Yep." Nope. Is there anything I'm sure of, other than my own mortality?

"Toklat is another twenty-three miles west," Brad says. "I can take you there."

"This is good."

"Okay then, have fun. Don't kill yourself."

I stare at him.

"I'm just saying it's a lot of paperwork when somebody dies in a national park. That's all. I gave you this ride. If you died, I'd be the last guy to have seen you alive, so I'd have to do all the paperwork."

"And stay in headquarters?"

"Yep."

"Not good?"

"No, not good."

"Okay, I'll stay alive." Promises, promises. The things I do for other people.

———

NO ENTRY. ROAD CLOSED BEYOND THIS POINT reads a sign on a gate on the far side of Teklanika River Bridge. Brad unlocks it. I open the gate so he can go through and close it behind him—the courteous thing to do—and watch him drive away, his big truck receding down the road. I hoist my bike and walk around the gate. The river rumbles, the mountains stare. Back in the saddle, I ride through Igloo Forest. It must get cold in here, I tell myself. The dark spruce press in, trees with little to say, a place of shadows, black on gray. I hear the murmur of my tires on the road, the occasional pebble striking a spoke. I ride hard, as if trying to escape something I cannot see.

I pass over Igloo Creek Bridge and begin a gradual ascent, the road wet from a recent rain, a patina of new snow on the soft shoulders. Mud grinds through the bike chain and gears, spatters up my legs and back, onto my face, into my mouth. I spit and stop to wash down the chain. I ride on, always on. Igloo Mountain rises to starboard, Cathedral Mountain to port. The entire place feels oceanic, deep in fathoms but also time, shaped by gales and storms and the workings of millennia that render alluvial terraces and misfit streams, braided rivers and kettle ponds. The tundra, streaked with fingers of snow, awakens from the last spell of winter.

Back at headquarters, rangers told me that Dall sheep inhabited Igloo Mountain. I see none. The sky is gunmetal gray and darkening. I estimate the temperature at forty degrees Fahrenheit, ten degrees lower with the wind chill. Already muddy and wet, I pull on a wool hat, a windbreaker, a thin pair of gloves and rain pants. The only thing that keeps me warm is the furnace of my own exertion.

Over Sable Pass, the bicycle troops on. I stop to drink and eat, to absorb the presence of the absence, stone upon stone, the land working its way into me as both storytelling and translation. Back on the bike, I coast down to the East Fork of the Toklat River, passing the spur road that drops down to the historic cabin where wildlife biologist Adolph Murie did his famous predator/prey research that—from what I'm beginning to learn—changed the young science of ecology. Wolves aren't evil, Murie concluded. They're four-legged echoes of the wise and cunning hunters we used to be; the sharp edge of natural selection that benefit prey populations by winnowing out the old, sick, and infirm.

This was heresy back in the 1940s, 1950s, and 1960s—and is still today, among some.

For centuries folklore flooded us with images of the Big Bad Wolf. Then along comes a soft-spoken man, small in stature but large in commitment. Adolph Murie was the younger half brother of Olaus Murie, a wildlife biologist and artist who'd already made a name for himself. The two half brothers married half sisters and devoted much of their lives to the study and defense of wild animals, and the defense of the vast tracts of wilderness lands those animals needed to survive. They spoke for the voiceless and helped to make wilderness conservation a social justice issue on par with civil rights. Standing before the false idols of industrial progress, they asked for a new environmental ethos, a new land ethic. To this day, Adolph Murie, who spent nearly fifty years in the park, coming and going and raising his daughters on the tundra, is remembered as the conscience of Denali.

———

ACROSS THE EAST FORK BRIDGE, I begin the climb up Polychrome Mountain, and stop and look back. There at the bottom of the spur road, on the other side of the river, tucked into the topography is the East Fork Cabin, resolute, alone, built by the Alaska Road Commission in 1928. Barely visible in the dimming light of the deepening night, it calls to me. I could turn around, recross the bridge, ride down to the cabin and have a better look, bivouac for a few hours, pay my quiet respects to Adolph Murie, or Ade, as his friends called him. It strikes me as a shrine, that little cabin, impossibly small yet bigger than its actual size, a place I might deserve to visit someday. Not today.

I ride on. Up and up. My heart jackhammers. The terrain falls away as the road cuts deep into beds of basalt and rhyolite, extrusive igneous rocks colored buff, orange, yellow, black, and gray, signatures of a fiery, superheated past. To my right, talus slopes climb skyward, poised on the angle of repose; to my left, everything plunges down to the Plains of Murie, river bars and tundra-scapes veiled in mist far below. I stop and wipe the mud from my cheeks and catch my hand on my chest, taking my pulse. Life, death, beauty, despair, anger, sorrow, trouble, joy, grace, rocks, rivers, the mountains, the sky. Nothing matters. Everything matters.

Is it madness that brings me here? A divine hand? Confusion or clarity? Knowledge or mystery? That which I know, or wish to know? Or simply that which I imagine? As if the imagination were simple. The night overtakes me. Back on the bike, I'm pumping hard when a wildcat wind nearly knocks me over. In the distance, approaching from the west, I see headlights. Somebody is out driving the road. I stare as the truck winds its way toward me, lonely lights poised above the void, negotiating the cliff like an alien ship out of *The Twilight Zone*, a celestial being. An angel, come to rescue me. It draws near. I know what to do. I'll do the sensible thing. I'll flag it down and get a ride back to a warm bed, a hot shower, a cold beer, a good laugh with new friends. I'll bring this crazy experiment to an end. Turn around. Go back. Be safe.

At the last minute, insanity strikes; I hide. Headlights wash over the cliff as I flatten myself against a shadowed face and pull in my bike to let the government truck go by, its diesel engine shattering the immense quiet. A minute passes, two, three, five. I stand dumbfounded as the twin red taillights recede down the road, eastbound. How quickly the night resumes, darker than before. Colder. Wetter. It begins to snow.

I shiver.

Time to pedal like hell, ride through my own discomfort and fear. If it's this cold in May, what's it like in January?

The road drops gently, rising and falling but mostly falling for seven miles from Polychrome Pass to the Toklat River. It's after midnight, I'm sure. The witching hour. I can't see a thing. The snow turns to rain. I should slow down. I should go fast and faster, as fast as I can. And turn around where? How to end this crazy ordeal? Whose idea was this? *I'm a fool on the hill with a ticket to ride on the long and winding road.*

Have I ever been more alive? More aware than I am right now on the rim of my own existence? The stoics were right.

When unafraid to die we can truly live, though it might not be for long. Everybody dies; we just don't want to be there when it happens.

From the Toklat River Bridge I can see dim lights to my right, downriver, a spur road leading to the Toklat Work Camp where Brad lives with other NPS employees. Kind people, no doubt. At this hour nobody will be awake. No matter. I'll take shelter on an empty porch, in a broom closet, under a truck.

But my bike has other plans. It takes me on, past the spur road, deeper into the park. Again we climb, my bike and me. Five miles up ahead is the high point of the road, Highway Pass, at 3,980 feet elevation. I'm tired, wet, cold. I might be hypothermic. But I'm not dead. I have free will. I could dismount the bike and let it go on by itself. We talk it over, the bike and me, and stop a few miles shy of Highway Pass. The snow is deep in places, with tall cut-banks rising on both sides where the graders have plowed. Their job—Brad's job—is to open the road as soon as possible for the tour buses and shuttle buses that will carry thousands of visitors in and out of their national park each day of summer.

I eat crackers and chocolate and stand numb-legged, half dazed from exhaustion. Up ahead, the road rises into a cold dawn that appears lighter than it did half an hour ago. Somewhere behind me, far to the northeast, a new day comes my way. Still, I face west. Bleary-eyed I see a bear come over the rise, profiled against the sky, right in the middle of the road, as if he owns it, walking my way. I step back, stumble over my bike, and fall. The bear comes nearer, moving toward me, head down, his exact size difficult to tell in the dimness of everything, above me now, coming over the rise. He looks small but big, determined in his movements. He could be a cub, followed soon by his aggressive, overprotective mother.

I gain my footing and scramble up a snowbank, my breathing hard and ragged. Heart pounding. From my low position on the road, half a minute ago, the bear appeared exaggerated. Now from an upper viewpoint, I see it for what it is: no bear at all, but an imposter, a porcupine. A ferocious, killer porcupine. *Ursus porcus.* Maybe sixteen inches tall, it weighs twenty-five pounds with rows of little teeth evolved to eat tree bark. It waddles by, stops to sniff my bike, and moves on, mumbling to itself.

What the hell? What am I doing? Where does it come from, this love of wild country? This affair with risk? Childhood. It comes from childhood.

SPOKANE, 1963.

Every kid should have a Wonder Dog that runs like the wind. A short little mutt blasting forth with his tongue out and ears back, his stubby legs moving so fast they're a blur.

I'd ride my Schwinn Red Racer with everything I had. Hot on my heels would be Max, the family pooch, a terrier of some kind running with all his might. We weren't fooling ourselves, Max and me. He was a mutt, a distant wolf. And I was a mutt too, an unremarkable kid from middle-class America, free-ranging, bike-zooming, as unmindful of my limitations as Max was of his.

Weaving past cars one summer day, we headed up Bernard Street to the end of Spokane's South Hill, where we crossed High Drive and stopped atop the bluff. I lifted my bike over the guardrail, then little Max, and turned my back to the traffic. Before me, the world fell away in a breathtaking slope of dry summer grasses and ponderosa pine that ended far below at a cliff. And below the cliff, another couple hundred feet down, a long sandy slope ran into Hangman Creek. I studied the clean, free-flowing waters that sparkled in the sun, and looked at Max; he looked at me, vaguely aware that I'd volunteered him for this dangerous mission. What a team we made: two buddies who'd never do alone what we were about to do together.

It was the summer of Bob Dylan and Joan Baez, the Beach Boys and muscle cars, Martin Luther King Jr. and "I have a dream." The summer before John Kennedy visited Dallas, and death grew a face. It was the summer after the Cuban Missile Crisis, the great Soviet threat and the much-talked-about eyeball-to-eyeball standoff that put Khrushchev in retreat and everybody on edge. The summer before the Beatles arrived.

I straddled my bike and faced down the bluff. Behind me, clawing the pavement was a river of Detroit metal and glass—mainstream America—going places that didn't interest me. I was a kid, after all. A nuthead goofball. Fear made a small fist in my throat as I fought it back and focused on the task at hand, something I'd thought about for months, years. How would it feel to race down the bluff and fly off the sand cliffs of Hangman Creek?

I felt the bike pulling, impatient, ready to go.

"Come home in one piece," Mom had said that morning. It's what she said every morning before she headed off to work. She knew me better than I knew myself.

I pushed off. In seconds my bike was a rocket. I tried both brakes. Nothing. It was all gravity and acceleration. *Holy shit.* Pines whipped past me. Grasses raked my ankles. A fleeting image of my own sensational death flashed before me, how my story would read: KID RIDES BIKE OFF CLIFF. In a split second I saw my funeral, everybody in black. And there was Foxy Felicity from down the street, the daughter of a retired Navy commander, her face wet with tears and regret for having never kissed me. A red rose in her hand. It was a perfect fantasy for a self-absorbed kid who like every other kid occupied the center of his own universe.

*Whoosh* . . . I sailed off the cliff and felt the earth fall away, my bike too, flying, falling, my heart in my throat, my skinny body twisting. Was I weightless? Everything was happening quickly yet slowly. Beside me I saw little Max, his legs pinwheeling against the blue sky, his tongue out, ears and tail high. He'd done it, the crazy mutt. He'd run down the slope and launched himself off the cliff with me. He was the coolest, stupidest dog in the world. Falling now with his cool, stupid master, twisting, spiraling, plummeting. Max and I hit the sand and tumbled down, down, down, coughing, spitting.

I stood up, laughing, a jester, a fool, a king. Max jumped into my arms and licked my face and we tumbled more. My bike was half buried in sand. The sun rode high, shining magnificently on us. I ran across the railroad tracks, stripped naked and jumped into the creek. Max joined me, splashing, frolicking. We dried ourselves on a big rock in the middle of the gentle current. I scratched his belly and he pulled back his lips in a cartoonish dog-grin. I laughed at him and he laughed at me and we laughed at ourselves. Damn, we were funny. We were hilarious. Look at us—rascals in paradise, ramblers and gamblers on the best day of summer, the best day ever. Had a freight train come by with Woody Guthrie in an open boxcar we'd have jumped aboard and gone wherever it was hoboes went. Had Huck Finn and Jim floated by on their raft, looking for America while hiding from the law, we'd have given them our last Snickers bar. Had Katharine Hepburn and Humphrey Bogart chugged by on the *African Queen*, the old riverboat belching black smoke, we'd have cheered them on. Had a Soviet sub slipped by, its sinister scope spying on Spokane, a city of strategic Cold War significance, we'd have stoned it and saved America and gotten medals for our bravery.

Had you asked me that day, sunstruck in the middle of Hangman Creek, what was the greatest source of my joy, I'd have said Super Max the Wonder Dog. I didn't know then—it would take me years to understand—that it was something much bigger, much deeper.

And fears? What were my fears back in the summer of 1963? Aside from global thermonuclear war and the annihilation of all life on earth, I had none. I was fearless. I was happy.

———

ENOUGH OF THIS. I have responsibilities. I have interpretive ranger training to attend, fifty-some miles to the east, at park headquarters, at eight sharp. So what am I doing out here? Yes, the road less traveled makes all the difference, and in wildness is the preservation of the world. But I'm tired of wildness, tired of roads less traveled and the preservation of the world. I want a warm bed.

Back across the Toklat River Bridge, over Polychrome Pass, over the East Fork River Bridge and Sable Pass, I ride, ride, ride. Tides of weather roll over me and bring the day, a beautiful day. Pockets of blue sky open and close and open again. Shafts of sunlight play like God's fingers on the Sistine Chapel, though out here it's the pristine chapel, the land shaped and colored with impossible grace. I have the entire place to myself. I laugh and cry and sing and ride, head down, mouth open, eating mud. Always mud. I'm covered in mud. My bike, somebody's bike, is covered in mud.

At Igloo Creek I stop and take shelter on the small wooden porch of Igloo Cabin, a ranger post. Too tired to shiver, I curl up and fall asleep. For three minutes? Thirty? It doesn't matter. Once awake, I feel refreshed and ride on. Nothing's going to stop me, except maybe a bear, a moose, a pack of wolves, a pride of lions. I can't be late for the first morning of training in this summer of 1981, the first summer that Denali National Park and Preserve is what it is, not Mount McKinley National Park, its previous name.

Six months earlier, in December 1980, in the eleventh hour of his presidency, after losing the November election to Ronald Reagan, Jimmy Carter did something Reagan would never have done: he signed the Alaska National Interest Lands Conservation Act (ANILCA), establishing more than one hundred million acres of new national parks, preserves, monuments, and wildlife refuges, more than doubling the acreage in the US National Park System.

Two-million-acre Mount McKinley National Park became six-million-acre Denali National Park and Preserve, its boundaries expanded to encompass Adolph Murie's vision of entire ecosystems, watersheds, and the home ranges of wildlife populations, specifically the summering and wintering grounds of caribou and wolves.

This is how it goes. The torch is passed from one visionary to another. Charles Sheldon had a dream. For nearly ten years he lobbied for the creation of a new national park. One week after Congress passed the bill, early in 1917, he hand-delivered it to President Wilson to be signed into law. Twenty years later, Adolph Murie had a theory: wolves were essential, even beneficial, to the park's ecosystem. Like grizzlies, they gave it vitality. To better protect them, the park needed enlarging. Forty years later, Jimmy Carter had a final act: he signed ANILCA and created a conservation legacy on par with Teddy Roosevelt. Don't-Tread-On-Me Alaskans hung him in effigy in the town of Eagle, on the Yukon River. They excoriated him in Seward, on Resurrection Bay. They burned a Park Service airplane in Glennallen. Carter didn't blink. He had the long view. He saved Alaska from those who would develop it to death, as they had so many places down south, caught in their own paradox, crowing platitudes about freedom and access while building another road here, a lodge there, a gold mine, coal mine, neon sign. It all began hundreds of years ago when we Americans learned our environmental stewardship from the conquistadors.

In the final weeks of Jimmy Carter's presidency, the gig was up.

———

PAST TEKLANIKA, only thirty miles to go. The rain stops. The road widens. I ride uphill and down, uphill and down. Who designed this thing? Over Sanctuary River. My legs are lead. An arctic ground squirrel stands at attention as I pass. "At ease," I tell him. A male willow ptarmigan calls from atop a spruce tree, its plumage half white, half brown. A truck comes alongside and paces me; the driver inquires with hand signals if I'd like a ride. I wave him on. Five minutes later another truck, another show of courtesy, another wave. Thanks guys, I'll finish this myself. If I'm late for training, I'll get a job next year at Tuzigoot National Monument, or Big Cypress National Preserve, or Delaware Water Gap— whatever that is.

At the Savage River Bridge, where the road turns from gravel to pavement. I hoist the bike, walk down to the river, and dunk it. I remove my windbreaker and rain pants, and dunk them too, washing them mud-free. My fingers ache in the cold water.

A clock in the Savage River Check Station tells me it's seven-twenty. I've got forty minutes to ride twelve miles, most of it downhill on pavement. I fly. Dropping into Hines Creek, I must be going thirty. I'm invincible as shafts of sunlight chase me; the sky dances with wind and great weather. I pull into headquarters with no time to shower or eat breakfast. I enter training looking like a scarecrow.

"Whoa?" asks Chuck Lennox, my cabinmate. Next to him stands Bruce Talbot, my other cabinmate, a cup of coffee in his hand. Both wear strange, inquiring smiles.

"Where you been?" asks Bruce.

"Out," I say. By going out we're really going in, said John Muir. Or was it Dylan? Or Thoreau? So many philosophers.

I take my seat and remember Yoda's advice to Luke Sky-walker, "Adventure, excitement, a Jedi craves not these things."

If I'm not a Jedi, who am I?

Jill Johnson, a pretty ranger, sits next to me and slips me notepaper, a pencil, and a hot cup of cocoa. She hands me her bandana and motions with her delicate finger toward my cheek. "Mud," she says.

I wipe it off, hand her back the bandana, and pull the cocoa to my lips. It tastes perfect.

Bill Truesdale, chief of interpretation, stands before us in his National Park Service uniform, US Department of the Interior. "Good morning, everybody," he says. "Welcome to Denali. I think it's safe to say that you're all lucky to be here, and that you're about to have the best summer of your lives."

# CHAPTER TWO

# Red Socks and Secretary Watt

JUNE IN THE SUBARCTIC, Interior Alaska, Denali National Park, a little shy of 64 degrees north, same latitude as the southern tips of Greenland and Canada's Baffin Island. Less than one percent of the world's human population lives this far north. The sun rises at 3:30 a.m. and sets at 12:30 a.m. Nobody sleeps a full night. There is no night. Only a dusky half-light of soft blues, warm pastels, and shifting grays that keep my fellow rangers and me up until midnight and well after, tired and wired, eating pizza, drinking beer, telling stories, playing music, chasing girls, climbing mountains.

Somebody put a sticker on our refrigerator door: Hike till you die. You can sleep forever in your grave.

On a day no different from any other, seven park visitors join me for a "discovery hike" up Mount Healy, a craggy sentinel that stands guard over the Nenana River at the east end of the park. The trail begins in a forest of spruce, aspen, and birch and climbs into alpine. It's warm out, but the air grows chilly when a cloud rolls across the sun, my favorite star. After three days of working in a double wide trailer that serves as a visitor center, assigning people their campsites and giving sled dog demonstrations (at the historic kennels, near headquarters) to explain the park's sixty-year-long tradition of winter ranger patrols, I've pulled the best duty of all, a four-hour discovery hike.

"What would you most like to see?" I ask the hikers as we begin working our way up the trail.

"Aminals," says five-year-old Oliver.

"Animals?" I ask.

"Yeah, aminals. Big aminals."

"How big?"

"Really big. Grizzly bear big."

Poor guy. Grizzlies and the other marquee animals (what park rangers casually call "charismatic megafauna") are common out west, deeper into the park, in the Sable Pass, Toklat River, Highway Pass, and Thorofare Pass areas. Tundra country. But one never knows. This time of year, beginning in late May, when moose cows gather in the forest to give birth, bears follow, eager to prey on the calves. We might see a bear after all. It's been estimated that in most years only about thirty percent of moose calves survive their first year. If the bears or wolves don't get them, winter will—deep snow and weeks at minus forty.

Oliver is accompanied by his mom and dad and older brother from California. Filling out the group is a couple from Australia, and Rick McIntyre, a fellow interpretive ranger along to photograph me as I walk and talk. Rick says the park needs additional photos of rangers doing their job. That's me, a ranger doing his job, risking his life—my life—to fulfill the dichotomous mission of the US National Park Service: to conserve the park's great scenery and plant and animal life, while also making the park available to growing numbers of visitors.

"You're wearing red socks," Rick says to me.

"So?"

"Red socks aren't standard issue uniform. How am I supposed to photograph you talking to visitors when you're wearing the wrong-colored socks?"

"I always wear red socks."

Rick shakes his head.

"I love the Red Sox, Ted Williams, Carl Yastrzemski, Fenway Park, all that."

More headshaking.

"Take your photos in black and white," I suggest.

"The world sees in color, Kim."

Oliver has a question. I get down on one knee to engage him. "How come the sky is blue?" he asks. I give the best answer I can. Over the next hour he asks, "How come birds fly? How come trees have different leaves? How tall is this mountain? How big is the universe?" He chews on each answer.

I hear Rick shooting, his camera set on rapid-fire motor drive, taking multiple images of Oliver and me and Oliver's brother. He positions himself to avoid my feet, those troublesome red socks.

"So the universe is really big," I say to Oliver.

"My dad says it's bigger than any of us can imagine."

And how big is the imagination? Albert Einstein said imagination is more important than knowledge. How then to make the universe seem big and wondrous without making Oliver feel small and insignificant? It's tough; I've yet to achieve it for myself.

Size is important; it's also relative. I once read that while Isaac Newton invented calculus and described the visible light spectrum and defined the law of gravity, he also wrote, "On the Distance of the Stars," and asked, how far away would our sun have to be to appear as faint as nearby stars? Writing with a quill dipped in oak gall ink, Newton correctly calculated that the star would be about one hundred thousand times farther away than our sun. That same distance would roughly separate each star from its closest neighbor, and so on. We know today that if the sun could be reduced to the size of a white blood cell, the Milky Way, reduced on the same scale, would be the size of the United States. Billions of stars billions of miles from each other, and billions of galaxies trillions of million miles from each other, the distances increasing, the universe expanding, countless patterns in the sky. Not only was the cosmos larger than anything ever before imagined, it's larger now than in Newton's time, and enlarging still.

Are we capable of understanding it, and ourselves in it?

Oliver watches me with dark, liquid eyes.

~~~

HIKING UP Mount Healy with worlds at our feet, we encounter our own patterns, a spatial order of sorts, constellations of things seen and unseen, flowers and grasses composed of tissues composed of cells and molecules down to atoms composed of who knows what, each a component of the next. Is it even knowable? This continuum, from one end of things to the other? Where along it do I engage Oliver? Can a spiral galaxy be found in lichen on a rock? Some men get down on their knees out of faith, others for flowers. Me? I find salvation in a saxifrage. On a good weekend in June, a serious field botanist can tally more than one hundred species of flowering plants in Denali: arnicas, saxifrages, poppies, cinquefoils, gentians, diapensias, harebells, heathers, moss campion, and more. Some in predictable places, others not.

"Maybe this flower is a universe too," I tell Oliver.

He squints. "It doesn't look like a flower."

"That's because it's just getting ready to bloom. See?" We get low to have a closer look. "Here are the sepals, and these are the petals. They're the different parts of the blossoms, where the plant makes flowers. The blossoms will open up in a day or two or three, or maybe in another week."

Oliver touches them gently.

"Different flowers bloom at different times," I tell him. "Some bloom now, in June; others bloom in July, others in August."

"Why?"

"Hmmm . . . I can't say for sure. Maybe because that's when the insects are out that pollinate them."

"What's pollinate?"

So it goes for the next hour as we make our way up Mount Healy, the sun dashing in and out, the Nenana River rumbling through its canyon far below. Tracing the river, we see the George Parks Highway that runs from Anchorage to Fairbanks. In the middle of the canyon is Glitter Gulch, a hive of hotels, chalets, art studios, gift shops, restaurants, and pizza joints that will grow with Denali's popularity. It's not unusual for a national park to have at its entrance a hungry commercial area. Every whale has its louse.

Oliver wants to know more about animals, bears in particular, but wolves, moose, and caribou as well. We walk and talk and join the rest of the group on an overlook high above where we began. We sit to eat lunch. Rick complains again about my red socks. I could go barefoot, or pick up Rick's camera, as I do now, and photograph him as he does the talking. "A naturalist," he says, "is a biologist with a short attention span." Rick claims to know "a little about a lot" as opposed to knowing "a lot about a little." He's been here many summers and has an easygoing style. He wears his hair long, like me, and talks about moose, the largest animals in the park, how ninety percent of their diet is willow. Yet pregnant moose appear to feed on springtime aspen and birch bark—"bark-stripping," he calls it—before giving birth, perhaps because the bark contains high levels of vitamin K that accelerates blood clotting and reduces bleeding. He expands on the feeding strategies of boreal and black-capped chickadees, at half an ounce each, among the smallest year-round vertebrates in the park. In winter, he says, their body temperatures drop nearly twenty degrees Fahrenheit each night (one third that amount would kill a human) to slow their metabolism to help survive the cold.

Their hippocampus, the part of the brain associated with memory, increases in size in late summer as the breeding season ends and seed caching begins. The better the memory, the more easily they'll find the cached seeds needed to survive the bitter cold.

Rick adds that Denali's black-capped chickadees have evolved to capture and metabolize fat much more efficiently than their counterparts down south. After shivering through a single night and losing ten percent of their body weight, the chickadees regain it from the cached seeds, eating all day. Then again, they lose it that night. If tough and ferociously determined, they'll gain it back. And don't forget the common redpoll that can tolerate even colder temperatures, in part because its plumage doubles in weight from summer to winter, and it can store daytime seeds in its esophagus to digest at night.

Oliver's older brother wants to know how nature got so smart.

I think, *Yes, we could spend the rest of our lives studying nature, forever amazed.*

Oliver wants to know if a hippopotamus has a hippocampus.

WHILE MOST rangers give evening campground programs with titles like "Migration and Adaptation: How to Survive in the Far North," or "Skins and Skulls: Piecing Together a Story of Predation," or "Climbing the High One: Mountaineering on Denali," Rick calls his program, "Why Arctic Ground Squirrels Are Such Jerks." His supervisors have asked him to change it. They're my supervisors too, cautious in brown socks. Rick says he'll change the program one day, though people tell me he's been saying that for years. Meanwhile his ground squirrel program is illuminating, irreverent, and funny, and packed every night.

"Competition and reproduction," Rick tells me privately. "That's what it's all about. Eat or be eaten, that's the game. We're not so different. Danger, sex, and food. You have to be alert to those things, know how to avoid them or find them. If not, you die. Your lineage dies. It's that simple. It's how our ancestors made it through the ice ages and times of hunger, drought, and disease. It's why we're here today."

I acknowledge Rick with a nod. Despite his rebel nature and mine, our rebel togetherness, my red socks make him uncomfortable. Some rebels go too far.

"Are you going to wear those socks when you talk to Secretary Watt?" he asks.

"What?" I'm still thinking about ground squirrels. And danger and sex and food, and the universe to be found in a flower, the distance between stars.

"Didn't you look at the duty schedule?" Rick says. "You're scheduled to give the sled dog demonstration for the new secretary of the interior, James Watt."

"I am?"

"You are. You might want to change your socks."

Little Oliver asks, "What's a Watt?"

—∽—

BALD AND BESPECTACLED, a tidy man raised on Wyoming oil and gas, seventh in line to the US presidency, flanked by young aides in tidy white shirts and grim-faced agents of the Secret Service, James Watt, attorney-at-law, our shiny new secretary of the interior, stands in the Denali Sled Dog Kennels with a practiced smile. Sunshine gleams off his brilliant forehead. If only he made it easier to dislike him. He says "please" and "thank you" all the time, too many times. With the firm grip of a high plains westerner he shakes my hand. "Good to meet you, Tim," he says, his narrow eyes darting about.

He has questions about the dogs, the kennels, the history of sled dog patrols in the park. Most are answered by Sandy Kogl, the kennels manager, a patient woman. A few fall to me, the rookie ranger in red socks, Kimmy the Kid. I say it like it is. Dogs have been used by the National Park Service in Denali since the 1920s, and long before that, by the Tanana and Koyukon Indians of Interior Alaska who used dogs in all aspects of their village lives, from hunting and fishing to year-round chores. The Tanana and Koyukon lived along rivers, and still do (they take their names from rivers), and enlivened their world with animal spirits and stories and a deep regard for all life. Anthropologist Richard Nelson observed that the Koyukon know all animals well, but they *understand* dogs. The same can be said of Sandy, I believe, and other storm-tough rangers who run the dogs on winter patrols.

Nelson wrote in 1977 while living in Huslia, 230 miles northwest of the park:

*Village dogs have their own subsociety, a world apart from the larger community of humans with which they also interact. I puzzle over which is most important to them and feel certain it is their private dog world. Their daily lives center on barking at loose dogs or passing teams, posing antagonistically toward their enemies, whooping at approaching visitors, urinating on the brush around their tethers, anticipating the day's feeding, and howling. . . . All that the dogs do fascinates me, but the howling absolutely captivates my senses. It is a wild shower of sound, as if voice were given to the quaver and pendulation of the aurora overhead. More than anything else, it epitomizes life here at the edge of the wildland, that separate world in nature that surrounds us but remains always beyond our grasp.*

⸺

SECRETARY WATT asks about the Iditarod Trail Sled Dog Race that happens every March, a race of over one thousand miles from Anchorage to Nome to commemorate the 1925 serum run to save children from a diphtheria outbreak. Winter set down hard that year, too cold for planes to fly, what few planes existed then, and none with landing skis. The serum had to be delivered to Nome by dog teams. Sandy tells the new secretary that just two years earlier, in 1979, Joe Redington, who founded the modern Iditarod Race, reached the top of Denali by sled dog team, together with a promising new musher named Susan Butcher. I notice that the secretary calls the mountain McKinley while we in the Park Service call it by its Native name, Denali.

I tell him that the name McKinley was given to the mountain in 1896 by James Dickey, a Princeton graduate with a winning personality and a good arm on the pitcher's mound. Dickey headed west, started a business in Seattle, lost it in a fire, and turned north to Alaska, gold-bound like other men. In the mudflats of the Susitna River, near Cook Inlet, where most would-be prospectors gave up, Dickey and his three companions whipsawed lumber into two Yukon-style riverboats and made their way more than one hundred miles upriver into what he called a "wonderful wilderness." Having admired Mount Rainier from Seattle, Dickey now regarded the great peak on the Alaska horizon. He estimated its height at over 20,000 feet, and named it after William McKinley of Ohio, who'd been nominated for the presidency. When asked later why he did this, Dickey, who wrote Alaska dispatches for the *New York Sun*, said that after receiving a verbal beating in Alaska from those who favored a free silver standard, he named the mountain after a champion of the gold standard.

"Thank you for that inspiring story, Tim," Secretary Watt says. He loves the idea of brave men going upriver in little boats to discover new country, to open it up, tame it, and create opportunities for others. "Entrepreneurship and Manifest Destiny, that's what America is all about. That's what makes us special. Lewis and Clark up the Missouri. Fremont and Carson up the Colorado. Washington up the Delaware."

What? Washington didn't go *up* the Delaware, he *crossed* it on Christmas night 1776 to surprise Hessian and British troops in Trenton and achieve a crucial victory in the American Revolutionary War. He was no explorer or gold prospector. He was a farmer and a slave owner, a soldier and a brilliant field commander who led a ragtag colonial army against the all-powerful British. Schoolchildren know this.

And Fremont and Carson up the Colorado? Never.

John Wesley Powell *down* the Colorado in 1869, yes. And Edward Abbey and Roderick Nash some one hundred years later, yes. But not John Fremont, not Kit Carson.

The secretary gestures and nods. He's President Reagan's choice to safeguard America's most cherished public lands, after all. As such, he has a gift for making broad assessments and tiny recastings of the truth. He smiles. His aides smile. I smile. What's going on? Any minute now I expect him to pat me on my head, another obedient husky.

Five months earlier, Ronald Reagan's selection of this man as his secretary of the interior was greeted by shouts of praise and howls of indignation. I was not one of them. I'd never heard of him. Like little Oliver, I wondered: What's a Watt?

Now I know. Since his Senate confirmation in early 1981, James Watt has shown himself to be a man on a mission, a sympathizer for the so-called Wise Use Movement that embraces the utilitarian maxim, "Conservation is the wise use of natural resources," an extraction approach to the natural world that calls for "the greatest good for the greatest number," as if the natural bounty will never end. Forget

John Muir's plea for wildlands preservation, his "let it be . . . any fool can destroy trees" approach. Secretary Watt, like his boss, is a free-market fundamentalist who wants the heavy-handed federal government to give the little guy a break. Set him loose in his bulldozer. He's just a little guy, after all, out there scraping by, digging and ditching, doing his best to feed his family and make a living.

—•—

THE SECRETARY speaks and I step away, my head spinning as I hear Sandy tell him about the park's sled dog program. How dog teams are used to haul out trash: fifty-five-gallon drums, two-hundred-pound bridge timbers, a coal car, Model A parts, culverts, discarded climbing gear, and metal roofing. "Performance is the key word," she says. "Handsome, traditional husky appearance is secondary to a dog's capability for pulling his share. Some of the best workers would not get viewing privileges at a dog show." Dogs don't break down, whereas trucks do. Yes, one dog might get sick or dehydrated and need a ride. But the whole team, unable to pull? Unlikely. If they refuse, they probably detect something you don't: overflow on the river, crevasses below, a moose on the trail ahead, snowbound and ready to rumble. She talks about "roughlocking," when she wraps chains around the sled runners for steep icy descents. Watch the dogs. Read them. Take their advice. That's the beauty of traveling the old way. It forces you to slow down, be attentive, listen. You need the dogs and they need you. You enter into an agreement, a pact, a trust.

Each backcountry patrol cabin stands a single day's mushing distance from the previous cabin. Etiquette requires that a cabin's wood-burning stove be left with a fire laid so arriving rangers can light it with one match, should they be debilitated by extreme cold. Winter patrols offer a chance to get out there and "drink up the silence, listen to the land, learn a thing or two."

Those are Sandy's words. She lives in a cabin she built at Carlo Creek, south of the park entrance, where she raises a small son and daughter at forty below, hauls water, chops wood, and doesn't suffer fools. Her words about silence appear to touch the secretary not at all. He thanks her and shakes her hand, and says something magisterial about all of us needing to work together to help make our national parks more "industry friendly." Another road, another hotel, maybe another gold mine or two, all in the name of progress. He shakes my hand and drifts away.

I walk over to the dogs, their names Tikchik, Toro, Suzi, Riley, Sandy, Joker, Tige, Mitts. They seem more genuine and honest-eyed, and happy to see me. Each has its own doghouse with a post in front to which it's chained, the chain long enough to give the dog a comfortable walking radius. This is where they spend their lives when not on winter patrol deep in the park, or when not being walked by Park Service personnel around the headquarters area. We rangers can adopt a dog for the summer for daily exercise. Longtimers in the park tell me the dogs are born to run.

Sandy finds me. "You okay?" she asks.

"I'm fine," I lie.

"Take a deep breath, Kim. We've had fruitcake secretaries of the interior before. Not many, but a few, and we've survived. We'll survive again."

I nod.

"What's with the red socks?"

"A protest."

"Against?"

"I don't know. I'm still trying to figure it out."

"So am I. So are a lot of us. I have something to show you." Inside her small, musty kennels office, Sandy pulls out a copy of a letter sent from the first director of the National Park Service, Stephen T. Mather, to the first superintendent of Mount McKinley National Park, Harry Karstens. It's dated

April 12, 1921, the day Karstens entered on duty (over four years after the park was established). She's highlighted a line where Mather reminds Karstens of the mining and hunting compromises that burdened the park's 1917 establishment act, and tells him to apply NPS policies with "tact, good judgment, firmness, fearlessness, and a cool head at all times."

"'A cool head at all times,'" I tell Sandy. "Not easy to do." She smiles. "The right thing never is."

TO CELEBRATE my thirtieth birthday, I hike to the Lower Savage River Cabin, and go alone. For weeks I've been discovering Denali with new friends, climbing high, taking photos, having good fun. This time I desire nobody's company but my own, and only a little of that. If only I could just leave myself behind, the chatter in my head. Ration my rationality. Indulge in old-fashioned intuition.

From the park road I hike north, downriver, in a heavy June rain. I cross the river many times, back and forth to avoid bedrock cliffs, each time stripping off my pants and plunging into the cold, swollen waters bare-legged, freezing my feet after tossing my boots to the opposite bank and slipping on a pair of dedicated "river shoes." That's the deal: fail to cross and I forfeit my boots.

The cabin waits, nestled in a spruce forest, patient, demure, rustic, dry. Inside I find a cozy space and a deep quiet, a teapot from the 1920s, a stack of *Life* magazines from the 1950s with ads featuring Hostess Cupcakes and the Marlboro Man out riding the range and breathing it all in. For three days I say nothing and burn candles and drink licorice tea, and read old novels and park journals, and write like a madman. Outside, the forest stirs with snowshoe hares and their chief predator, the lynx—Alaska's only wild cat—a furtive animal that dances to the mysterious oscillations and rhythms of the north, their numbers rising and falling on an eleven-year cycle. Up go the hares, up go the lynx; down go the hares, down go the lynx. Hour after hour I watch and listen and see nothing. How many times do they see me while I don't see them?

The rain abates. I leave the cabin with a fire laid in the wood-burning stove, and return to a national park in shock.

A tour bus has rolled off the road at Thorofare Pass. Sandy tells me the inexperienced driver caught a wheel on the soft shoulder; rather than back up, he tried to go forward. The bus rolled, the windows popped, and visitors tumbled out. Five died.

Newspaper and television crews are here from Anchorage and Fairbanks.

Over the next few days, politicians question the Park Service's decision of nine years before, in 1972, to close the park road to private vehicle traffic and initiate a shuttle bus system. That same year, construction was completed on the George Parks Highway, between Anchorage and Fairbanks, and visitation to the park promised to explode. The NPS reasoned that a bus system would minimize traffic and preserve wildlife along the road; that forty pairs of eyes in a single bus would see more than one or two pairs of eyes in a private car. The buses would stop, and everybody would see the bear, the caribou, the Dall sheep in steep terrain, the bull moose shaking his antlers in a thicket of willow, the mighty roadside pika atop his talus domain.

In other words, travel by bus would enhance rather than erode the visitor experience; it would accommodate increased visitation and help to preserve the wild integrity of the park. Around every bend would be another vista that demanded we be right here, right now, in this place and no other.

It worked.

"Driver, stop the bus. I see a bear."

The bus stops. Everybody looks.

"That's not a bear," the driver says. "It's a rock."

"No, it's a bear. I'm sure it's a bear."

People jostle, looking, staring. Binoculars, cameras.

"It's a rock," the driver says. "From this angle, I know, it looks like a bear, but it's a rock."

"But I saw it move." the visitor says, earnest, persuasive. "It has to be a bear."

Everybody wants it to be a bear.

"It's a rock," the driver says, exasperated.

"It can't be. It's too big to be rock."

Accidents were bound to happen, fender benders here and there, but nobody expected a single accident to take the lives of five people.

Such is the bitter taste of irony: that we invite people to Denali and put them in a bus to enhance their experience, and this happens. It's one thing to climb a mountain or cross a crevasse, to barter in the currency of extreme risk and not come home. It's another to get rolled over and killed by a bus.

The park's critics—I'm always surprised by their numbers and vehemence—attack the Park Service as another manifestation of an inept federal government. The private sector should run our national parks, they say.

————

ON A RAINY DAY soon after the accident, I fail as a park ranger. I'm on duty at the Riley Creek Campground, in a double-wide trailer that serves as the park's makeshift visitor center. Flanked by my fellow interpretive rangers behind the visitor center desk, I am a Spartan at Thermopylae, outnumbered ten to one by visitors hustling for campsites before the afternoon ends and the weekend begins and the campground is full. It's Friday. They line up. A man moves forward and soon stands before me, dark-faced, determined. Having waited his turn, he tells me that he's secured campsite number 81 for himself and his family. He has an accent, Middle Eastern of some kind. Obsidian eyes. He's Xerxes with a neatly trimmed moustache above perfect teeth.

"Great," I say to him. "Did you follow the instructions and secure the campsite by leaving something there on the picnic table? An empty cooler, a waterproof bag, something, anything?" *A wallet, a checkbook, a child.*

"Not at all," he announces. "It's raining. The campsite's empty. We drove by. We saw it. We want it. It's ours."

"Yes, but without leaving something there to secure it, somebody else could be there right now taking that site."

"I saw the site first. It's open, I want it. It's mine."

"It *was* open. But now it's probably gone." *Taken by somebody who followed the instructions.*

"What kind of business is this?"

"Look, go back through the campground quickly, on foot, find an open site, any site, and put something on the table to hold it. You have to hurry. Every site will be taken in the next few minutes."

He hustles out the door with his two teenage boys.

IN TRUTH, I'm not a Spartan.

Growing up in Spokane, that title belonged to my brother Mick. Fourteen years older than me, he loved guns, books, and the ukulele. He'd walk around the house singing "The Ballad of the Green Berets." At eighteen he joined the Coast Guard. At twenty-six he became a career army officer. Everything he did was exotic to me: sailing the world's oceans and sending home postcards from Hong Kong and Spain of women in bikinis and matadors with swords. How worldly he looked in his blue uniform, the sailor's white cap tipped jauntily on his head. I'd sit at his feet while he told stories with the cut and swagger of another Mick, Mickey Mantle, the great Yankee center fielder who personified everything right and strong about America.

Brother Mick taught me to play baseball aggressively, cleverly, to use all my wits. Most of them anyway. I wanted to be like him and play third base, but was a lefty and couldn't charge ground balls and make a strong throw to first. Mick decided I should be a pitcher. I had a good fastball. So we worked my sidearm into a crazy curving-slinging-zinging-screwball mudball that struck out hundreds of kids, hit a few, and walked hundreds of others. I always felt bad about it. Mick told me to suck it up. Get tough. Dreams of grandeur ran through my head. Soon I'd play in Yankee Stadium.

One day Mick took me to the bluff. I figured he'd decided my pitch was so wild I couldn't throw safely at Comstock Park. He had another reason: guns. We drove along High Drive past Manito Golf and Country Club and down Hatch Hill Road. We parked and hiked into the wilderness not far from the sand cliffs where Max and I had flown into legend. Max came along thinking we might go skinny-dipping. The minute we started shooting, he ran off. We began with .22 rimfire revolvers and quickly moved to Remington .270 and 30.06 bolt-action rifles, some with scopes. Anything was fair game. Soup cans, Coke bottles, pine cones, flowers, we killed them all. Such marksmanship and rapid fire. We were ready to defend the Alamo or storm San Juan Hill. Let the commies or liberals try to take Spokane. They'd never get by us. I improved quickly and Mick rewarded me by notching things up to .44 and .45 Colt revolvers and pistols. Miniature cannons. He'd pin my forearms to the ground while I lay prone and squeezed the trigger. Boom . . . boom . . . boom. Did I hit anything? My head rang like a bell. Did we wear ear protection? Eye goggles? Ha. Did American insurgents wear sissy stuff like that on Bunker Hill? Those scrappy colonists that one frustrated British officer called "a rabble in arms," did they give a damn about ear protection?

"Shoot faster," Mick would tell me.

Every time he came home, this was our gig: go shooting but never hunting. Max wanted no part of it. After a while, neither did I. The thrill was gone. But could I say this to my big brother, my hero?

"I don't want him out shooting guns all day," Mom told Mick upon our return one afternoon. I think that's what she said. My ears were still ringing.

Mick bristled. He probably thought me a mama's boy who enjoyed too much privilege. I was the final son, "the caboose," many years younger than my brothers, pampered like an only child. Mick and Bill had grown up on Idaho logging roads and cut their teeth on the cougar-filled Bitterroot Mountains, and listened to Elvis Presley and Buddy Holly in the years before we could afford money. By the time I became a teenager the world was something new. Buddy Holly was dead. Elvis was fat.

Then one day Mick brought home a cat he'd named G-2, a golden tom that slept all day, prowled all night, and left little dead birds everywhere. Not exactly a cuddly lap cat, G-2 became a legendary lion of Spokane's South Hill. Mick boasted that he was the cat who took other cats' nine lives. Every night we'd hear horrendous cat screaming out in the street, metal garbage cans falling over, the lids rolling across pavement. More screaming and hissing. The next morning G-2 would be on the porch, untouched, sleeping it off. We'd let him in and watch him go to his cat bowl slowly, like a gladiator, pieces of shredded skin between his claws. A cat with an ego, image conscious about eating under less-than-lion-like circumstances, he didn't touch his food until after we left. Give him a gazelle and he'd run it down, kill it, and pull it up into an African acacia tree for the world to see. But give him Purina Kitty Chow in a plastic bowl on a linoleum floor in a modern American kitchen and he'd act as if it were beneath him.

Max took special care to avoid him.

After a while Mick and I didn't go shooting anymore. I'd find him down in his basement bedroom reading or playing the ukulele that he'd bought in Hawaii, or oiling his guns, spinning the chambers. I loved the smell of gun oil and would help him run the cloth over the barrels and the wooden stocks until each weapon was a marvel to look at and touch. My favorite was a Colt single-action Army .38 Special revolver like Little Joe Cartwright used on *Bonanza*. Mick would tell stories about each gun, its history and evolution. I found him encyclopedic and fiercely intelligent.

Like Xerxes.

⸻

FIVE MINUTES later he's back, and in my line. Why not Jill's line? Or Bruce's? Chuck's? They're rangers, too. Better rangers than me, easier on the eyes. Jill anyway. The Riley Creek Campground campsite board is nearly full. Xerxes inches forward. He has all the intensity of an older brother who always wins. "Campsite 81 was taken," he announces in his thick accent, "but we found campsite 35."

"And you left something there to hold it?" I ask him.

"No, anything we leave might get stolen. We are here now to claim it."

At that moment another park visitor in another line claims the last campsite, number 35, and the board closes. Chuck announces that the campground is full.

"Sorry," I tell the determined man standing before me. "You lost the site to somebody else. There are other campgrounds outside the park, north and south of the park entrance, along the highway and near the Nenana River. Nice places. From there you can drive into the park and catch a shuttle bus west and see all kinds of cool stuff."

"This is ridiculous." He pounds his fist onto the counter. The visitor center goes silent. Everybody freezes. I take a step back. He says, "I am a successful businessman who employes thousands of people. Thousands. If ever I ran my corporation like you run this park, I'd be out of business in a week. One week."

"Oh?" I say, stunned.

"That's all you have to say, is 'Oh'?"

"I'm sorry, sir. The campground is full. You can stay outside the park and check in with us when we open at seven o'clock tomorrow morning, get in line then if you'd like and maybe get a campsite as soon as one opens. But none may open until late in the morning, if at all. It's a busy weekend."

"And you think this is an efficient way to run things?"

"It's the best way we've come up with so far. We're always fine-tuning it."

"Fine-tuning it? Are you joking me? Tell me you are joking me."

"I'm not joking you. I'm being serious." *A cool head at all times.*

"I would never run a business like this, so inefficiently, so stupidly."

Such anger. Was this man once a bright-faced innocent boy like little Oliver, a boy in search of *aminals* and flowers and stars and his own imagination, his dark eyes filled with wonder instead of rage? I should feel sorry for him, show him compassion. I'd heard once that we're never more disappointed in others than when we're disappointed in ourselves. Or I could fight him, sword to sword, the Spartan and the Persian. Be a jerk, an arctic ground squirrel. Danger, sex, food.

"It must be nice to be such a successful businessman," I say. *Careful.*

"Imagine one hundred percent efficiency, if you can. Can you do that?"

"Yes."

"This is what I do. I operate at one hundred percent efficiency, until I run into something like this, like what you have here. Something inefficient."

"One hundred percent efficiency? Your corporation runs that well?"

"If it did not, I would not be successful."

"Does it really run at one hundred percent efficiency all the time?"

"All the time? No. Most of the time? Yes."

"So your corporation runs at just under one hundred percent efficiency. Say, ninety-nine percent efficiency?"

"Yes."

"Well, so does our operation here at Denali. And you're our one percent." *Oops.*

---

THE NEXT DAY my supervisor calls me into his office and tells me I'm finished working in the Riley Creek Visitor Center. I have a new job in Denali.

# CHAPTER THREE

# Not Recommended for Rehire

SNOW IN AUGUST. A big storm rolls off the Gulf of Alaska, soaks Anchorage in heavy rain, and slams into the Alaska Range. Clouds billow over the highest peaks. The summit of North America disappears; all summits disappear. In hours the park turns white, goes silent. Only the wind has something to say as wildcat gusts rip down the north-flowing Savage, Sanctuary, Teklanika, and Toklat Rivers.

I trudge on, my pack heavy, the straps digging into my shoulders, the wind pushing me from behind. Why all this stuff? Ice axe, stove, cook kit, camera, lenses, film, tripod, processed food, synthetic clothes, plastic tarp, rip-stop tent and sleeping bag—wet, everything wet. I'm a walking, staggering slave to my possessions. I follow my feet, one step at a time over the Thorofare River Bar, my sodden boots taking me home after three days camping in the backcountry. At this lower elevation the snow melts when it alights on the riverside cobbles and rocks, each stone a wet, glistening window into the park's distant past. I love the names: gabbro, argillite, graywacke, and granite; micaceous sandstone, serpentine, actinolite schist, and radiolarian chert; granodiorite, limestone, green tuff, and metarhyolite. Speaking them softly deludes me into thinking I understand their stories and history. All three major rock types are represented here: sedimentary, igneous, and metamorphic, excavated from the tortured, weathered spine of the Alaska Range, the rounded cobbles tumbled by water, the angular rocks dropped by ice. They exist in a freeze-frame in time to me, but in fact they have their own clock, older and more patient than mine. If millennia were minutes they'd move as fast as I do, probably faster, en route from the mountains to the sea. And they'd break up as they go, rocks to sand, silt, and clay. The fine sediments accumulating in deep marine beds, baking and hardening under the weight and pressure of more sediments, and more, thousands of feet thick, millions of years in the making. Erosion and deposition. Continents drifting, colliding, subducting. Tectonics and volcanism building the mountains up; glaciers and rivers tearing them down. This is the study of deep time, the drama of epochs, a never-ending story; this is the science that got Darwin out of the ministry and onto HMS *Beagle*, which took him around the world.

This is geology.

About 400 feet elevation above me, on mile 66 of the park road, Eielson Visitor Center moves in and out of the clouds like an illusion; it's the clouds that move, of course, always going, always late, chased by more clouds and more after that, the storm exhausting itself. Now and then a piece of blue sky opens up.

I leave the river bar and begin to climb, working my way through thick willow and dwarf birch. Still in full leaf, they bow heavy under their new burden of wet snow. On wind-swept tundra I find a gentian and an arctic poppy rising through the whiteness, impossibly resolute. Arctic ground squirrels peek out from their burrows. More blue sky. I hear birdsong. A fox sparrow? Lincoln's sparrow? (I should know my sparrows, their songs and preferred habitats.) As I gain elevation, the snow deepens in some places up to my knees; I avoid the worst of it by following windblown areas. By the time I reach the visitor center the storm has mostly cleared and sunlight dances off white peaks all around me.

The Thorofare River shines below—a braided beauty. I can see the road has been recently plowed east and west by the maintenance gang, Brad Ebel and his boys. Rick McIntyre opens the visitor center door.

"Hey," he says, "you're not dead?"

"Not yet."

"You will be one day, though."

"You too, amigo."

He shrugs. "How was it out there?"

"Wet."

"And cold, too, I'll bet."

"A little."

"Come on in and dry out."

"Where are the buses?"

"They're coming. You want something hot to drink?"

Rick has the best interpretive job in the park. He lives in a basement apartment at Eielson Visitor Center, with a full window view of the Alaska Range and the surrounding foothills and tundra-scape. He wakes up at times to see caribou or grizzlies looking in, making sure he's okay. Five days a week he reports for duty upstairs, and greets visitors with his wit and deep knowledge. Rather than be a permanent career ranger with the National Park Service, he'll remain a seasonal with no benefits or retirement, which is fine with him, near as I can tell. He spends his summers in Denali and his winters down south in Death Valley and Big Bend. At Eielson, he leads daily hour-long hikes, and once a week a four-hour-long discovery hike in the coveted west end of the park. He also gives his popular arctic ground squirrel program at Wonder Lake Campground.

My job is almost as good. I too work at Eielson, and lead hikes, but I live at the Toklat Work Camp, at mile 53, with two dozen other NPS employees. For screwing up at Riley Creek Visitor Center and failing as a park ranger, this is my reward. A better job. In fact, I've been sent out here to write a road guide, a mile-by-mile description of what visitors can expect to see in the park. It's not Hemingway in Cuba but it is a writing assignment. In my own American expat way I can say things beyond the descriptive, according to Bill Truesdale, chief of interpretation. Have at it, he tells me. Say what needs to be said. Tell the readers where they are and what they're looking at. But also provoke them, challenge them; go ahead and get philosophical if you'd like. Make them think.

"Really?" I say.

"Really," Bill says.

"Thinking is no easy thing."

"Exactly."

"I'm going to have to think about how to make the readers think."

"Take your time."

I like Bill. He's an old school park ranger. "It's important to remind people that national parks don't happen by accident," he tells me. "They're established and defended through great commitment, vision, and force of character. They show us another kind of wealth, one that cools the fevered money culture of American capitalism. Big, wild national parks are the best thing we got going. Don't let people forget that. Never let them forget that."

"Hit them over the head with it?"

"No. Massage it into them."

"How do I do that?"

"Delicately."

"So, I still have a job?"

"Yes, but no more confrontations . . . and no more red socks."

―――❦―――

RICK HANDS ME a cup of tea. I warm my bones as we watch the mountains come out one cloud at a time: Scott Peak above the headwaters of the Thorofare River, followed by Mount Eielson to the west, then Mount Mather, Mount Brooks, and Denali itself, much larger and higher than the others, a giant, a guardian, its twin peaks, the south and north summits, two miles apart, separated by the high reaches of the Harper Glacier. Below the north summit, on the right flank of Denali, the Wickersham Wall drops 14,000 vertical feet in one of the most daunting mountaineering challenges in the world. Rick points out the Muldrow Glacier, one of forty named glaciers on the mountain, the largest on its north side. Twenty thousand years ago, when glaciers ruled much of Alaska's mountainous regions, the Muldrow reached north into the Kantishna Hills, twelve miles beyond its present terminus. With its lower reaches today covered by rock, soil, and vegetation, the Muldrow looks nothing like a river of ice. "What glacier?" people ask. For reasons not entirely understood, the Muldrow "galloped" forward in the summer of 1956, advancing up to 1,100 feet per day. It came to within a mile of the park road and slowed down, and by 1957 returned to relative dormancy. Rick says he's waiting for it to gallop again.

"When will that be?" I ask.

He looks at his watch. "Hard to say."

"So glaciers 'gallop'?"

"Not many, but some."

"They don't charge or race or blitz or sprint? Why is that?"

"I don't know. They 'gallop' and 'surge.' Those are the terms glaciologists use. Don't ask me why. The Bering Glacier surges, I think. So does the Hubbard. The Black Rapids Glacier galloped some years back and almost ran over the Richardson Highway."

Galloping glaciers. I'd heard of them. Prior to Denali, I'd worked two summers as an interpretive park ranger in Glacier Bay National Monument (now a national park) and knew a little about glaciers—just enough to make me want to know more. Glacier Bay itself, seventy miles long, ten miles wide, was entombed by a surging glacier back in the mid-1700s, and many times before that over hundreds of thousands and perhaps millions of years. Study glaciology and you quickly learn that ice has its own metronome, a tempo. It floods and ebbs, advances and retreats. Many things oscillate in the far north: lynx, hares, caribou, glaciers; the populations up and down, the icy rivers flexing back and forth, the land itself beating to a rhythm we may never fully understand, the music of the high latitudes.

Sitting there drinking my tea, I tell Rick that what intrigues me about Interior Alaska is its history of an *absence* of glaciation. While ice covered much of northern North America twenty thousand years ago and dominated the mountainous coasts of south-central and southeast Alaska, the low-lying regions of Interior Alaska, along the Tanana, Yukon, and Kuskokwim Rivers, while cold, had no nearby mountains, no places to accumulate great amounts of snow. And so remained glacier-free.

"And filled with cool Pleistocene megafauna," Rick says. "Woolly mammoths, mastodons, North American camels, short-faced bears, and saber-toothed cats, to name a few."

There's only so much water in the world, after all. It's a closed system. With more of it invested in glacial ice twenty millennia ago, sea level dropped three hundred feet. A land bridge opened between Asia and Alaska where the shallow Bering Sea is today. As best we know, the first humans to arrive in North America came by that bridge from Asia, hunting and gathering, and fishing along the coast. It wasn't so much a bridge as a causeway, hundreds of miles wide.

Rick and I talk about what it must have been like to hunt mammoths and bring one down, to be pagan, primitive yet not crude, but deeply content and in love with the people around you, respecting them and their skills as they in turn respected you and yours; to survive as a family, a tribe, a little band of humanity living through times of bounty and want, always facing death and as such always acutely alive, alert, robust, making music and fire and stories and love to stay warm. A far cry from shopping at Safeway. How easily we in our modern world, seduced by our clever devices and aisles of disposable consumer goods, blithely plunder nature and crow about progress and regard the distant past as feudal and brutal and backward. For many, life long ago was difficult and filled with suffering. Yet for many others life was simple, beautiful, and bountiful, the days filled with flowers and birdsong, clean water and air. Bring those people forward to today, stuff them in tight shoes and a cubicle office, have them commute in traffic and eat microwave dinners off plastic trays while watching loud sitcoms on a big TV, and they'd curl up and soon die. Worried about the unlivable future? We're already there.

"You ever think about progress?" I ask Rick.

"Not a lot."

"Neither do I."

"What? You think about progress all the time."

"You're right, I do."

"It's a writer's curse to think about things too much."

"Maybe I'll be a carpenter. Jesus was a carpenter."

"And look what happened to him."

"I know . . . sad."

"Check out that cloud over Pioneer Ridge."

I check it out; for a while we say nothing, Rick and I. We let Denali do the talking. Words only get in the way. But words will soon be required. The buses are coming, buses filled with people hungry to *see*, to bask in the American landscape. We have the privilege to help them do that.

"You think this park can make the world a better place?" I ask Rick.

"Absolutely."

We grow silent again and drink it in, as if the land could nourish us. Blue sky, new snow, ancient rocks, the topography etched perfectly into our hearts. Not a bad deal. A truck arrives from Toklat with a couple of maintenance guys. I throw on my NPS uniform; it's time to go to work.

I look down at my socks. They're brown.

A CROWD gathers as Rick talks about Denali, the High One, the mountain that commands the visitor center's large west-facing window; sacred to the Tanana and Koyukon peoples. The first recorded reference occurred in 1794, Rick says, when Captain George Vancouver, charting Cook Inlet near present-day Anchorage, described "distant stupendous peaks" to the north. Throughout the 1800s, Russian and American trappers, prospectors, and army surveyors noted how the mountain dominated the horizon. In 1902 Alfred Hulse Brooks of the US Geological Survey led an expedition of seven men and twenty packhorses, and wrote:

> *The task before us was to find a route across the swampy lowland, traverse the mountains, and, following their northern front, approach from the inland slope as near the base of this culminating peak of the continent as conditions and means would permit; we must map the country and incidentally explore a route which some time could be used by that mountaineer to whom should fall the honor of first setting foot on Mount McKinley.*

Brooks did this, covering eight hundred difficult miles in 105 days, from Cook Inlet to the village of Rampart, on the Yukon River. At one point, while off climbing alone, he fell under the mountain's spell, moving up treacherous slopes of ice:

> *Convinced at length that it would be utterly foolhardy, alone as I was, to attempt to reach the shoulder for which I was headed, at 7,500 feet*

*I turned and cautiously retraced my steps, finding the descent to bare ground more perilous than the ascent.*

Near where he turned around, he built a cairn and buried a cartridge shell from his pistol that contained a brief account of his journey, and a roster of his party.

Others followed. McKinley was a prize, the undisputed crown of the continent.

In 1903 Alaska Territorial Judge James Wickersham, having set up a district court in Eagle, and civil offices in the new gold strike town of Fairbanks, made an assault on what he called "the monarch of North American mountains." He and his party traveled by boat—first a steamer called the *Tanana Chief*, later a poling boat called *Mudlark*—down the Tanana River and then up the Kantishna River. Marching overland, they passed lakes brimming with waterfowl, hunted caribou, made jerky, and in the northern reaches of the Kantishna Hills, on Chitsia Creek, they staked ten placer gold mining claims. While not impressive in quantity, the claims would nonetheless contribute to a stampede and help write an entire chapter of Denali's history.

Wickersham and party climbed the mountain's northwest buttress, a difficult route, and soon found themselves high above the Peters Glacier, stymied by "a tremendous precipice beyond which we cannot go," Wickersham wrote. "Our only line of further ascent would be to climb the vertical wall of the mountain at our left, and that is impossible." They were at 10,000 feet, face to face with what today is called the Wickersham Wall.

Two months after Wickersham's climb, Frederick Cook, a medical doctor with a winning personality, attempted Mount McKinley by roughly the same route, and reached an elevation of 11,000 feet, over halfway to the top. He received high praise, and his reputation would have remained stellar had he stopped there. But three years later, in 1906, Dr.

Cook, a veteran of the Arctic and the Antarctic, returned to climb McKinley with another team, including Herschel C. Parker, a Columbia University physics professor, and Belmore Browne, an artist, hunter, poet, scholar, and lumberjack. After two months slogging up the Susitna River into the Alaska Range, finding the terrain vexing at best, the expedition members turned back while the doctor stayed in the mountains with his horse packer, Robert Barrill.

In an unexpected September telegram to his East Coast backers, Cook announced: A LAST DESPERATE ATTEMPT ON MOUNT MCKINLEY.

Moving fast up the Ruth Glacier, he bagged the great mountain in two weeks, he said; up and back, simple as that. He had a photograph to prove it. Sure enough, there he stood alone on bedrock, triumphant, shot from below, backdropped by nothing but sky. The claim provoked immediate skepticism.

Rick tells the crowd, "The photo was actually taken on a granite knob above the Ruth Glacier, at fifty-five hundred feet elevation, only about one-fourth as high as the summit of Denali. Today it's called Fake Peak."

The crowd is mildly stunned. People don't know what to think. Rick smirks as he sweeps his long red hair out of his eyes. A good joke, the crowd agrees. Fake Peak. Two young men laugh. "It's true," Rick says.

Dr. Cook did it again in 1908 when he claimed the North Pole with a sudden dash from Nansen Sound, off the north coast of Ellesmere Island, in an impossibly short period of time. Again, skepticism ensued.

About Cook's outrageous McKinley claim, C. E. Rusk of the Oregon Mazama Mountaineering Club wrote, "That man does not live who can perform such a feat. Let us draw the mantle of charity around him and believe, if we can, that there is a thread of insanity running through the woof of his brilliant mind. . . . If he is mentally imbalanced, he is entitled to the pity of mankind. If he is not, there is no corner of the earth where he can hide from his past." Cook never admitted wrongdoing. He was dropped from the Explorer's Club, where he was a past president, and from the American Alpine Club and other prestigious societies.

—◦—

BURDENED by Cook's story, I walk out the visitor center doors, wondering why a man would do such a thing. Climb so high, and risk falling so far.

Forty or fifty people stand outside in the parking lot, in the brilliant sunshine, most of them silent. As if the park were a holy place, the mountain a religious icon, they look about, warmed in the sun. Some stand atop picnic tables and take photos. Others hold loved ones and speak quietly. There's no wind.

I say nothing; nobody approaches me.

South of the visitor center, where the topography falls away to the Thorofare River, a young man trudges determinedly through deep snow, headed for a clean white north-facing slope. He's by himself, moving with conviction. I watch him but think little of his actions, his willfulness. After a minute I go back inside where Rick still has a crowd. "The Brooks, Wickersham, and Cook expeditions were merely reconnoiters. None got close to the summit," I hear him say. "But they set the stage for three expeditions that did: the Sourdough Expedition, the Parker-Browne Expedition, and the Stuck-Karstens Expedition that finally reached the summit."

—◦—

IT OCCURS TO ME, watching Rick hold a crowd: people love a good story. Facts are nice and especially useful when manipulated. Art and photography have their persuasions. Music brings people together; wars tear them apart. Demagoguery

53

can turn entire nations upside down. And don't forget oratory and rhetoric. But there's nothing like a good story, well told, rich in content and delivery. Rick excels at it.

He ticks off the three mountaineering expeditions, one at a time.

The 1910 Sourdough Expedition. Believing that Alaskans, not outsiders, should be the first atop Mount McKinley, four Fairbanks prospectors—Billy Taylor, Pete Anderson, Charley McGonagall, and Tom Lloyd—wagered a bet that they could do it. Wearing bib overalls and "light duck parkees" (light parkas without fur lining), they followed the Muldrow Glacier and established a base camp at 11,000 feet. On summit day, three men (the overweight Tom Lloyd stayed at camp) climbed in subzero temperatures and consumed nothing more than hot chocolate and donuts as they ascended today's Pioneer Ridge, the sinuous northeast route that knifes between the Wickersham Wall and the Muldrow Glacier. Covering 8,500 vertical feet in an eighteen-hour ascent and return, Taylor and Anderson reached the north peak (while McGonagall dropped out not far below) and planted a fourteen-foot spruce pole (with a six-by-twelve-foot American flag) as evidence of their success. Could the two men see that the south peak, two miles distant, was in fact 850 feet higher, the true summit? When asked about this nearly three decades later, Billy Taylor would respond, "It didn't seem to have any elevation more." Besides, the north peak, the one visible from Fairbanks, had been their objective, and they'd succeeded with remarkable pluck.

But when Lloyd returned to Fairbanks before the other three, and boasted that all four men had climbed both summits, his false testimony clouded the expedition's true achievement. For awhile the Sourdough Party was regarded as just another Cook-like fantasy. People in Fairbanks shook their heads. The most powerful spotting scopes strained 170 miles to the southwest and showed no flagpole.

The 1912 Parker-Browne Expedition. Herschel Parker and Belmore Browne, former colleagues turned critics of Frederick Cook, attempted McKinley via the Muldrow Glacier. While relaying supplies up the glacier by dog team, Browne did double duty after a third member of the party, Merl LaVoy of Seattle, injured his knee. As they gained altitude, snow blindness plagued them. They found that their bodies, starved for oxygen in the thin air, could not metabolize the fat in their pemmican; they resorted to a starvation diet of tea, sugar, raisins, and hardtack (crackers). A stabbing cold hounded them. They pushed on, higher, higher. Browne wrote that the summit rose "as innocently as a snow-covered tennis court and as we looked it over we grinned with relief—we knew the peak was ours." It was not.

The wind intensified, the sky darkened. A storm advanced from the south. Less than two hundred feet below the summit, hurricane force winds pinned them in place, and showed no sign of abating. "The game's up," Browne screamed to Parker and LaVoy. "We've got to get back down." If they didn't, they'd die. Browne later called it "a cruel and heartbreaking day."

The next day they recovered at a high camp, ate hardtack and raisins, and applied boracic acid for snow blindness. Then they tried again, leaving for the summit at 3 a.m. And again a fierce storm pinned them just below their objective, leaving Browne with "only a feeling of weakness and dumb despair."

Later, while recovering at Cache Creek after descending the Muldrow Glacier, the three men were nearly knocked off their feet when a massive earthquake shook the Alaska Range. Geologist Michael Collier would later write: "The ground around them pitched like a ship at sea. As they watched, the western flank of Mount Brooks was swept clean by a miles-long avalanche. A cloud of snow four thousand feet high swept over the climbers in an icy sixty-mile-an-hour blast. Summit or no summit, the men, still alive, counted themselves lucky to be off the mountain." Later, the climbers would learn that the earthquake was an aftermath of the cataclysmic eruption of Novarupta, in today's Katmai National Park, three hundred miles to the south-southwest, that created the Valley of Ten Thousand Smokes, darkened the skies of Kodiak Island, and blasted volcanic ash high enough into the upper atmosphere that it circled the world many times.

The 1913 Stuck-Karstens Expedition. Alaska's Episcopal Archdeacon Hudson Stuck, a traveling missionary, organized an expedition and went looking for a partner who could lead "in the face of difficulty and danger." And so he found the indomitable Harry Karstens, former wilderness guide for hunter/conservationist Charles Sheldon in 1906–1908. They recruited Walter Harper, Stuck's aide, and Robert Tatum, a theology student, both strong young men. Like Karstens, Stuck was no stranger to what Teddy Roosevelt called the "strenuous life," a toughness and wisdom gained by learning from the Natives, knowing the land, sleeping on the ground. Still, Stuck failed to do his share of camp chores, and he erringly regarded Karstens at times as an assistant, even though Karstens was the key to the expedition's success. Through his skills and tenacity, it was Karstens, not Stuck, who repeatedly saved the day and kept the party together, though Stuck would later take credit.

A campfire on the Muldrow Glacier destroyed or damaged their mitts, socks, and tent. Despair set in. Maybe they should turn back. "Forget it," Karstens said. They advanced upward and discovered a bewildering maze of tumbled, jumbled ice blocks larger than buildings, the entire scene created by the previous year's great earthquake. For twenty days Karstens and Harper cut three miles of ice steps into the concrete-hard ice. Karstens noted that some of the ice blocks, balanced precariously against each other in defiance of gravity, appeared ready to fall if somebody whispered. At an elevation of about 16,000 feet, they spotted the spruce pole planted three years earlier by the Sourdough Party on the north peak. At 17,500 feet they set up their final camp. Fifty-year-old Stuck struggled in the thin air. The summit day dawned clear and cold; at minus four degrees Fahrenheit Karstens assigned Walter Harper to lead the assault. Many times Stuck blacked out; he had to rest to recover and would be relieved of the mercury barometer he carried to make scientific measurements.

It was Harper then, the smallest man in the party, a robustly built half-Athabascan Native, who on June 7, 1913, first set foot on the top of the highest mountain in North America. The others followed, and for ninety minutes they looked about, took measurements, and congratulated each other. Stuck attributed the benevolent weather—a perfect day—to God's design. "There was no pride of conquest," he later wrote,

> . . . *no trace of that exultation of victory some enjoy upon the first ascent of a lofty peak, no gloating over good fortune that had hoisted us a few hundred feet higher than others who had struggled and been discomfited. Rather was the feeling that a privileged communion with the high places of the earth had been granted; that not only had we been permitted to lift up eager eyes to these summits, secret and solitary since the world began, but to enter boldly upon them, to take place, as it were, domestically hitherto in their sealed chambers, to inhabit them, and to cast our eyes down from them seeing all things as they spread out from the windows of heaven itself.*

RICK FINISHES, and everybody takes a moment to regard the three-dimensional map of Alaska before them, the long arc of rugged peaks that comprise the Alaska Range, and the crowning mountain itself out the west-facing window, bathed in sunlight and new snow.

"Hey," somebody says, "what's that guy doing?"

Everybody looks out the south-facing window. The man I'd seen earlier marching with determined willfulness below the visitor center toward a north-facing slope is now kicking large, bold letters into the snow, making a proclamation to the world:

*JESUS SAVES*

I am not a godless man. I appreciate the mysteries of the universe, the possibility that things are ordered by a divine power, a maestro, a simple carpenter or a musician, a minstrel. I've read some of the Bible and caught myself praying now and then, a few times fervently. So when I see the man writing in the snow and I look at Rick and he looks back at me as if to say, "Hey, I'm on break. You go tell him to erase what he's just written into the pristine Denali landscape," I know I'm about to be tested. Again.

I go.

Perhaps this crusader should be in advertising: the billboard business. His handiwork preempts everybody's view of the Alaska Range. The lettering is perfect in the angel-white snow. Visitors who previously stood about and enjoyed their national park, each in his or her own private way, what Hudson Stuck might call a "privileged communion" with nature—a beauty beyond improvement—now watch me as I walk out onto the visitor center deck and wave at the billboard man. The communion has been broken. For us all. He waves back. He's about three hundred meters away. I shake my head at him. He raises his arms in a questioning manner, palms up, as if to say, "What?"

"Erase it," I yell; my voice abrasive by its volume. I wish I could whisper to him, tell him to please undo what he's done. Get on my knees if I have to. Treat him like a flower.

Again he raises his arms in a "What do you want me to do?" gesture.

"Erase it," I yell. I might have to go down there and do it myself.

But he gets it. He spends a good ten minutes tracking through his own lettering, obliterating it. He walks back upslope to where I wait.

"Thank you," I say.

"I apologize if I did anything wrong," he says.

"Apology accepted."

He's so young and sincere, not so much a man as a boy, not a day over twenty. Short haired, clean-shaven, clear-eyed, the smile of a salesman, the heart of a missionary, he puts his hand on my shoulder and says, "You know, a single lifetime is very short, while eternity is forever. Without a Heaven, all we have is the Earth."

～～

TWO WEEKS LATER autumn arrives and I am tested for a third time. Snow has melted from the tundra yet persists on the high peaks. Bearberry leaves color the land crimson while dwarf birch makes it russet orange. Caribou and moose wear thick, luminous coats burnished by the hormones of the rut, the bulls feisty with full antlers. Grizzlies spend all day with their heads down, eating soapberries and blueberries. For many people who love Denali National Park, this is their favorite time of year.

Once again I'm on duty at Eielson Visitor Center when a couple approaches me. The wife says, "Ranger, there's a man over there, down off the trail, with a camera, sneaking up on a bear, getting really close."

They lead me to an overlook and point down. Sure enough, about four hundred meters away a man is sneaking up on a bear that's got its head down, facing away, eating berries, fattening up for the long winter. What to do? Let the man proceed and see what happens? Watch the bear finish eating berries and start eating him? Yell at him to back off? Run down there and grab him and pull him back and risk my life with his? Start a betting pool? A memorial fund?

Every passing second brings the man closer to the bear. I yell.

He doesn't hear me, or he ignores me.

He steps closer.

I yell again. "Hey, get away from that bear. RIGHT NOW."

The man turns and glares up at me. He looks back at the bear, back at me, back at the bear, his head snapping to and fro. I motion him to get back up here. He resumes his crouched position, camera at his face, and makes two more steps toward the bear, now very near, maybe only about twenty meters away.

A few years ago a backpacker in Glacier Bay encountered a coastal brown bear on White Thunder Ridge and took two photos of the bear before the bear killed him. All that remained days later when the rangers arrived was a ravaged campsite, a few scattered bones of the backpacker, his boots, torn clothing, and his camera.

"Stop," I scream. "Get away from that bear and get back up here. NOW."

The man stops and stands upright, turns and walks back upslope, his eyes fixed on me. The entire time the bear, busily eating, hasn't lifted its head. Here comes Mister Camera Man, Mister Wildlife Photographer of the Year. He's about to thank me for saving his life, nominate me for an award, give me a big hug. I'm his hero. In full stride now, he comes at me, a bear himself. A crowd gathers for my award ceremony.

"Wow," I hear somebody say, "he's really angry."

Bill Truesdale's caveat comes to mind: *No more confrontations.*

How far do we have to go to find out who we are? Our family cat, G-2, never left Spokane's South Hill; he considered himself a king until the night he lost his first fight and turned up on the porch with one ear chewed off, his golden fur matted in dried blood. It stunned me and felt like the end of an era, the fall of an empire. My brother Mick was overseas. "Who's going to tell him?" I asked. Mom did. Should we lock G-2 indoors to keep him safe? "No," Mick said. "Let him go." On a cold moonless night a few months later G-2 went out and never came back. We could only guess his fate. Mortally wounded, he probably crawled under a bush to die alone; his final victim not some other cat, but himself.

Mr. Wildlife Photographer of the Year strides up to me and says, "Are you insane?"

"No."

"What's your name?"

"Kim."

"Rangers are supposed to protect people in a national park, not endanger them."

"That's what I just did."

"You could have gotten me killed yelling like that, so close to that bear."

I sigh. *Next time I'll do better.*

―――

THERE IS NO NEXT TIME. The Charles Darwin Research Station in the Galapagos Islands offers me a position in a naturalist training course and I accept, leaving Denali early. Because of this and perhaps other matters, my final evaluation doesn't read "highly recommended for rehire," which most rangers get, or even "recommended for rehire." Instead, I get "not recommended for rehire."

Bill Truesdale drives me to the train station. He says, "If a ranger leaves early, Kim, that's the final evaluation I'm required to give. I hope you understand."

"I do." I don't.

Out the window of Bill's truck, aspens and birches flash by, the leaves golden medallions in the sun. Silver clouds sail over the peaks of the Alaska Range. I roll down the window to let the cool air wash my hair, feel the sharp stab of winter's approach.

*Bill,* I want to say, *turn this truck around, take me back. Keep me here. I'll sleep with the sled dogs and eat hardtack and never complain.* But I say nothing. We see a cow moose and her grown calf. She should have two; a bear probably got the other one. Eat or be eaten. Danger, sex, food. Music, fire, love.

"Keep writing," Bill tells me.

"I will."

My heart is breaking. Mountains, tundra, forests, flowers, braided rivers and galloping glaciers, golden eagles and golden bears, sandhill cranes and sudden rains, the quilt of life so thin yet robust, resilient yet vulnerable. A tear lodges behind my eye. Will it all still be here when I return?

If I return?

# TEN YEARS LATER:

# TOLKAT RIVER

# CHAPTER FOUR

# The Presence of Absence

HERE I AM AGAIN, on the run from civilization, tundra underfoot, open sky above, Toklat River far below, silver in the sun. It's nice to be back, to remember how to breathe, listen, live. Sometimes you find yourself in the middle of nowhere. And sometimes in the middle of nowhere you find yourself. This is one of those times.

The wind stills, and I calm myself high atop Divide Mountain. I can hear the Toklat singing its distant melody. Scanning north, I see the park road running east to west, dotted by shuttle buses bringing visitors into a national park that Stephen Mather said should be "readily accessible to all." As first director of the National Park Service, Mather believed it was important to build a constituency for all the parks, to get people out there on "family vacations." He aimed to build roads and make the parks a distinctive part of our national experience, an American tradition, something new back in the 1920s.

He succeeded.

Too much so, some said.

"Mather goes too far," announced his own publicist, Robert Sterling Yard, a founding member of The Wilderness Society (along with Robert Marshall, Olaus Murie, and Aldo Leopold) who criticized an excess of road building. Yard lamented, "While we are fighting for the protection of the national park system from its enemies, we may also have to protect it from its friends." He wanted national "primal" parks.

And so we have Denali, a national park the size of Massachusetts with only one road, some ninety miles long, most of it unpaved, designed by men who were engineers—and artists.

FOR REASONS I'm just beginning to understand, reasons I didn't ponder until I hit my forties, I am drawn to the high latitudes, those hungry landscapes shaped by ice and cold. Yes, I've been to the tropics, face-to-face with howler monkeys and three-toed sloths, waxy-leafed figs and frisky epiphytes and all that hot photosynthetic plant sex going on day and night, ten million bazillion ants going about their business, moving single file to T. H. White's dictum: "Everything not forbidden is compulsory." I understand why the tropics attract ecologists and other defenders of biodiversity who've determined that nearly half of the world's terrestrial species live on about two percent of the earth's land area, and we'd better save it. Their goal is simple: preserve the heart of our planet's genetic library, one hundred million years of evolution. It is hard, noble work.

Up here the land is rugged, rocky, and damn near roadless. A hundred-acre parcel of virgin Brazilian rainforest can boast more species of *everything* than can all of Denali National Park. But who's counting? Denali matters. It teaches and inspires; it slows me down. It opens my lungs. I love the intimate distance, the raw existence, the unexpected avens, the furtive lynx, the stoic moose, the resilient birch, the poetry of water over stones; I love pulling my sleeping bag up to my chin and wondering: how far away is the nearest bear? The farthest star? I love the sunrises and sunsets, the only gold rush I care to be a part of. I love the survival amid hardship, the warm embrace of indifferent mountains, the simple but profound freedoms; I love the dream-tossed nights when, according to comedian George Carlin, "the wolves are silent and the moon howls."

---

UNLIKE MANY memoirists these days, I cannot claim any addictions or mistreatment by my parents. Raised in rural North Dakota with farm dirt under their nails and no scars or resentments of their own, Mom and Dad imparted none on me. They didn't shoot up heroin or rob banks or insist that I go to Harvard or Yale, or that I be a doctor or a lawyer. I didn't shatter into a million little pieces or run with scissors. I might have run with a meat cleaver once, but just once.

Dad loved his Monday night Montgomery Ward Bowling League, his Saturday afternoon major league baseball and beer, and his daily Jim Beam on ice after six. As alcoholics went, he was a gentle man, always good to Mom and my brothers and me. He'd sit at the dining room table and smoke his pipe and devour Louis L'Amour novels like candy. Mom favored the one-thousand-page James Michener epics about faraway places. Tired after a long day, she'd read in the bathtub, and come out with the book soaking wet and twice its normal size, having fallen asleep and dropped it in the water. Dad would say, "Reading is supposed to expand your mind, Virgie, not the book." She'd take the novel down to the furnace room to dry it out, separating the wet pages one by one so they didn't stick or tear. Never would she buy the same paperback twice, or a new hardcover. We didn't have the money.

Our first television was a magic box that cost exactly what we had and told us when to laugh and worry, what to think, what to buy and why. We loved it. "Stay right where you are," it said. "We'll be right back." And back it came, faithful as a friend. It gave us our favorite movies, and Walter Cronkite, a real newsman, and regularly scheduled programming, and told us to see the USA in our Chevrolet.

We had an old Buick with whitewall tires and a dinosaur engine that drank gas like water. About the best we could do to see the USA was a trip west to Seattle. For a bumpkin kid from Spokane, Seattle was Paris. It had the ocean and Pike Place and the Public Market where fishmongers threw salmon across selling stalls and bantered with buyers. Best of all, Seattle had the Space Needle, Washington State's Eiffel Tower, with a restaurant on top. I could see everything from up there—Mount Rainier, Mount Olympus, the entire Emerald City spread out below, perfect in its proportions, humming, thrumming, and growing, always growing.

En route back home, Dad sometimes got off the interstate to drive the back roads, as he put it, "to see what we might see." I sat up front—with Max the dog—to sing with the radio and watch every curve in the road and what new places it might reveal. That's how it was: the road, like television, revealed new worlds. It took us places. One time we followed the mighty Columbia River as it coursed its ancient way east of the Cascades, a great artery framed by bone-dry scablands and imposing black walls of basalt colonnade: so much water running through brown, thirsty country. I wondered: *Where does all the water come from?*

Nothing prepared me for Grand Coulee Dam, a tall, graceful, imposing concrete plug set into a bedrock gorge as if by aliens, a divine hand, an extraordinary power. Behind it was a large lake where a river used to be, Lake Roosevelt, named for Franklin Delano Roosevelt. I stared. Even little Max was without words.

Dad lit his pipe and spoke solemnly about the men who built the great dam back in the 1930s, how some fell into the concrete and remained there, entombed, sacrificed to progress. He talked about turbine power and kilowatt hours, more in numbers than in words. Big numbers. No salmon swam past that dam, he said. The Bureau of Reclamation built fish ladders to assist salmon on all the other dams, but not Grand Coulee. It was so big, so tall, they didn't bother. It was the new geography, the new beginning, the new end.

I had no reason to question it. Everything we did in America we did for good reason, to make us stronger, bigger, better. Deep in the basement of the local library, books told me stories about people who belonged to the land once, Indians and all that. But TV said that romance was just that, a romance, a silly nostalgia. The land belonged to us now, you and me and John Wayne on his big horse as Woody Guthrie sang "This land was made for you and me" and we all sang along. The land, having been made for you and me, should be harnessed and put to work. Nature wasn't a community we belonged to. It was a commodity we owned. And like all commodities, it was here to be consumed.

I stood beside my dad a bit bewildered, a happy twelve-year-old kid who didn't know what he didn't know. Grand Coulee Dam didn't charm or impress me like the Space Needle. It made me sad, and that sadness embarrassed me.

Everybody else admired Grand Coulee Dam. Why didn't I?

BACK HOME, I pulled out a map of Washington State and found Hangman Creek where it flowed into the Spokane River, which flowed into the Columbia, which flowed into the Pacific Ocean. Not like it once did, though. What would Huck Finn say? And Lewis and Clark, who crossed the Rocky Mountains and followed the time-honored, free-flowing Columbia to the Pacific?

Progress, they'd say. There's no stopping it.

One morning in school as I stood at attention and faced the flag and recited the "Pledge of Allegiance" with my hand over my heart, I felt my mind forced narrowly upwards. A good citizen, I was enthralled with America and American exceptionalism, the shining ideals of liberty and justice for all, the powers of creativity, innovation, and higher learning;

summertime apple pies, hot dogs, and baseball, the crisp originality of rock 'n' roll, bluegrass, and the twelve-bar blues. I was also enthralled with the girl down the street, Felicity, whose father would sit in his dark basement and insist that I sit with him while he played stirring military anthems on his scratchy old record player. And I did as he commanded because he had authority and I could stare at his daughter's soft curls and deep brown eyes as she coyly winked and drove me crazy.

My sixth-grade teacher reminded my classmates and me (Felicity to my left, hand over her heart) that we had good reason to be proud. We were civilized Americans who lived in the greatest nation on earth, in modern homes with soft beds, electricity, ovens, radio, and television. Grand Coulee Dam gave us that comfort, that convenience. It turned night into day. It lit our future. Yes, it was an end of some things. But it was the beginning of so much more. Every dam on the Columbia River was a great engineering feat and con-servation project, she said, a tribute to human ingenuity, a bold step forward that improved our daily lives. Foxy Felicity nodded her pretty head. All the kids nodded. *Think about it,* the teacher added. All that water that once ran to the ocean unused as a river, going to waste, now turned turbines to make the desert green with alfalfa, to make our homes glow blue with television.

Maybe it was something loose in my head. I told nobody about how weird I felt upon first seeing Grand Coulee Dam, or my adventure with Super Max the Wonder Dog, flying off the sand cliffs of Hangman Creek. Like a make-believe hero in my own secret movie, I alone carried the knowledge of my achievements as I struggled to fit in. The only thing other-worldly in my life was my imagination.

Then the Beatles arrived.

THEY CROSSED the North Atlantic and landed in New York City in early February 1964 with America still in shock less than three months after the assassination of President Kennedy. "Please join me in welcoming these fine youngsters from Liverpool," said Ed Sullivan, the host of his own variety show. He waved his hand and the music began, "All My Loving," "Till There Was You," "She Loves You, yeah, yeah, yeah . . ." I sat transfixed by the mop-top hair, knife-sharp suits, black boots, and youthful, easy smiles. Mom tapped her foot. It was the first time I'd seen her come alive since Kennedy's killing. Max cocked his head. Dad said they looked funny and didn't sing like Bing Crosby or Frank Sinatra; Mom said they didn't sing like Roy Orbison. I thought, Nobody sings like Roy Orbison. They had their own sound, a tight, bright beat that juiced things up ten degrees into—what? I didn't know. Did anybody? Such vitality and originality. Such compelling melodies and harmonies. Never mind the lollipop lyrics. The music seemed to render everything that came before it obsolete. It would take one night for America to know their names (and soon, their traits): John Lennon (clever), Paul McCartney (cute), George Harrison (quiet), and Ringo Starr (funny).

"How do you find America?" a reporter asked John.

"Turn left at Greenland."

"What do you think of Beethoven?"

"He's great, especially his poems."

Seventy-three million Americans watched that performance and stepped from darkness into the light, a national epiphany that acknowledged music heals, it transforms. It makes us feel and think in ways we never have. It's not a luxury; it's a necessity, a profound way to express our humanity, the deepest part of ourselves. To some, the Beatles were a simple pop band, all sugar, no salt. But many critics quickly grasped that what ran below the playful lyrics was a musical sophistication to rival Cole Porter and Irving

Berlin. Bob Dylan would observe, "They were doing things nobody else was doing. Their chords were outrageous, just outrageous, and their harmonies made it all valid. . . . They had staying power. I knew they were pointed in the direction of where music had to go."

All that winter I listened to Mom hum their songs.

When they returned to America for a concert tour the next year, Paul soloed with "Yesterday," the song that had come to him in his sleep, and John belted out "Twist and Shout" with a voice one observer said came from "leather tonsils in a steel throat." Later, American television aired the 1963 Royal Command Performance, attended by Queen Elizabeth II, when John invited the people in the "cheap seats" to clap their hands. "And the rest of you, if you'll just rattle your jewelry."

⌒

MY DREAMS changed after that. My school essays too. A small wolf took up residence in my heart. Call it rapid cognition or the adaptive unconscious or the crazy ability to know a thing without thought or explanation. I'm not sure what it was, but something was born in me the day I heard John Lennon stand before the world and challenge a queen. I began to question things and feel more alive than I did when flying off a cliff.

I started to sing, quietly at first, then with more gusto while riding my bike or mowing the Manito Golf Course, my summer job. On perfect putting greens I'd jam my heel into the soft earth to make divots, fulfilling my apprenticeship into the School of Civil Disobedience, inspired not so much by the soft-spoken Henry David Thoreau—who went into the woods to "live deliberately" and later spent a night in jail to protest a war—as by John Lennon, the tough, cynical, crude, creative, funny, brilliant, vulnerable son of an absent sailor and a loving mother who like John was insecure and would die too young. Stepping from a hedgerow into a street, she was struck and killed by a speeding off-duty policeman who paid no fine and served no jail time.

Life presented itself then as something infinitely wondrous, beautiful and unfair. A defiant little seed took root, watered with images of insurrection. I decided it wasn't the divots in putting greens that were wrong. It was the golf course itself, a big lawn where a forest used to be. And a dam? Could an entire dam be wrong? I listened to Bob Dylan sing about becoming a "suck-cess," and wondered, *Is he talking to me?*

When my stern sixth-grade teacher told me to stop humming and start writing my assigned exercise, I wrote the music in my head. "Write an essay about one of your heroes," she told my classmates and me. I chose Paul McCartney and John Lennon, unaware that television had clouded my ability to differentiate between a hero and a celebrity. "Your hero should be one person," the teacher announced. "And an American."

"Bob Dylan?" I inquired.

"A patriot," she added. "Somebody with wisdom."

I wrote about Pete Seeger with his banjo and guitar, out there inspiring people to sing. Felicity wrote about Jesus Christ and smiled smugly when she got an A and I got a C. *Jesus of Nazareth? Wait a minute. What instrument did he play? When did he get his US citizenship?*

I responded by writing more. It appealed to me, pulling a pencil across paper to give birth to words, ideas, a story, a voice, maybe even a truth, whatever a truth might be.

 ◆ 

CLOUDS. RAIN. WIND. Weather moving in.

Time to go. I hoist my pack. It must weigh fifty pounds. Again, too much stuff.

I hike north along the spine of Divide Mountain and begin to drop down its nose, a steep descent. Ahead and directly below, veiled in wisps of cloud, is Melanie, my wife of five years. A bandana swings off her waist belt as she picks her route, measuring each step, careful not to turn an ankle and take a fall. There are no emergency rooms out here. No designated trails. No warning signs. You find a route, or make one, and go. In places the slope feels so steep that if I were to jump—or better, sail away on a bike—I'd feel as though I could fly. For an instant a shaft of light dances off the Toklat River and I'm a kid again, studying Hangman Creek before I push off with Super Max the Wonder Dog.

"Howya doin', Sweetie?" I yell down to Melanie.

"Good."

She's humming, making her own music, like the river. I can't make it out; a John Denver song maybe, or Peter, Paul and Mary. Melanie's more of a folk gal while I'm a rock 'n' roll guy. Friends tease me that I can't go a day without talking about or singing the Beatles. Yeah, yeah, yeah, I tell them.

My pack digs into my back. I sit for a spell and watch Melanie descend, getting smaller in the immensity. At one point she stops and looks back, raises her arm and waves, then makes a sign with her fingers: You okay? She's fluent in American Sign Language. I signal back: I'm okay. She smiles, turns and continues down, arms swinging, legs pumping. Stephen Mather once noted that this is a good way—not the only way, certainly—but one good way to make better citizens. Cool their fevered minds. Get them outdoors. Set them free in their national parks.

All around me is a harmony of motion and sound, the land and sky, river and clouds, songbirds and deep silence. I'm thrilled by what's here and what's not, the presence of absence: no phones or malls, no ten-minute parking, thirty-year mortgages, or ninety-nine-cent bargains. Nothing I see is for sale, yet it's all mine. All I have to do is leave it as I found it, for those who will follow.

How ironic. We spend thousands of hours tidying our houses and tending our lawns while in the wilderness everything is right where it belongs: no raptor is too high or flower too low, no river is out of place or mountain ill-designed, no stone is too angular or round. Nobody complains of leaves unraked, trees unpruned, grasses uncut. Everything is in order, and not always convenient. I like that.

Nobody ever discovered himself through convenience.

Melanie recedes into the distance. She's almost to the river, where she'll wait for me so we can cross together, our arms interlocked and pants rolled to our thighs, our boots tied together and hanging off our backpacks as we brace against the strong current. The cold, silt-laden water will roil up to our knees, pounding us as we work our way across, one step at a time, one channel at a time.

"Are we almost there?" she'll ask, her teeth clenched against the cold.

"Where?"

"The other side."

"No."

"I think we are."

"Okay, we're almost there."

"I can't feel my feet."

—◆—

HIGH SCHOOL, senior year. John and Bobby Kennedy gone. Martin Luther King Jr. gone. Vietnam bombed and burning. Richard Nixon lying. Thousands of sleepless mothers crying in the middle of the night, angry and scared, one of them mine.

"I hate this war," Mom told me. "When they come for you, I'm taking you to Canada."

Maple leaf flag, great national anthem, hockey crazy. Pizza with bacon on it. Gordon Lightfoot and his twelve-string guitar. Joni Mitchell and her long hair. Neil Young and *his* long hair. *I could live in Canada*, I thought.

Mom already had two sons in 'Nam: Mick, an army first lieutenant in the napalmed jungle, his M-16 at his side day and night. And Bill, a navy flight navigator based in Japan, logging missions over North Vietnam, his plane designed to detect communist SAMs—surface to air missiles. His objective: get the commies to shoot at him, dodge the missile, plot its firing site, and call it into the B-52s so they could bomb it to hell.

So began Mom's disillusionment. And mine.

Where to find escape?

IN MUSIC. The Beatles defined my youth. I loved their free spirits and daring style, their catchy melodies and clever, sometimes nonsensical lyrics, their foreignness and wild creativity, how John and Paul competed with each other but also complemented each other. Song after ingenious song born from collaboration and bold experimentation. A string octet on "Eleanor Rigby." A French horn on "For No One." A sitar—George's idea—on "Norwegian Wood." Separate call-and-answer voices, one belonging to a runaway girl, the other to her heartbroken parents, in "She's Leaving Home." A dozen chords in "Sexy Sadie" when most songs don't have half that many. Alternating measures of reflection and angst in "Michelle" and "A Day in the Life." A brooding overtone in "I Am the Walrus" while using not a single minor chord. An alter ego group, Sgt. Pepper's Lonely Hearts Club Band, filling an album and reminding me—reminding us all—that we get by with a little help from our friends.

When John sang the opening line of "Girl" on *Rubber Soul* and asked if anybody out there would listen to his story, his pain was my pain; it was everybody's pain.

In senior English we wrote essays on the Beatles, what they said and how they said it, the power of paradox, innuendo, and love, always love; the importance of critical thinking and reflective self-expression. Near the end of spring semester, with graduation nearly upon us, our teacher, Mrs. Jovanovich, said, "If only our political leaders were as open-minded and creative in solving world problems as these four young men are in making music, we'd save ourselves a lot of trouble."

Creative young men. Open-mindedness.

I would never forget that.

Could creativity and open-mindedness save the world? Not a world left in tatters and table scraps after a careless, oily, money-fevered feast, but a world rich in beauty, bounty, and diversity, where we learned to live more simply so others might simply live; where we found a deep connection to nature, and sang together as if it were a moral and ethical action, no longer beguiled by illusions of dominion. Was this achievable?

Five months earlier, during the Christmas holiday, 1968, Apollo 8 had whipped around the dark side of the moon and sent back photographs of Earthrise in space, something we'd never seen before: our little blue planet afloat in infinite blackness, white clouds like ribbons around the continents, as if we lived in a gift-wrapped place, the whole thing ascending over the sterile, gray, lifeless surface of our nearest heavenly neighbor. The photos spoke volumes: Look at our beautiful home. It's precious, priceless, the ultimate real estate deal, no interest, nothing down, a hustler's paradise. A scientist on the radio said NASA was created to win the space race against the Soviets and was doing just that. But also—and more important—NASA was created to preserve humanity, which was "too restless and destructive to survive as a one-planet species."

His warning: We'd better learn how to leave Earth now while it's still inhabitable because one day, given who we are, we'll make it otherwise. We'll use it up. We'll trash it.

Of course I turned a deaf ear. Why listen to NASA when I could listen to the Beatles? I was in high school, after all, a slave to my hormones, heartbroken that Foxy Felicity showed interest in every boy in Spokane except me. Her father had died from a heart attack. The terrible loss filled her eyes with tears that made her all the more beautiful. I imagined him down in his dark basement marching to cadence songs (left, right . . . left, right . . .) when he collapsed. Crazy guy. He smoked like a chimney, but nobody said it killed him. It was heresy back then to say cigarette smoking caused lung cancer and heart attacks. Better to say he marched into the afterlife, a good soldier to the end.

—◆—

AS ALWAYS, I retreated into my sanctuaries of music and secret wild places. Not that I wanted somebody to eradicate death, sadness, or pain. They were here to stay, I knew. What I wanted was somebody to explain them. Some kids might hear what they want to hear from a parent or teacher. They might find comfort in their faith and church: revelations of convenience that promised eternal life, angels in the clouds, dessert before dinner. For me it was music, the earthbound magic of lyrics and melody, timbre and tone, flower and stone, river and stream, inflection and syncopation, how folk music blended into rock 'n' roll that blended into the blues and back into folk.

I listened with my friend Kelly Bogan, who played Chopin etudes and Beethoven sonatas and showed me how it worked on the blacks and whites, the sharps and flats, minor thirds and major thirds, fourths and fifths, dominants and subdominants, sevenths and major sevenths, full octaves and ninths, a geography of music waiting to be explored, a place to improvise and create in a million clever ways. He explained how a major chord was a sunny day, a minor chord a cloudy day. How a seventh was Ray

Charles; a major seventh, Stevie Wonder. He introduced me to Rachmaninoff and Tchaikovsky, Schubert and Brahms, the great left-handed American bluesman, Art Tatum, and the ragtime king, Scott Joplin.

Like millions of other high school kids, Kelly and I faced the prospect of being lambs to the slaughter, drafted and killed in the next two years in Vietnam. If the bad guys had been Nazis marching across France and bombing London we'd have signed up at age fourteen, eager to fight like our fathers in 1942. But commies in the rice paddies of their own country? What had they done to us? What had they done to our allies, our friends? Were they the invaders, or were we?

Mom said the Pentagon generals were mighty stupid getting us into a land war in Asia and were too proud and pigheaded to get us out. They too, it seemed, were still in high school.

In the locker room, football kids a few years older than Kelly and me read *Leatherneck* and *Soldier of Fortune* and boasted about going to 'Nam to kick commie butt, and got their own butts kicked instead and came home in coffins. Once a month we students would gather in the courtyard of Ferris High School and hold hands as the principal lowered the flag and offered a prayer.

"Our Father who art in Heaven . . ."

\~\~\~

I REMEMBER it all, the geologic epoch called high school, voices in the hall, the mischief and laughter, the music and sports, the algebra exam I barely passed thanks to the quadratic equation that made no sense back then and makes none today. I can still see the one-page career questionnaire that landed on my desk in spring semester of my senior year, how it took my stare and turned it back on me. Three columns of thirty-three professions each, ninety-nine total.

All I had to do was mark the one I wanted, the title I would wear the rest of my life, once I became a grown-up, an adult, a real person. A suckcess.

How hard could it be?

"Choose carefully," the career counselor said. "Everything is there to make you a productive citizen." Doctor, lawyer, banker, accountant, teacher, secretary, salesman, policeman, fireman, minister, nurse, carpenter, armed services . . .

But wait. What about rock star? Could I be a Beatle? A minstrel, a hobo, a writer, a traveler, a tramp? Did Huckleberry Finn have to fill out one of these? Tom Sawyer? Mark Twain, Pete Seeger, John Steinbeck, John Lennon, John Muir? And what's this? In the lower right-hand corner at the bottom of column three, the last profession, number ninety-nine, was marked "other." Next to it a blank line invited a short description, a space to be filled in with—what? My imagination? An essay, a novella, a manifesto? Such temptation. What to say? Who was I to become—who were any of us to become?—on this journey where the beginning so profoundly shapes the end?

I hesitated.

What did it mean to be number ninety-nine, other? To stride into new ways of seeing and being? What did it mean to stand at the edge of the known world and be something you've never been?

———

WITH THE RIVER behind us, our legs numb with cold, we sit on rocks and massage each other's bare feet to get the blood running. It takes a while. Melanie's toes are kernels of ice. Mine too. Our hands, cold as they are, feel warm on each other's feet. The rain has stopped. A steady wind blows. We roll down our pants, pull on our socks and boots, and hike hob-footed to the park road, nearly a mile away. From there it's fifteen minutes into Toklat Work Camp, where Melanie, as the new West District supervisory naturalist in charge of Eielson Visitor Center, has a small A-frame cabin, our summer home, three hundred square feet of joy.

We make a taco dinner and join Brad and the maintenance gang at the new recreation center for a big night. Melanie and the naturalists have agreed to watch the new James Cameron film, *Terminator 2*, and pretend to enjoy it only if Brad and his gang will watch *Beauty and the Beast* and pretend to be equally charmed. Brad wants to know if he has to sing all the sappy songs. Melanie says he doesn't.

Still, Brad falls asleep. He tells Melanie the next day that if Disney wants to keep his attention they should use more motorcycles, machine guns, and tanks. And explosions. Lots of explosions.

It worked for television the previous year when Bush the Elder sent General Norman Schwarzkopf into Kuwait to kick out Saddam Hussein's Republican Guard. Hunkered inside our Healy house, hiding from the cold, we watched him do it on the steady news feed. The general could have run all the way into Baghdad, he said, moving his tanks through Iraqi sand at sixty miles per hour; he could have taken Saddam hostage, easy. Bush stopped him, though, against the protests of Dick Cheney, Donald Rumsfeld, and Paul Wolfowitz, the "Crazies," as Brent Scowcroft, Bush's national security advisor, called them. Twelve years later, with Bush the Younger in the White House, the Crazies would be in charge.

The beat goes on. In every war is an element of sport, and in every sport an element of war.

◆～◆

UNABLE TO SLEEP, I leave Melanie warm in bed in the A-frame and walk down to the Toklat River, always there, northbound and free, timeless yet timely, never early but never late. On the slope opposite, pale in the early morning light, twenty Dall sheep ewes and lambs move like white confetti on the green tundra. Tendrils of clouds race over them, carried by a strong wind. Even at this hour they are up grazing. The highest ewe, stationary on a rocky promontory, might be on lookout duty for wolves or bears, her manner more circumspect than the others. I cannot say. Can anyone?

Such mystery and grace, the elegant beauty of the unknown.

So focused am I on the Dall sheep, I fail to see a bull caribou coming straight at me, off my right shoulder. Sitting motionless on river rocks, I hear him before I see him. Turning my head slowly is all it takes. He stops, stone still. We stare. He's maybe thirty feet away, trying to decide if I warrant a quick getaway. And quick he is, for good reason.

An hour after birth, a caribou calf can follow its mother. In one day it can outrun a human. If still alive and in good condition after one month, it's considered safe from wolves. In its first two weeks it will double its birth weight and be ready to swim powerful rivers. This fellow near me is a barren-ground caribou, agile, sleek, almost regal in his posture compared to the larger, stockier woodland caribou found in the boreal forests of Canada. Biologists recognize fourteen major caribou herds in Alaska. The largest, the western arctic herd, oscillates between roughly 200,000 and 500,000 animals over thirty to forty years, though the herd can boom and bust on much faster timelines.

Why caribou herds fluctuate so dramatically nobody knows. There's no shortage of theories, ranging from food to predation to climate. The Denali herd is so small that some biologists don't even regard it as a herd, though it offers an important baseline, being the only herd in Alaska that's not hunted. In the 1920s and 1930s the park had around twenty thousand caribou. By the 1970s, the number had dropped to as few as one thousand. It began to increase by ten percent per year and had nearly tripled in size before a couple hard winters of heavy snowfall knocked it back.

All in all, it's not easy being a caribou. Predation, winter, and disease sharpen their edge and make them strong. They must forever move to find adequate food. Still, in summer I've seen them stand under the Toklat Bridge where strong winds relieve them of bothersome mosquitoes, bot flies, and other insects. That's probably where this guy came from.

When he walks, I can hear the castanet-like sounds of tendons rubbing over the bones in his feet. Suddenly he runs right past me, continuing north. And like a dream, he's gone. Silence.

No traffic. No heavy machinery up and moving. Only the river, clouds, rocks, and wind; the sky blushing with the approach of another day. Dall sheep on high. Caribou on the move. Wolves and bears out of sight but never out of mind.

Two ravens wing by, calling in conversation. How much do they know that I do not? If this isn't music, an ancient rhythm of some kind, I don't know what is. If this isn't number ninety-nine, "other," I don't know what is. If this isn't primal and purifying, a window into our deepest selves, the best thing we got going, then please show me what is.

# CHAPTER FIVE

# Alexander Supertramp

WINTER, forty below, darkness twenty hours a day. I could be in Brazil right now, or Bali. Thailand's nice this time of year, I've been told. Birds go south. Why not me? This is why: Alaska, deep silence, open space, feathers of hoarfrost, winter's mint blue shadows and ballets of northern lights, spokes of January pastels shooting through mountains carved against a brittle sky; a male willow ptarmigan motionless, watching me as I pretend not to watch him; Dall sheep off-white on white; tracks of lynx and snowshoe hares dancing to rhythms only they can hear, a thousand quiet dramas, a time of reckoning when the land goes dormant but doesn't die, when rivers run beneath great slabs of ice, when neighbors check in on each other, when bears sleep and wolves howl and I acknowledge their survival every time I pull my fingers into fists inside my gloves to keep them warm, every time I close a door behind me and confront Denali: cold, beautiful, authentic, unforgiving, just as it should be. If it were warm and easy to live here, it'd be Orlando.

Melanie and I own a small ranch-style house a short distance north of the park entrance, in the town of Healy, home to some two hundred snowmobiles (what Alaskans call "snowmachines"), three hundred all-terrain vehicles, four hundred dogs (many of them sled dogs) and seven hundred people, many of them employed at Usibelli Coal Mine, east of town. Our house sits on State of Alaska land that's leased to the Alaska Railroad that in turn is leased to Usibelli, or some-thing like that. So maybe we don't own our house. We attend high school basketball games and local hockey games and find the people friendly, conservative, and easygoing. A com-pany town, Healy has one of the highest per capita incomes in a state that's awash in money, where eighty to ninety percent of the state's operating revenue comes from oil, and there's no state income tax, and in many places no property tax. Add to that the Permanent Fund that pays every state resident a dividend check of $800 to $2,000 every year. Business lead-ers say Alaska has more coal than oil; it's the Saudi Arabia of coal. So relax, breathe deep. The future is bright.

I'm not so sure. Maybe because I studied science instead of business, and learned about glaciers, wolves, the car-bon cycle, and the Paleocene-Eocene Thermal Maximum and met professors who gifted me and burdened me with an ecological awareness. Maybe because I read Humboldt, Darwin, and Muir. Not that I plunged into the Amazon Basin or climbed equatorial volcanoes as Humboldt did, or had a keen intellect and a naturalist's eye like Darwin, or walked a thousand miles from northern Kentucky to Florida through the post–Civil War South, following Muir. I merely pulled a high number in the draft lottery, escaped Vietnam, and grieved when the Beatles disbanded. And grieved again when I buried my pet dog.

What to do? I sharpened my hitchhiking thumb and left Spokane looking for that most mysterious creature of all: myself.

It was the mid-1970s. I could have headed north at first, in search of the "last frontier," Jack London's land of "the masterful and incommunicable wisdom of eternity laugh-ing at the futility of life and the effort of life." A temptation, for sure, to laugh at life. But I was fencepost thin and had trouble staying warm, so I went south.

It didn't work.

SOMEWHERE between Butte and Idaho Falls my toes went numb. Hoarfrost covered my moustache. The January sky, drained of color, was a dead thing as I stood on I-15, the loneliest piece of interstate in America, and waited. The last guy to give me a ride, a Blackfoot Indian with a gold-tooth smile and a loaded Smith & Wesson, said as he dropped me off, "You should have a new name, white man. One that fits your journey. Coyote Freezes. That's you. You're Coyote Freezes."

That was me, Coyote Freezes, a failed hitchhiker, thinking about dying, or ready to write that I was ready to think about dying. For a young man determined to better the world, writing had more significance than dying right then. If only I could get a little farther south. If only a car would come by with a soft seat, a big heater, and lots of food. Writing was "a good way to starve," Dad had told me. "There's no money in it, no survival, unless you eat manuscripts."

I curled into myself, thinking: this is where they'll find me, on the snowy shoulder of the interstate, blue-lipped and brittle-boned, the little thermometer on my jacket at minus ten, a manuscript in my mouth.

I screamed from the pain. The windswept land, pounded flat by winter, made no reply. I worked my gloved hands in and out of fists. No water. No food. A Mercedes came and went. A Cutlass with Confederate license plates. An Audi going eighty. Faceless, graceless cars. Cold iron and tinted glass. Two eighteen-wheelers passed by with such brute force they seemed to suck the interstate off the ground, and me with it. Tectonic drive-bys. Each followed by long moments of silence, stillness, emptiness.

I made a pillow of my backpack, stacked my banjo and guitar for a windbreak, folded myself into my parka and found meager shelter in the growing darkness. How to explain the banjo? My pianist friend Kelly had digressed from Beethoven into bluegrass—shelving "Moonlight Sonata" for "Foggy Mountain Breakdown"—and taken me with him. Together we had bought five-string banjos, studied Earl Scruggs, put metal picks on our fingers, and delivered the Kentucky sound to Spokane. We practically drooled when we played. It made no sense. But neither did Kent State, Richard Nixon, the New York Mets, the Nuclear Arms Race, Tex Ritter, Big Macs, Patty Hearst, the Symbionese Liberation Army, or America mourning the death of its chief spook and spy, J. Edgar Hoover. Six years had passed since my high school graduation, and here I was a college graduate, educated but not smart, freezing to death in Idaho, burdened with a banjo, and looking for number ninety-nine: other.

Did I fall asleep? Into a stupor?

"Hey," a voice called, "you looking for a ride?"

Dazed, I turned. A Volkswagen hippie van had pulled over and now idled on the shoulder, facing south. A long-haired guy had his head out the door. The van sported a Sierra Club decal and a bumper sticker: "IMPEACH NIXON."

I got in.

Half an hour later I began to thaw out, sandwiched between two men and five women bound for the slick rock canyon country of southern Utah. "Cactus Ed Country," said their apparent leader, his name Beast, Feast, Priest . . . something like that. I still had ice in my ears. The van smelled of incense and insurrection. Neil Young sang on the tape deck. Issues of *Rolling Stone* lay about, dog-eared, coffee-stained. The heater blasted on full. The driver snapped gum with her big teeth. In military fatigues and wire-rim glasses, Beast looked part Che Guevara, part John Lennon. He asked about me. I told him I was a runaway writer from Spokane. "Read this," he said as he thrust into my hands a copy of *The Monkey Wrench Gang*, the comic eco-novel by Edward Abbey.

I'd heard of him. On the back of *The Monkey Wrench Gang*—or was it Abbey's memoir, *Desert Solitaire*?—novelist Larry McMurtry had said he was the Thoreau of the American West. No small mantle. I cracked it open as the miles rolled by and a million ideas rumbled through me, planted there by Abbey, his satire and savage wit, his flowers and thorns, his double helix of anger and joy, his unabashed love of a threatened American landscape. He made me laugh and think and question a thousand cherished beliefs. "Life is too tragic for sadness," he said. "Let us rejoice." He had Beast and the others—and soon me—throwing our empty beer cans out the van windows. Beer cans aren't ugly, Abbey said. They're beautiful. The highway is ugly. Beer cans improve it. A Coors here, a Rainier there. As for Samuel Johnson's observation, "It is always a writer's duty to make the world better," Abbey responded, "Well now, that should keep him busy for a while."

❧

"HEY SPOKANE," Beast asked me (I'd told him my name but he called me Spokane). "You say you're from Spokane, right?"

"Raised there; born in Idaho, in the Bitterroot Mountains."

My last time in Spokane, I'd walked to where Max and I flew off the sand cliffs a dozen years before. I carried a shovel and the little dog's lifeless body wrapped in his favorite blanket, and found everything as I'd hoped, filled with beauty and mystery. A fresh wind blew through the pines. A belted kingfisher flew the length of Hangman Creek. Mallards circled in an eddy behind the rock where Max and I had sunbathed. A great blue heron stood on shore, still as stone, fishing. I dug a hole and buried Max and sat alone. Time was water then, moving on. "It's the end of an era, my little friend," I said. "I'll never forget you. You were a great companion. You had some wolf in you, you know. Don't let anybody tell you otherwise. People say developers intend to put houses on this bluff, if you can believe that. Watch for survey stakes from up there in Dog Heaven. Pull them out, every one. We have to keep this place wild."

When I turned to walk away, the heron was gone.

———

"THE BITTERROOT MOUNTAINS," Beast mused as he handed me a flask of wine and I felt the blood returning to my cold limbs. He rolled a joint and asked, "What kind of mother names her son Kim?"

What kind of guy calls himself Beast? I said nothing, grateful as I was for the ride. The wine was sweet, the hippie women were sweet, even Neil Young sounded sweet as he sang about cinnamon girls and ten silver saxes and a bass with a bow. I was still half frozen and had to get my mouth working. The wine went down like water. The women were goddesses. Beast said something and I said something back and he laughed. They all laughed. What the hell? I laughed too. The joke was on me, Spokane Kim, Coyote Freezes.

The VW van crossed into Utah as I took my first drag on what looked like marijuana but was Moroccan hashish. The hippie woman next to me in blue jeans and a low-buttoned denim shirt whispered that she called herself the Butterfly of Love and she was a child of God and wanted to be my pillow. Never one to argue, I took another drag and flew through the rings of Saturn and handed the joint to the Butterfly and found that my hand wasn't my hand anymore, it belonged to somebody else. Were these guys at Woodstock? Neil Young sang about castles burning as I watched another guy—Beast called him Karma—pull out my guitar and play along while an angel-faced hippie woman bowed a violin and another woman beat on a conga.

Nobody touched the banjo.

"You a train nut?" Beast asked me as he smoked the joint down to his fingers.

"What?" My voice sounded a thousand miles away. I saw myself floating above the others as the original me lay below, glassy-eyed, one leg over my banjo, my tired head folded into the Butterfly. Her fingers in my hair.

"The Burlington Northern runs through Spokane," Beast said. "You like trains?"

"I love trains," I heard myself say. I loved everything just then.

"What about dams?"

"Dams?"

"You know, dams? Dams on rivers?"

"I don't like dams."

"Good. Cactus Ed doesn't like them either. Neither do we. That's why we're heading south. To take them out."

"Take them out?"

~~~

THE VAN ROLLED ON: Honeyville, Brigham City, Roy, Bountiful. Midnight waffles at Denny's. Peeing on rest stop pavement at 3 a.m. More Moroccan hashish and red wine, a case of Coors, a case of Rainier. Joni Mitchell sang "I could drink a case of you" and soul man Gregg Allman belted out "Southbound" followed by guitarist Dickey Betts ripping into "Ramblin' Man" and "Jessica." They took us over a mountain and back, fingers flying. The van flew too; it was a rocket, the fastest VW on the planet. Signs on the interstate asked motorists to be "Prudent and Polite." Beast bought six dozen eggs. In the middle of the night we stopped and threw them at a huge illuminated billboard: "WELCOME TO UTAH: LAND OF SALVATION. OPEN FOR BUSINESS." We laughed until we could hardly breathe, and breathed, it seemed, only to laugh.

"Let's cut it down," Beast said. "The billboard. We should cut the fucker down."

"With what?" asked the angel-faced violinist.

"Anything we can find."

We found nothing. No axe, no chainsaw, not even a butter knife. Maybe we could cut it down with a banjo string. Torch it with a Bic lighter. Chew it down with our teeth, beaver-style. Stoned and stupid, we stood in the darkness and did nothing. We didn't even pull up survey stakes.

Wheeling past the Wasatch Range, a crescent moon over the mountains, the stars watchful, I read *The Monkey Wrench Gang* with my head on the Butterfly's warm thigh. By the end of the book, with George Washington Hayduke about to dynamite Glen Canyon Dam, the Butterfly offered to be my girlfriend. I told her I had a girlfriend already, a Lebanese woman from Albuquerque studying French literature at the University of Utah, or a French woman studying Lebanese literature at the University of Albuquerque. I couldn't remember. Beast and the others dropped me off and wished me luck and drove away with the Butterfly leaning out the window and waving as only a woman could. It took me one night to discover that my French/Lebanese girlfriend wasn't my girlfriend anymore, and northern Utah in January was no warmer than southern Idaho. What to do? What any sensible person would do. I got a copy of *Desert Solitaire* and headed south to find Edward Abbey.

The first chapter said it all:

*I am here not only to evade for a while the clamor and filth and confusion of the cultural apparatus but also to confront, immediately and directly if it's possible, the bare bones of existence, the elemental and fundamental, the bedrock which sustains us. . . . I dream of a hard and brutal mysticism in which the naked self merges with a nonhuman world and yet somehow survives intact, individual, separate. Paradox and bedrock.*

Who was this guy?

He was Thoreau tunneling out of jail, not waiting for

Emerson's visit. He was Mark Twain in his own golden age of sarcasm, incendiary, insightful, the white suit traded for dusty jeans and a brown corduroy jacket. He was a man of rivers, not oceans or ponds, camped out amid agaves, cacti, and hoodoos, shooting televisions with a shotgun, chewing on the bones of his dogma, any dogma, yours and mine. "Is there a God?" he asked. "Who knows? Is there an angry unicorn on the dark side of the moon?"

ACROSS THE COLORADO PLATEAU he was everywhere and nowhere, this river rat, desert dweller, half rascal, half ghost, this Abbey, a storied man, a phantom, a dusty Huckleberry Finn with an attitude and a beard. In a canyon or up a mountain, he was out there somewhere, a vulture, a twister, kicking things up and writing in his journal and playing his flute naked atop a mountain where he worked as a fire lookout, or pretended to work while his wife or girlfriend or femme du jour awakened in perfect morning light. Everybody talked about him but nobody seemed to know him, not well anyway, except through his books. Which was enough.

And his aphorisms. On nature: "Concrete is heavy; iron is hard—but the grass will prevail." On music: "Music begins where words leave off. Music expresses the inexpressible. If there is a Kingdom of Heaven, it lies in music." On adventure: "May your trails be crooked, winding, dangerous, leading to the most amazing view. May your mountains rise into and above the clouds. May your rivers flow without end . . . where storms come and go as lightning clangs upon the high crags, where something strange and more beautiful and more full of wonder than your deepest dreams awaits you." On activism: "Sentiment without action is the ruin of the soul." And on writing: "The writer concerned more with technique than truth becomes a technician, not an artist."

Outside Moab I pitched my pup tent near the Colorado River and felt a pup myself, an apprentice to strange shapes and eternal processes. The stars told me their names and I told them mine as I spread out on great formations of sandstone and stared at the Milky Way above the black shapes of canyon walls. The sun rose each morning different but the same, cast in an ancient prism of light and rock.

In a Moab café I met the nine-fingered blues guitarist who said he knew Abbey. Meaning he knew a guy who knew a guy who knew another guy named Ken Somebody who inspired one of Abbey's fictional characters in *The Monkey Wrench Gang*. This Ken, who floated rivers with Abbey, described him as a fiercely loyal friend, a brilliant, defiant bastard who's more reserved in person than you might think.

Back in the 1950s, Abbey studied philosophy at the University of New Mexico and wrote his master's thesis on anarchism and the morality of violence. Hospitalized in Albuquerque after damaging his knee, he watched horrified as nurses injected old men with tubes and chemicals to keep them alive. He resolved to die right one day, not in a hospital but in the desert, amid the brutal beauty of wild nature. A Baptist minister visited and told him he'd better repent soon or he'd burn in Hell.

"Hell?" Abbey said. "How hot could it be?"

The minister tried to paint a picture. "Imagine bacon frying."

"Smells good," Abbey replied.

NINE FINGERS and I jammed down by the river that night, our hands warmed by a large fire. Other musicians came and went, sandal-footed women in long dresses and wool sweaters, whiskered vets in military fatigues and tattered coats, the shoulder stripes ripped off, faces half in firelight, half in shadow, eyes still lost in the jungles of Vietnam. How different time and space were then, worlds away from quarterly statements and annual reports.

We passed around guitars, a ukulele, a mandolin, a flask of wine, a roach. The guy next to me, from Brazil, had a pack half the size of mine and had been traveling for twice as long. Next to him was an Israeli whose pack was even smaller; he'd been away for a year or more. And across from him was another guy, his hair in thick ropey braids, his brown face a map of distance and time. He'd been away the longest—five years. He came from Australia and looked remotely Aborigine, as if he wrote song lines and studied ancient runes and knew every star in the sky. He had no pack, only a small burlap bag filled with books and smooth stones. His name was Zed. He played the guitar as if it were a drum, beating it gently as he strummed and sang with a voice made of salt and light. He finished a song I vaguely recognized. For a long moment nobody spoke. Finally I asked, "Is that a Paul McCartney song?"

"No, John Lennon."

"Lennon, you sure?"

"Oh yeah." He repeated the final line, "Fixing a hole in the ocean . . ."

Yes, "Glass Onion," from the *White Album*, the double album filled with songs the Beatles wrote while in India. But what's Lennon saying? "How can you have a hole in the ocean, and fix it?"

"You can't," Zed said. "Lennon writes in ellipses and metaphor."

I stared at him.

"The ocean he's talking about is the human ocean," Zed explained. "The hole is in each of us separately and in all of us as one, you see? We're driven by dissatisfaction; incapable of deep gratitude. No matter how much we have, we want more. Even in paradise. We dig and dig and keep trying

to reach some crazy-ass thing we never can and never will."
He took a drag and passed it along. "Pretty stupid, don't you
think? How easily we get addicted and forget who we used to
be. How we mistake vast amounts of money for real wealth.
You ever been to India? Seen all the poor people who smile
and the rich people who frown? It's one big fucking paradox. People were happy long before we invented our modern
notions of progress and prosperity."

I had to think about that. "Peasants in feudal Europe?
Black slaves in the South? I doubt they were happy, or felt
very prosperous."

"Or kids working fourteen hours a day in the slaughter-
houses of Upton Sinclair's Chicago." Nine Fingers added.

"All victims of modern progress, the money machine,"
Zed announced. "You have to go back thousands of years,
before religion got in the way of spirituality, before cities
and agriculture created hierarchies and human subjuga-
tion. Before pollution and overpopulation. You have to go
back to when people lived close to nature."

"And close to death."

"Which made them acutely alive."

"And dead at age thirty of an abscessed tooth."

"Or at any age of starvation."

"'I would rather be ashes than dust . . . I would rather be
a superb meteor, every atom of me in magnificent glow, than
a sleepy and permanent planet.' That's what Jack London
said."

"He died at forty, an alcoholic."

"He's really not dead, though, is he? Thousands of people
read his books every year. Same with Abbey and Thoreau."

All that night we talked philosophy and books, drank
cheap wine and shared songs, Nine Fingers and Zed the
Aborigine, and me. If in fact I was still me, and Zed was an
Aborigine. I didn't know who I was anymore.

SOMETIME LATER, after Zed disappeared and the hippie women disappeared and daylight brought everything into better focus, I showed Nine Fingers a photo of the Beatles, an end-of-summer image taken on John's estate thirty miles outside London, in a northern field of fireweed, the blossoms fading. It was the last picture made of the four men together. I kept a tattered copy in my guitar case, torn from an issue of Time dated August 22, 1969. George stands far to the left and looks at the others with poorly veiled contempt, hands jammed into his jeans. He and John wear dark broad-brimmed hats from what looks like a turn-of-the-century bank robber's wardrobe. Ringo wears a psychedelic tie, not around his collar but his bare neck. Only John, in wire-rim glasses, is without a long-tailed coat. Only Paul, who most wants to hold the band together, is without a beard and shoulder-length hair. There's nothing boyish about him anymore. He stands with his right hand tucked into his breast lapel as if he were an Edwardian duke posing for what he knows is the end of an era.

"Look at that," Nine Fingers said, pointing not at the Beatles but at the flowers surrounding them. "Fireweed. It looks like McKinley Park."

"Where?"

"Mount McKinley National Park, in Alaska."

"You've been to Alaska?"

"I was born there, in Fairbanks, two hundred miles from the Arctic Circle." He had the frostbitten toes to prove it, he said, from what he called "time in the mountains." Maybe he'd lost his finger there, too; I never asked. He added that he'd go back one day. "Once you've lived in Alaska, it ruins you. It ruins everything. Every other place that used to be vast and wild seems small and tame and crowded, like all these postage stamp parks and boutique wildernesses in

Utah and Montana and Colorado and the rest of the lower forty-eight. Pretty places; nice for photography and meeting girls, but surrounded by too many roads, too much agriculture, too many people. I'm telling you, man; it's dangerous. It's incredible. Alaska is what America was."

"A time machine?"

"Yeah. It'll kick your butt and steal your heart and shape your imagination like nothing else."

I could still remember that March day, six weeks after the Beatles first came to America, when the Great Alaska Earthquake displaced shorelines in Prince William Sound by twelve vertical feet, killed more than one hundred people in Alaska, sent a deadly tsunami across the Pacific Ocean (that killed people in Oregon and northern California), and shook our Spokane house so hard that rocking chairs rocked and glassware fell to the floor. I was twelve; I thought, *Why would anybody want to live in Alaska?*

"It's cold," Nine Fingers added as he packed up, preparing to go his way as I'd go mine. "Had Ed Abbey been a mountaintop fire lookout in Alaska, he would have had grizzlies on his porch and wolves in his dreams."

IN HEALY, many years later, Melanie and I watch the spring of 1992 come fitfully to subarctic Alaska. An early April thaw is followed by severe cold. Brad and his maintenance gang work hard to open the park road in time for summer tourists. Melanie greets her seasonal naturalists and trains them for another summer in the West District. By early June she's in the A-frame cabin at the Toklat Work Camp. It's a fine summer, a little cloudy and wet. Hundreds of thousands of visitors come and go, riding buses, taking photos, making memories, unaware, as we all are, of tragic events unfolding nearby. By the second week of September, the crimson tundra has faded to brown; aspens and birches dance in yellows and gold along Riley Creek, and moose hunters find a young man dead in an abandoned bus along the historic Stampede Trail, just north of the park, some twenty-five miles (as the raven flies) due west of Healy. Taped on the door of the bus is a note written in block letters:

*S.O.S. I NEED YOUR HELP. I AM INJURED, NEAR DEATH, AND TOO WEAK TO HIKE OUT OF HERE. I AM ALL ALONE, THIS IS NO JOKE. IN THE NAME OF GOD, PLEASE REMAIN TO SAVE ME. I AM OUT COLLECTING BERRIES CLOSE BY AND SHALL RETURN THIS EVENING. THANK YOU, CHRIS MCCANDLESS. AUGUST ?*

One of the hunters makes a successful radio call, and the next morning a police helicopter flies into the site and troopers remove the dead body, the note, a camera and film, and what appears to be the man's tersely written diary in the back of a field guide to edible plants.

At the time of the autopsy, the badly decomposed remains weigh only sixty-seven pounds. The victim carries no identification. The coroner finds no severe injuries or signs of foul play; the young man apparently died of starvation and/or poisoning, probably in the third week of August.

Alaskans are quick to say he was reckless, naive, inexperienced, a real dumb-ass.

My first response is: *Oh, no.*

My second: *That could have been me.*

My third: *What's an abandoned bus doing on the Stampede Trail?*

Everybody has an opinion. The story is high voltage and a living origami of sorts, unfolding one fold at a time, first in newspapers, then feature articles in magazines: Chip Brown writing in the *New Yorker*, Jon Krakauer in *Outside*, and Kris Capps in *Alaska*. While the *New Yorker* story will give Brown the greatest cachet among large publishers, he'll decline to capitalize off a book, perhaps seeing it as blood money, the wrong road to fame. Krakauer will jump at it, and write a bestseller, *Into the Wild*.

The young man, our victim, it seems, was out to reinvent himself. He'd given himself a new name, Alexander Super-tramp, and embarked on what he considered his "great Alaska odyssey."

He had abandoned his car and burned the last of his money, hoping to repudiate modern civilization and "kill the false being inside." Pulled by the beauty of wilderness and the allure of risk, perhaps even the mask of death, he intended to gather roots and berries, hunt game, and live close to the marrow of life. Never mind national parks with their rangers and regulations. National parks feed the soul, not the stomach; they're wonderlands and playgrounds, not hunting grounds or proving grounds. Not in the deepest sense, anyway.

A star cross-country runner in high school, razor sharp in academics, raised in affluent America by accomplished yet complicated parents, Alex (as he introduced himself) had graduated from Emory University in Atlanta, Georgia, given his life savings to charity, and headed west in his old reliable Datsun (that he'd reluctantly abandon in an arroyo after it was caked in mud by a flash flood). Everywhere he went, working itinerant jobs from South Dakota to Nevada, he was well liked and in some cases deeply loved. Friends tried to keep him, but the road kept calling, first west, then north. He wanted to live by his hands and wits, be the "Dominant Primordial Beast," use the sharp edge of the knife, taste the sweetness of a successful hunt. By all accounts later pieced together, Alex wanted to know himself as only raw self-reliance could teach.

"He was alone," James Joyce wrote in his first novel, *A Portrait of the Artist as a Young Man*, "unheeded, happy, and near to the wild heart of life."

With Alaska for a canvas, Alex, too, was an artist. And so he wrote to a friend before he departed Fairbanks in late April, "I walk into the wild." Nobody knew he was out there.

Except one man, a union electrician named Jim Gallien who'd picked him up hitchhiking on the George Parks Highway, south of Fairbanks, and dropped him off as far down the Stampede Road as he could drive, about ten miles west of Healy. This Alex—he refused to give a full name—had a small caliber rifle, a ten-pound bag of rice, several novels, and a book on the edible plants of the area. He said he intended to "live off the land for a few months." Considering the task at hand and the country ahead, Jim sized him up as book smart yet naive, another dreamer who'd come to Alaska to test himself and could end up in big trouble. Jim tried to talk him out of it; Alex wouldn't listen. Jim's wife had packed him two sandwiches, which he insisted Alex take, along with a pair of oversized rubber boots. Wear extra socks, he told the kid. Stay dry and warm. Alex in turn gave Jim his comb and watch, saying, "I don't want to know what day it is or where I am. None of that matters."

In the end it mattered greatly.

HIS REAL NAME was Chris McCandless.

He's all I think about as I squeeze in one last hike in late September. Morning frost lingers on willows and dwarf birch when I leave the park road at the Teklanika Bridge and move north toward the Outer Range, tracing the river that now runs with less volume than it did in midsummer, swollen as it was then with meltwater from glaciers and snowfields in the Alaska Range. A dozen miles or so ahead, I should find where the Teklanika intersects the Stampede Trail, where in late April our tragic hero crossed his Rubicon, westbound, early in his grand adventure, eager to prove so much. The river then would have been much as it is now, braided into many channels, perhaps thigh deep at most. He crossed it, and a day later found the old bus—a rusted International Harvester from the 1940s, retrofitted with bunks and a stove; the floor littered with broken whiskey bottles and busted out windows—and took up residence, making it his rudimentary home.

After living there for nearly three months, eating roots, squirrels, ptarmigan, porcupine, and a young moose he butchered poorly, Chris headed back east, jubilant, his experiment a success. We know this from his journal entries. But the Teklanika River in late July was a raging beast compared to the docile stream he'd encountered in April. Had he tried to cross it in full flow, Chris (our Alex), already weak and undernourished, would have been swept downriver and into a canyon and probably killed. Had he carried a USGS topographical map, he would have seen that a cable car was strung over the river one mile to the north. Deliverance. He could have just as well followed the river south and hit the park road—walking the same route I do now, in the opposite direction—and saved himself. A simple park brochure would have told him this. But he had no topo map. He had no brochure. Ignorant of his options, he returned to the bus, his home. His trap.

WHO AM I to judge? I've taken risks, done foolish things, pushed myself beyond reason, hitchhiked through an Idaho winter, tempted the billboard business gods of Utah, ridden my bike off the sand cliffs of Hangman Creek, given my tender heart to Foxy Felicity. I even kissed the Butterfly of Love. Or did she kiss me?

John Muir stranded himself on a rock face on Mount Ritter, in the Sierra Nevada, and got down only after a good bruising and perhaps a strong prayer. Later, he tied himself high in a giant Douglas fir, "like a bobolink on a reed," he said, to feel a violent windstorm, the full glory of wild nature.

Edward Abbey found himself alone on a sandstone precipice once, with no easy escape, nothing but a long fall and hard rocks below. He'd put himself in peril, and only by staying cool did he get himself out. Later, Abbey joined a search party that found a tourist dead of heatstroke on Grandview Point, in the Canyonlands, a place so unpeopled and remote he called it "land's end, the shore of the world." The poor man, dehydrated and delirious, must have gotten lost. Giving up, he sat down to die. "Looking out on this panorama of light, space, rock and silence," Abbey wrote in *Desert Solitaire*, "I am inclined to congratulate the dead man on his choice of jumping off place; he had good taste. He had good luck—I envy him the manner of his going; to die alone, on a rock under the sun at the brink of the unknown, like a wolf, like a great bird, seems to me to be very good fortune indeed. To die in the open, under the sky, far from the insolent interference of leech and priest, before this desert vastness opening like a window onto eternity—that surely was an overwhelming stroke of rare good luck."

Was it?

I'M THINKING ABOUT THIS—only about this—as I hike north along the Teklanika River. Meaning I'm thinking too much, living only in my head, so in my head that I'm unaware of the country around me, what it has to say. The river makes an easy course, and I follow, a blind man preoccupied by death, my pack made too heavy by photographic gear: lenses for wildlife, landscapes, macros; bricks of film, a tripod, extra batteries, blah, blah, blah.

The topography begins to pinch the river into a canyon. An alluvial terrace rises to my left, well above my head. A rudimentary trail climbs the embankment at a low angle. Making no noise, mindless of the faint tracks in front of me,

I angle up and crest the terrace. I raise my head and come face to face with a grizzly, *Ursus arctos.*

"Whoa!" I stumble back and catch my right ankle between two large rocks and fall. I'm hanging upside down, my back to the ground, pinned by my stuff. My heart jackhammers. My leg hurts.

He appears. The Bear. Standing at the edge of the terrace, he looks down. I'm his for the taking. I have no pepper spray, rifle, or ax. My left hand finds a rock of perfect shape and size. "Take one step toward me," I say, "and I'll bean you. I swear." The bear appears suitably well fed, ready to den up for the winter. He continues his assessment, his beady eyes sizing me up; his wet, sensitive nose taking me in. His ears small yet alert. If I have to be killed by a bear, this one's a beauty. "Hey," I yell as I pull my arms free of my pack straps and sit up as best I can, my leg throbbing, "back off, NOW."

THAT EVENING I arrive back at park headquarters with a twisted ankle and wounded pride. It's snowing.

Melanie hugs me. "Kimmy, are you okay? What happened?"

All I can think is: *Why him and not me? Why Chris and not me?*

Rumor has it that sometime in August, as Chris McCandless was dying of starvation and/or poisoning (slowly paralyzed from ingesting the seeds of wild potato), his mother, Billie, some four thousand miles away in Virginia, sat up in bed and heard her son call for help. He'd been out of contact for two years, and his family worried about him every day. When his sister, Carine, heard of his death, she curled into a fetal position and wailed with grief for five straight hours. His father, Walt, a brilliant scientist who wanted so much for his son, maybe too much, would wonder aloud with Jon

Krakauer, "How is it that a kid with so much compassion could cause his parents so much pain?"

In the last book he read, Boris Pasternak's *Doctor Zhivago*, Chris underlined this passage:

> *Oh, how one wishes sometimes to escape from the meaningless dullness of human eloquence, from all those sublime phrases, to take refuge in nature, apparently so inarticulate, or in the wordlessness of long grinding labor, of sound sleep, of true music, or of a human understanding rendered speechless by emotion.*

He circled and starred "refuge in nature." Farther along, he marked, "And so it turned out that only a life similar to the life of those around us, merging with it without a ripple, is genuine life, and that an unshared happiness is not happiness. . . . And this was most vexing of all."

Here Chris had written, "HAPPINESS ONLY REAL WHEN SHARED."

THAT NIGHT in Healy, in the shadows of train whistles softened by the first snows of winter, I hold Melanie and fall into a deep sleep.

# CHAPTER SIX

# Kantishna Gold and Usibelli Coal

HALLOWEEN IN HEALY. Melanie and I are ready with a bowl of mini Snickers bars and dozens of small packets of M&M's, plus apple and orange slices and a few grapes. It's Melanie's idea to give the kids some healthy choices. I suggest brussels sprouts and broccoli. Melanie shakes her head.

"Tofu?"

She rolls her eyes.

"Sushi?"

Our little house has no arctic entryway and no wood-burning stove. Every time we open the front door, warm air spills out and cold air floods in. The boiler runs all the time and burns through four to five gallons of heating oil every day when it's this cold. Night falls early. Soon big trucks and SUVs come rumbling down our driveway, their high beams on. Parents keep the engines running as the doors open and kids spill out amidst billowing clouds of steam. They run to our house, talking, laughing. Dressed head to toe in arctic gear—RefrigiWear, bunny boots, down parkas with wolf fur-lined hoods—they look nothing like pirates, vampires, and dragons.

"Who are you?" I ask one little guy in a black helmet. I already know the answer.

"I'm Darth Vader."

"You're Darth Vader? Where's your light saber?"

"I left it out in the truck with my mom."

They demolish the M&M's and leave the apple and orange slices, every one.

"See," I tell Melanie, "we should have offered them broccoli."

Into November and December, darkness descends and the temperatures drop. Small glaciers form on the insides of our windows, complete with bergschrunds and crevasses. It wouldn't be so bad, Melanie says, if we stopped breathing and filling the house with water vapor. It makes me think of Chris McCandless out in the old bus, alone, burrowed deep in his sleeping bag the moment he stopped breathing. Did he go peacefully, beyond fear? Too weak to panic?

Out on the George Parks Highway, the local gas station and foodmart does a brisk business selling chips and renting movies, and we contribute. And I wonder—I even worry, as a child might worry about monsters under the bed—if one day people will stop reading and only watch movies and sitcoms and football, and shuffle about their seam-sealed homes between the kitchen, bathroom, and sofa. Warrior fans in their bathrobes and soft slippers, beer in one hand, channel changer in the other. Maybe not. Maybe books will live forever. Halfway around the world a down-on-her-luck single mother has just written her first of seven fantasy novels about a young wizard that will soon create a whole new generation of readers.

As I write my own fantasy stories, late at night, and Melanie sleeps, and the darkness feeds my imagination, I hear the train roll through town, its whistle a comfort. It stops at the coal mine, loads up, and follows the Nenana River through the Alaska Range and on down toward Anchorage and beyond, all the way to Seward, the end of the line on the Kenai Peninsula. There the coal is loaded onto vessels bound for South America and South Korea.

Nobody questions this. It's the way it is and ought to be. It's progress: burning oil to deliver coal. It's jobs, happiness, prosperity, and warmth.

As Harper Lee wrote in *To Kill a Mockingbird*, "In the secret court of men's hearts, no amount of evidence could make them see otherwise."

~~~

FIVE MORNINGS a week Melanie gets up early and drives to work at the national park, fifteen miles to the south. Past Otto Lake, she enters the Nenana River Canyon as gusts blast her little Subaru and shake the windsock on Windy Bridge. Snow blows over the highway in wild, mesmerizing patterns she calls "the swirlies." She downshifts into third gear and four-wheel drive, and with both hands on the wheel charges through snowdrifts as if she were an eighteen-wheeler minus fourteen wheels and big mud flaps and a CB radio. When the temperature drops to minus twenty, the local schoolchildren have recess in the gym. When it drops to minus fifty, Melanie and other park employees work at home. The coal mine, gas station, and foodmart stay open.

"Capitalism runs regardless of nature," a businessman once told me.

Does it?

It's a complicated matter to question one's own society, government, and, most compelling of all, the long and rocky road we affectionately call civilization. And it's a privilege. It wasn't the Persians or Spartans who condemned Socrates to death. It was his own people, the citizens of Athens, the birthplace of democracy. Here old man, they told him. Drink this. You're asking too many questions. You're challenging too many ideals. You're "corrupting the youth of Athens." He drank and he died.

And what of Rosa Parks, thrown in jail for the simple act of sitting down, for refusing to give up her seat on a Montgomery bus? And Rachel Carson, called before a Senate committee for writing a seditious book that challenged the pesticide industry? And Margaret Sanger, jailed in Brooklyn for writing a pamphlet—later a book—on family planning and birth control? Why make trouble? And don't forget Galileo, Martin Luther, and George Washington who had the gall to fight the British in an ungentlemanly manner, crossing rivers under darkness, sneaking in, sneaking out.

*Stand up and fight*, the British said. *Stand up and get shot.*

Washington had other plans. He let the British stand up, wear red, march in a straight line, and get shot.

And of course there was that other troublemaker from two thousand years ago, long-haired, poorly dressed, out cleansing lepers, making people see things anew.

It was on All Saints' Eve, Halloween night, when the troublesome monk Martin Luther posted his ninety-five grievances against the Catholic Church and kicked off the Great Schism, the Protestant Reformation. It nearly got him killed.

＊＊＊

PRIOR TO MOVING to Healy, Melanie and I lived in Anchorage and enjoyed the university classes, restaurants, and movies, the evening sun that danced off sterile malls and big box stores and most distinctive of all, the stately glass-fronted oil buildings like you'd find in any charming petropolis. Houston, Riyadh, Dubai. We loved the elegant ski trails in Kincaid and Russian Jack parks, the way winter played on stands of birch. We met hundreds of gracious people, made new friends, and reconnected with old friends, including Bruce Talbot and Jill Johnson from my first summer in Denali. A graduate of Cornell, Bruce had found a good career as a recreational planner with the State of Alaska. Jill had prospered too, moving into medicine as a physician assistant.

We had survived Rambo and Ronbo, eight years of Ronald Reagan, who as governor of California once quipped, "If you've seen one redwood, you've seen them all." James Watt had gone back to wherever he came from, and Edward Abbey, like John Lennon, had died too young. Knowing the end was near, Cactus Ed arranged his own kidnapping from a Tucson hospital after doctors said they could do nothing more. Friends and family brought him home and made him comfortable on a foldout bed in his small writing cabin behind his house.

Having rhapsodized about the lost tourist at Grandview Point, years before, in Utah's Canyonlands, Abbey conjectured that the man might have stumbled through the heat and come to rest beneath a lone juniper, and there in the meager shade, he "died in his sleep, dreaming of the edge of things, of flight into space, of soaring."

Now it was Ed's time.

He went quietly, without complaint, friends said.

They loaded his body into the truck, drove out into the desert and got stuck. This always happened when they went camping with Ed: they got the damn truck stuck, axle deep in the sand. Only this time Ed wasn't going to help them dig out. Lazy buzzard. It took a couple days to find the right site and bury him deep, covered with what one friend said was "a ton of desert soil, piling rocks on top."

"He died well," said another. No overpriced coffin or sermons. Just a funky pine box and a small band of friends who buried him in such a way that he could join the great cycle of things. Fulfilling his last wish, they inscribed on a black volcanic gravestone: "Edward Paul Abbey, 1927–1989. No Comment."

THE DESERT RAT had already said it all. In his final nonfiction book, *One Life at a Time, Please,* written when he knew he was dying, he made more than a comment. In an essay titled "A Writer's Credo" he issued a call to arms: "It is my belief that the writer, the freelance author, should be and must be a critic of the society in which he lives."

I sat in my crackerbox Anchorage apartment, his book in my hands, and wondered: *Is he talking to me?* I think he is. I *know* he is, damn it. This is the problem with writers, some anyway: Mark Twain, Henry David Thoreau, Joseph Heller, Harper Lee, Rachel Carson, and the old man himself, Socrates. They shake the tree; they rain apples on our heads. They make trouble. They provoke. They reach out beyond their mortal lives and burden us with ideas.

What to do with Abbey's credo? I loved my country and its turbulent history, the American Revolution that gave us those daring sons of the Enlightenment, men fluent in Latin and Greek who pledged their lives, fortunes, and sacred honors—if caught by the British they could have been hanged—to give us a new nation built on greatness, on the idea that we will be *a nation of ideas.*

Compare our revolution with the ones in Russia and France where the revolutionaries quickly became more monstrous than the monarchies they deposed. We had no guillotines, firing squads, or labor camps. No Napoleon, Lenin, or Stalin, thank God. It took France eighty-five years to get a working democracy. Russia, with its tyranny and corruption, still isn't there. Six years after defeating the British at Yorktown, we created a constitution, and four years after that, the Bill of Rights. We separated church and state, and eventually abolished slavery, addressed civil rights, and welcomed millions of immigrants to help make their dreams come true. We gave women and blacks the vote, defeated fascism, liberated Western Europe, stopped Imperial Japan and saved South Korea, all at great cost. We invented hundreds of things that would have astounded Leonardo da Vinci. We created the American Red Cross, the American Civil Liberties Union, the Peace Corps, and Earth Day. We invented national parks, wildlife refuges, and the idea of public lands as a good thing, beneficial to all. We passed the Freedom of Information Act, Civil Rights Act, Wilderness

Act, Clean Air Act, Clean Water Act, and the Endangered Species Act. Not a bad resume, one to be proud of. Maybe that was the problem. Maybe pride blinded us.

"It is easy enough, and always profitable," Abbey continued, "to rail away at national enemies beyond the sea, at foreign powers beyond our borders and at those within our borders who question the prevailing order. Easy. And it pays. . . . The moral duty of the free writer is to begin his work at home: to be a critic of his own community, his own country, his own government, his own culture. The more freedom the writer possesses the greater the moral obligation to play the role of critic."

HERE was this Abbey, vexing me again. Couldn't I make a little money first, then become a critic?

One day a publisher called and offered me a book assignment: Twenty thousand words in six months for twenty thousand dollars. A fortune. The subject: Arctic Alaska.

"Arctic Alaska?" I said. "Wow."

"Yes, Kim. Let me tell you, this is a great opportunity."

"I've never been to Arctic Alaska."

"Not a problem. We'll fly you up to Prudhoe Bay and then fly you around by industry helicopter so you can meet everybody and see everything."

"Industry helicopter?"

"The oil industry. They're bankrolling this book. But that doesn't mean it's going to be written from their point of view."

"What does it mean?"

"It means you get to write what you want to write. About the land, the people, the wildlife, ocean, history, weather, climate, everything, the pipeline and exploration, how it all fits. We want a complete investigation into the region and why it's so special, why it's such a great place to live and work. And we want you to write it. We like your style."

Twenty thousand dollars. All I heard was twenty thousand dollars.

And they liked my style. I didn't even know I had a style. Madonna had style. Bruce Willis and Mister Rogers had style. But me? Since when did I have style?

Melanie came home that night and I told her about the offer. "The publisher says the book will be a straightforward piece of journalism, an investigation of sorts, but also a celebration of everything that makes Arctic Alaska so special."

She listened. I'd never seen her so quiet. We ate cheap pasta and drank Zinfandel from a box and stared at our feet. I talked more about the book, the money, the time I'd spend in a helicopter. She looked sullen. Outside, traffic pounded the Anchorage streets. A dog barked. A siren screamed.

"I miss Denali," I said softly.

"I know."

"I'd like to live there again, one day."

"So would I."

"I haven't played my guitar in years."

"I know, it's sad."

The next day the publisher called back and added that it would be a large coffee table book with many photographs, and I could be the chief photographer if I'd like, for another twenty thousand dollars or so. I'd keep the copyright to my photos and could market them through stock photo agencies. In six months I'd make more money than my fledgling freelance business had earned in the previous three years combined. I'd fly all over Arctic Alaska and meet people and shake hands and give out my business cards.

I didn't have business cards. No matter. I'd get some. I'd become a make-it-happen, wheeling, dealing American wheeler-dealer like a guy I'd recently met who, like me, thought Alaska was great.

"AIN'T ALASKA GREAT?"

Everybody smiled and nodded and I did too. It was the right thing to do as the president of an Alaska oil company told a story in his lavish home on the hillside above Anchorage, praising Alaska as a great place to live. The previous weekend he'd gone camping on the Copper River and tried a little catch-and-release salmon fishing with his twelve-year-old son.

"Look, Dad," his son said, holding up a sockeye, "number thirty. I've caught thirty fish and it's not even lunchtime yet."

"Good job, son."

A couple hours later, "Look, Dad, number fifty . . ." and later, "number eighty . . ." And so on into the evening until . . . "Dad, I did it. Number one hundred. I caught one hundred fish in one day."

"That's super, son. Ain't Alaska great? Where else can you catch and release one hundred wild salmon in one day? Not in Oklahoma, that's for sure."

Boy howdy. Good thing we've got someone to remind us how lucky we are in the last frontier, with everybody drinking expensive wine and having a great time. A fine host, this captain of American industry, so personable, sincere, and welcoming in the way he shook our hands and clasped our arms and repeated our names as if he were a politician. Or funeral director.

I walked out onto the large redwood deck. Below me spread Anchorage, the lights winking on as the June sun descended far to the northwest, its ocher rays dancing off hundreds of large homes and commercial buildings. I could see steady traffic on the Seward Highway: motorhomes and camper trucks bound for good fishing on the Kenai Peninsula. Planes landing on Merrill Field. The whole city vibrant, busy, alive.

*What am I doing here?*

"How are you?" asked Susan Ruddy, the Alaska state director of The Nature Conservancy, suddenly at my elbow.

"Fine," I lied.

I'd been invited to this soiree as a "corporate sponsor" to The Nature Conservancy (TNC). Not because I had the money, but because I donated hundreds of photographs that TNC used in its promotional literature. Susan sipped the same wine I gulped. I was having a better time by the minute. She told me about the oil company president, his family and career, his dedication to TNC's habitat protection programs. Was he the president of ARCO, British Petroleum, Conoco-Phillips, Tesoro, or Shell? I couldn't recall. Was the wine from California or France? Somebody said he got it in Africa during an oil deal, in a former French colony. What I did remember was the fish story, and trying to find the bathroom.

"Down the hall, third door on your left," the president's wife told me. "Or up the stairs, fifth door on the right." Or I could just pee off the deck, freestyle, the way people peed before we got modern. I cruised the hallway and found a bathroom, and on my way back sighted a bedroom built for a boy king. Plastic toys everywhere. Out a window I saw a boat, a Hummer, a motorhome, and four ATVs parked in the backyard.

As the party ended, I departed in line with the other guests, everybody gushing their appreciation and admiration, shaking hands with the host and hostess, one hand in the palm, the other on the elbow. Some guests getting hugs and kisses.

"Nice house," I said. "Very clean."

- ~ -

MELANIE AND I lived in a little one-bedroom basement apartment for four hundred dollars a month. We drove an old Subaru, ate tacos three nights a week, bought things used, counted every dollar and saved what we could. Rent was cheap because the price of oil had fallen below ten dollars a barrel. For a while a single Copper River sockeye salmon was worth more than a barrel of North Slope crude, and Alaskans were not happy about it. They drove big diesel trucks and talked about "surviving the tough times," how business and industry weren't growing and that wasn't American. Recession was the new depression, security the new freedom. In churches and corporate offices the liturgy was the same: We shall rebound and grow our economy and make a better Alaska for our children and their children's children. This was the growth mantra, as if Alaska wasn't good enough, big enough, or bountiful enough to begin with.

Alaska's most powerful politician, Senator Ted Stevens, spoke with conviction about a bright economic future despite all the new national parks foisted upon us by "extreme environmentalists." Not once did I hear him say anything about "extreme capitalists," "extreme businessmen," or "extreme developers."

～～

ON A HOT DAY in June 1988, the last summer of Reagan's presidency, NASA scientist James Hansen sat before a Senate committee in Washington, DC. Wiping the sweat from his brow, he testified about rising temperatures, saying, "There is only a one percent chance of an accidental warming of this magnitude. . . . The greenhouse effect has been detected and it is changing our climate now." We the people of the United States, who comprise five percent of the planet's human population, burn twenty-five percent of the world's energy. As a result, we burden the atmosphere with $CO^2$, a greenhouse gas that captures heat from the sun and holds it for a long time. The science is irrefutable, Hansen said.

The genie was out of the bottle.

One year later, the year Ed Abbey died, Bill McKibben, a twenty-nine-year-old former staff writer at the *New Yorker*, authored *The End of Nature*, the first popular book to sound an alarm on global warming. Printed in seventeen languages on six continents, it was an instant bestseller. He began with two observations. First, we tell time badly. We think the earth changes slowly over thousands of years, which it does. But every so often it changes quickly and violently, and is doing so now because industrialized nations have been burning fossil fuels—first coal, then oil—at accelerating rates since the mid-1700s.

Second, our sense of scale is wrong. We think of ourselves as small and the world big, which was true for tens of thousands of years. But not anymore. We live in a new time now, the Hydrocarbon Age, wherein humanity is large and the earth small. We are not making the world a better place anymore; we are imperiling it.

For those in love with American exceptionalism, this was heresy.

Still, Hansen and McKibben got people talking. More than a few magazine and newspaper columnists posed this scenario: If an alien species invaded us, took our precious natural resources, and imperiled the stability of our planet, every high school kid in America would enlist to stop it. Instead, we give subsidies to Exxon.

In church we learn *what* to think; in school we learn *how* to think. One is indoctrination, the other education. One requires obedience, the other experimentation; one faith, the other skepticism. In church we find a young impressionable Sarah Palin; in science, a wise Rachel Carson. "So you're the little lady who started this whole thing," Abraham Lincoln said during the Civil War to Harriet Beecher Stowe, who dared to write *Uncle Tom's Cabin*, an unvarnished novel about slavery.

One hundred years later, at the beginning of another conflict, this one between industry and ecology, Senator

Abraham Ribicoff echoed Lincoln when he welcomed Rachel Carson and said, "Miss Carson, you are the lady who started all this." The lady who showed us the dark side of our cleverness. Dying of cancer, Carson wrote the book no other writer had the courage to write, *Silent Spring*, an eloquent deconstruction of the wonders of modern technology, in particular, pesticides that kill bugs and raise agricultural productivity but also kill other things, slowly, quietly, such as butterflies and bees, and us.

Did this make Carson un-American? An extreme environmentalist? And Edward Abbey? James Hansen? Bill McKibben? As the evidence for global warming mounted and the crisis deepened, the denials went from strident to absurd.

I shook my head.

IN TEARS one night Melanie said, "Don't write it, Kim." I looked at her, uncertain what to say. She was talking about the Arctic Alaska book. "We don't need the money. It's an oil book. They say it isn't, but it is."

I found myself defiant at first, then thawing, slowly, as if coming out of a trance. That's how the oil industry—any large industry—works. It seduces people; it buys them. Psychologists call it "industry capture," the buying of the human conscience. From the outside looking in, it's obvious. But once inside—once you're an employee or a contractor, bought and paid for and beyond the point of no return—it's different. It's the hand that feeds you. Everything is rationalized in the brilliant light of loyalty, duty, and little ampules of greed sold as need, in a comfort that affords you a nice home and a new car every three years. What could be wrong with that? A bonus here, a golf junket there. A hundred salmon caught and released in a single day. Ain't Alaska great?

Upton Sinclair once observed that if a man's salary depends upon him not understanding something, he's never going to understand it.

The publisher called with a final offer.

I said, No thank you. You'll need to find another writer.

Shortly before Melanie and I left Anchorage and moved to Denali, the publisher, a goodhearted man, sent me a copy of the finished book. It was so big it could have been a coffee table itself. All those warm images of a cold place. Among them: a striking photograph of caribou standing next to the oil pipeline in a modern northern tableau; a drilling facility in radiant winter light; waterfowl nesting near wellheads; a fox on a road; Arctic Alaska as one big compatibility story: oil and tundra, industry and wilderness.

———

DENALI SAVED US. It slowed us down and rearranged our chemistry with its infinite landscapes and cosmic stillness.

We arrived in the bitter cold of midwinter, our little Subaru stuffed with houseplants, the car heater on high, a U-Haul trailer following behind, filled with sofas, lamps, pots and pans, a big desk, and a newfangled thing to go on top of it: a desktop computer. Yessiree, I was a modern state-of-the-art living word-processor, a hard-driving, soft-waring, floppy-disking, take-a-risk storyteller and scribe. And my typewriter? Left behind to be pondered over by an archaeologist a thousand years from now.

When did life stop being so simple? When did I end up with more stuff than I could fit in my car? Melanie wondered the same thing. Our first challenge in Denali: get the house-plants from the heated Subaru into our little heated apartment (at park headquarters) without flash-freezing them. First, position the Subaru as close as possible to the apartment door. Second, run. It should only take half a minute or so. We ran. The plants froze. They died.

Note to self: don't move at forty below.

The next summer we bought our house in Healy and Melanie began her duties at Eielson Visitor Center, living at the Toklat Work Camp from June to September.

⌐ ⌐

A PORCUPINE lives under our Toklat A-frame cabin. Melanie thinks the names "Porky" and "Pork Chop" too rude. "Little Bear" comes to mind, as this guy might be an offspring of the porcupine that frightened me during my midnight bike ride a dozen years before and had me believing for a moment that he was a bear. What to call him? We commission a committee to compare and contrast and conclude conclusively, in the end, after great deliberation and more wine from a cardboard box, to call our new little friend "Bristles." He's not a friend, though. He's a loner who'd prefer we live elsewhere so he can go about his duties and chores.

In *Make Prayers to the Raven*, an ethnology of the Koyukon people of Interior Alaska, Richard Nelson describes porcupines as "great wanderers, despite their labored gait, as anyone knows who has followed their tracks winding almost aimlessly through the forest. They are given a special power to know the landscape, I was told, and this is why people should never set traps for them." They make excellent eating in the fall, and taste like pork, and are best killed by a swift club to the head. A woman did set a trap once, and paid dearly. The porcupine escaped, and the woman later became crippled and lost all function in one of her legs.

"For the Koyukon," Nelson says, "no animal is just that and nothing more. Even the least imposing creatures, those that seem insignificant from the lofty perspective of humanity, have dimensions of being that extend far beyond the realm and power of the senses."

Not many visitors come to Denali National Park to see the mighty porcupine. They want the marquee species: grizzly bears, wolves, barren-ground caribou, Dall sheep, and the largest member of the deer family, the Alaska moose, in roughly that order. Bus drivers call these species the "Big Five." A single grizzly that spends its summer near the park road, in full view, eating berries, chasing ground squirrels, scratching its back on road signs and knocking over orange plastic traffic cones, brings great joy and satisfaction, and countless photographs and memories, to thousands of people. No exact dollar amount can sum up the value of such a bear. It's priceless, timeless. That single bear is worth—what? Ten, fifty, perhaps one hundred times more money to the Alaska economy than the luckless bear shot by a trophy hunter. And if the Denali bear has cubs, it's priceless times two or three.

It falls to Melanie and me then to bestow upon our cabin-mate Bristles our sense of appreciation for the smaller animals of Denali. He appears most often at dusk, and regards us with irritation and intrigue. He often speaks to himself, his head down as he mumbles his way through his day. Other people have dogs and cats, a parrot or two. We have a porcupine. On late summer nights, while Melanie is out west closing down Eielson Visitor Center, I take my dinners outside and listen for him, this little philosopher made of quills and padded feet. We know from Nelson that the Koyukon find him a powerful animal, low to the ground but knowledgeable, a good meal. Chris McCandless ate at least three in his experiment with survival. I try to imagine; I've never been so hungry as to discover who I really am, the predator within. A local joke goes: How do you cook a porcupine? Get a big pot of water. Throw in a porcupine and a rock. Boil until the porcupine is soft. Throw away the porcupine and eat the rock.

❧

ONE DAY, I'm deep in thought about this and other important matters when Secretary of the Interior Bruce Babbitt arrives. From my little cabin I see half a dozen government trucks and fancy law enforcement vehicles—a real convoy—pull into the Toklat Work Camp. Rangers with radios and guns stand ready to protect President Clinton's newly appointed defender of our public lands as he gets out and stretches and looks around. I muster up great courage and walk down to say howdy. Given my ambassadorial history with James Watt, this should be easy.

Assistant Superintendent Linda Toms stops me and interrogates me—Is my hair too long? Are my socks red?—when Secretary Babbitt hears my name and walks over.

He's gracious, like James Watt, but all similarities end there. First, Babbitt has hair. Second, he has honest eyes that reflect the country around him. Third, he fits. The mountains and rivers seem to embrace him in how he moves about and engages people. A graduate of Harvard Law School, he's the former governor of Arizona, and now, as secretary of the interior, he's deeply engaged in an effort to reintroduce wolves into Yellowstone National Park. He knows of my writing, a little, and appears genuinely grateful to be in "this magnificent place." He's headed west to see what he can, in particular, to inspect the historic gold mining district of Kantishna, due north of Wonder Lake.

"Why do we romanticize the gold miner and not the coal miner?" I ask him. I've seen many ranger interpretive programs over the years rhapsodize about Joe and Fanny Quigley and many other "colorful" prospectors who in the early 1900s lived in Kantishna and loved it. Fanny as a real can-do gal, a skilled cook, keen on embroidery, tough and resourceful, with her sinewy arms and booming voice— "Foghorn Annie," they called her—out netting grayling, kind to strangers, foul-mouthed and wise in her own way, not about to let society dictate what she can and cannot do. And of course tall Joe, easygoing, tough as nails, a good dog musher, able to hike thirty miles a day while carrying a thirty-pound pack. A capable prospector too, taking seriously the practice of using cyanide and mercury to separate gold from quartz. Back then it was an "unscrupulous" trapper who poisoned a wild animal for its fur but a "resourceful" prospector who poisoned pristine land and water to get a soft yellow metal.

And to what purpose do we apply that soft yellow metal? To cure disease? Improve education? No. We make jewelry.

Why romanticize this?

Secretary Babbitt studies the mountains before he turns to me with an answer. "The gold miner of old," he says, "the lone prospector . . . fits into our idealized image of the rugged pioneer heroically working his way over the mountains."

The coal miner does not. Black-faced and often tunneling, the coal miner works his way underground, and is heroic in his own way. Or is he? Regardless, he's not a pioneer.

And America loves its pioneers.

The Denali road corridor is bookended by extraction industries: Kantishna gold to the west, Usibelli coal to the east, one historical, one contemporary, each lucrative in its own way, and destructive. The boundaries of the original 1917 Mount McKinley National Park were drawn specifically to exclude Kantishna. But with the park's enlargement in 1980, the historic mining district became an enclave within the enlarged park, and we today are left to survey the claims, buy them, and clean them up. Around the world, every gold ring comes at a cost of roughly twenty tons of toxic mine tailings, and all waters run to the sea. Today, most major seafood in every ocean contains mercury that's absorbed (as methylmercury) and concentrated via bioaccumulation through the food chain.

Yes, mercury occurs naturally. Nobody invented it. But we elevate it, sometimes to dangerous levels. We vaporize it and spread it around the world, all from a history of irresponsible prospecting, hard rock mining, and, worst of all, today's continued practice of burning coal in large power plants. Coal contains mercury that drifts skyward as it's burned; mercury that later rains into rivers and streams *everywhere.*

I wish it weren't so. I wish an abundant black rock was there for our taking, and once burned, turned into protein-rich food to feed the poor. I wish the new Healy Clean Coal Plant, constructed near the Nenana River, was all that it promised. Usibelli's low-mercury, low-nitrogen, low-chlorine, and low-sulfur coal makes it among the best to burn. Its high calcium content gives it excellent performance in equipment designed to clean exhaust emissions.

Still, the mercury is there.

According to the United Nations Environmental Programme (UNEP), mercury and its compounds are highly toxic and pose a "global environmental threat to humans and wildlife."

"All gold is fool's gold," wrote Edward Abbey. To which I add, All coal is dirty coal.

Of course this will rain criticism on my not-so-pretty head. Yes, I like my electric heat. Nearly half of the electricity generated in the United States comes from burning coal. Yes, I have gold in my mouth. I'll do my best not to choke on it. As a voice for change, as a critic of the system, I step into the mudhole called hypocrisy. How much easier it is to simply conform. "The opposite of courage is not cowardice," says Texan Jim Hightower, "it is conformity. Even a dead fish can go with the flow."

Consider the Quakers who opposed slavery while wearing shirts made of cotton picked by slaves. Did this invalidate their beliefs? Their activism? We could sit meekly in the corner and make no trouble at all; let pollution and tyranny run free. Witness those comfortable white novelists in the Old South who romanticized the happy slave and his kind owner. Or the boy so modest he was awarded the Most

Humble badge only to have it taken away the minute he put it on. So the question arises: Who am I—who are any of us—to be in this free society? A lion, or a lamb?

A lion, says Edward Abbey.

A lamb, says the bureaucrat, the artful dodger of controversy, positioning himself for the next promotion, looking good while doing nothing.

"Keep writing," Secretary Babbitt tells me as he departs. It's the same thing Bill Truesdale told me a dozen years earlier.

Socrates could have shut up. Rachel Carson and Ed Abbey could have stopped writing. John Lennon could have stopped singing. Charles Sheldon could have stayed home and sold grain, or gold, or anything else. Huck Finn, too.

But they did not.

And we today benefit from their courage.

"I believe that words count," Abbey wrote, "that writing matters, that poems, essays and novels—in the long run—make a difference. If they do not, then in the words of my exemplar Aleksandr Solzhenitsyn, the writer's work is of no more importance than the barking of village dogs at night. The hack writer, the temporizer, the toady and the sycophant, the journalistic courtier (and what is a courtier but a male courtesan?), all those in the word trade who simply go with the flow, who never oppose the rich and powerful, are no better in my view than Solzhenitsyn's village dogs. The dogs bark, the caravan moves on."

WHEN WE moved from Anchorage to Denali three years ago, and killed our houseplants, Melanie's boss was George Wagner, a former Rocky Mountain National Park wrangler who knew a little about interpretation but a lot about human nature, as if horse sense worked with people. Melanie loved his wisdom and easygoing manner. While other rangers read crime and mystery novels, George read Bernard DeVoto and Wallace Stegner. He lasted only a couple years before he retired, but in that time he fell in love with the incomparable Sandy Kogl, manager of the Denali Sled Dog Kennels, and joined her on many long backcountry mushing trips, cabin-hopping through winter's mountains. Melanie admitted to George one day that she too found the bureaucracy a tightening noose of micromanagement, small decisions and petty squabbles. "Don't work for anybody who doesn't inspire you," George told her.

OUR DECISION to leave comes easier when we receive job offers as shipboard naturalists in Antarctica: the big chest freezer at the bottom of the world, home to ninety percent of the world's ice. The following summer we'll be back in Gustavus, the little town next to Glacier Bay, where we met as rangers and were married. We'll build an energy-efficient home with a good arctic entryway, add a south-facing sunroom, and hope for passive solar heat and rambunctious kids at Halloween.

"I'm always leaving this place," I say as we watch Mount Healy recede in the rearview mirror that spring.

North to Fairbanks, then southeast to Tok and Haines Junction, the miles tick by. Flocks of snow buntings erupt off the shoulder of the highway as we pass. Our little gray Subaru—we call her "Grayling"—purrs along. Melanie has tears in her eyes.

"I won't miss the cold," I add.

"But you'll miss everything else."

"Such as?"

"Bristles."

"Okay, I'll miss Bristles. But what else?"

"Dall sheep and caribou."

And bears, wolves, mountains, rivers, the land itself, the

ocean of land, the way it rolls and crests and falls away and climbs again like it's stormy in one place and calm in another and has a poetry and energy all its own. And summer's flowers, and autumn's colors, and winter's pure white peace, the way the wolves howl and the sled dogs howl back and the wolves howl more as if they're telling stories from a thousand years ago.

Yes, it's the cold that defines Denali, what poet John Haines calls winter's shadow language "spoken by things that have gone by and will come again." I'll miss the tiny tracks of the ferocious shrew, a riot of moose hair on crystal sharp snow, the imprint of a raven's wing, a perfect ski trail cutting through a forest of spruce, the arctic ground squirrel deep in his burrow, asleep, his heart beating only once a minute; the mighty chickadees and redpolls toughing it out at fifty below.

"Most birds simply fly away," writes historian Bill Brown. "The living things that stay must go dormant, living on stored energy, or be so tough that they can run the merciless gauntlet of cold, wind, and dark hunger and still come out alive the next spring."

Tough and alive, that's Denali.

I'll miss the kids too, the little Darth Vaders bundled up like cabbages as they rifle through the M&M's and leave their light sabers out in the truck.

With their moms.

# ANOTHER TEN YEARS LATER:

# WONDER LAKE

# CHAPTER SEVEN

# One Degree North of Heaven

HELLO OLD FRIEND. It's been too long. The great mountain stands as I remember it, a mighty pyramid-shaped bastion born from the ages—magma, actually—deep in the earth's crust. Slowly it cooled, giving elements ample time to come together to form the compounds, minerals, and crystals necessary to make granite. As such, the entire mass hardened and uplifted, higher and higher for more than fifty million years, all while being sculpted by tectonics and later shaped by ice.

As our little shuttle bus rumbles west, I strain for a good view through the dusty windows and many bobbing heads, seated in the back like a delinquent schoolboy with my fellow Alaskans Larry Bright, Stan Carrick, and Richard Steele. We haven't even started hiking and already we're dirty.

"Are we there yet?" Richard asks me.

"Patience, Grasshopper."

BOUND FOR Wonder Lake, we're little over halfway there, with thirty-some miles to go; two or three more hours of riding and looking, including a rest stop at Eielson Visitor Center, all before we reach what is perhaps the most photographed lake in Alaska. From there we'll hike west into the Kantishna Hills and set up camp in the backcountry, due north of the giant mountain Richard calls "Big Mac," and "Mount BeKindly."

Because I'm something of a nature photographer, Richard calls me "Tonsil Adams," after Ansel Adams, who came to Alaska on a Guggenheim Fellowship in the summer of 1947. Accompanied by his fourteen-year-old son, Michael, Adams shot an iconic black and white of the mountain from above Wonder Lake, decades before Photoshop and digital photography. "I was stunned by the vision of Mount McKinley . . . ," Adams wrote, "Wonder Lake was pearlescent against the dark embracing arms of the shoreline. I made what I visualized as an inevitable image." An image famous today, taken at 1:30 in the morning, with a large-format, field-view camera, shot from a location now called Ansel Adams Point, not far from Reflection Pond.

Richard carries a copy of my 1992 book of essays and photos, *In Denali*, that he says is too pretty and "puuuurrrfect," to accurately represent the park: too many colorful, oversaturated, sharply focused images of flowers, rivers, and wild animals. Is he crazy? I tell Richard that many photos these days are doctored and embellished. Adams did some of his best work in the darkroom, dodging and burning.

Honestly, I have no idea what I'm talking about. I've never been in a dark room.

Richard shakes his head. Denali doesn't work on a postcard, he says; it doesn't fit in a photo book. It's beautiful and immense, for sure. It's also gritty and raw, predator and prey, eat or be eaten, die now or die later. He says he'll publish his own book someday, *Blurred Denali*, with every image shot at a slow shutter speed from a moving bus to capture the real visitor experience. Rub a little mud on each photo as well to give it the seen-through-a-dirty-window look, make it *puuuurrrfect* for the visitor-on-the-go, here today, gone tomorrow, the tourist on tour, courtesy of corporate America and the cult of money, everybody moving too fast to learn anything of any substance. If this is Tuesday it must be Denali. Tomorrow, Fairbanks. And the next day? Classic Richard, he sings a ditty that swings from Johnny Cash into Clint Eastwood: "Talkeetna glad to meet ya', Skagway whaddya' say . . . I've been everywhere, man, Ketchikan to Garbage Can, Prudhoe Bay, hey, hey, hey . . . Oil Town makes me frown . . . Rollin', rollin', rollin' . . . don't try to understand 'em, just rope, throw, and brand 'em . . . rawhide."

If he takes a photo while he's off the bus, Richard plans to shake the camera violently while snapping the shutter to get a point-of-view image as things might be seen by a caribou when taken down by wolves, or an arctic ground squirrel when snarfed by a grizzly. *Blurred Denali* will be the real deal, he says, a bestseller from Cantwell to Healy.

THREE HOURS LATER we stagger under heavy packs through ankle-twisting tussocks, northwest of Wonder Lake. The terrain we thought would be easy walking on dry tundra is not. Our boots are soaked; our legs, wobbly. We're not even making one mile an hour.

Such is Interior Alaska, a landscape built for wings, a seemingly endless maze of tussocks, ponds, sedge flats, lakes, thickets, and bogs and other expressions of wetlands. While no picnic for summer travel, it's ideal for nesting waterfowl. Here, where the mountains end, the land runs flat for hundreds of miles and boasts several national wildlife refuges. One, Yukon Delta NWR, at nineteen million acres, is nearly nine times larger than Yellowstone National Park.

In winter, when the ducks and geese have gone, the country "opens up," as Alaskans say. It freezes over and makes for inviting travel by dog team and snowmachine. We hike now at its southern margin, where the Alaska Range— a province of rocky verticality—abruptly surrenders to a horizontal domain of standing water. The best we can do is aim high for dry ground atop the Kantishna Hills.

By evening we're there, alone, with our tents pitched and socks drying and dinner hot and the great mountain bathed in pink pastels playing on the Wickersham Wall. Out comes the whiskey and jokes. The more we drink the funnier we become. By the time the bottle is empty, we're hilarious.

Two hours later, long after all direct light has left the mountain, it continues to glow, luminous, alive, a white diamond against the indigo sky. The stars make faint appearances and dance into the night. We four friends tell stories and laugh and turn silent, mindful perhaps of something greater than ourselves: the mountain, the rivers, the little flowers all about, blue harebells, arctic bell heather, whitish gentian that have their own cosmic quality and stories to tell.

I find myself thinking about the mighty purple mountain saxifrage that grows to 7,000 feet elevation in rocky outcroppings in the Alaska Range; the highest flowering species in Alaska is also the northernmost flower in the world, found against all odds on the north coast of Greenland. And let us not forget the heliotropic arctic poppy that like a little radar dish tracks the sun throughout the day, warming itself to attract pollinating insects. Or the seeds of a ten-thousand-year-old tundra lupine found frozen in permafrost that germinated within forty-eight hours of being planted. Is this not astounding? A miracle? The greatest show on earth isn't the circus, it's wild nature, where every participant, large and small, deserves our deepest regard. In a time when we never have enough time, and our gadgets hoodwink us into thinking we are many places at once, it's nice to fully inhabit one place at one moment, right here and now, off-grid and off-line, hyperconnected to the present. That's why it's called a "present." That's why we have national parks and open spaces.

Does an hour go by? Two? Do hours exist anymore?

Slowly my companions rise and trundle off to bed. Larry and Stan occupy one tent; Richard and I share another.

———

UP EARLY, I find Richard on the tundra, a wool hat on his disheveled head. He's sitting cross-legged, sock-footed and bootless, like a monk, facing Mount BeKindly. A small stove purrs nearby. Water boils in a metal pot.

"Tea?" he asks.

"Sure. Thanks."

The sun, having set in the northwest, will soon rise in the northeast, its first light anointing high peaks along the range. Richard and I talk about the big mountain, the summit fever that infects many men and women who climb it, men unlike ourselves. Richard doesn't take risks like he used to. He's a father now. Between him, Larry, and Stan, they have five daughters. I'm the only one who's childless. And still, I have no desire to climb. I honestly doubt it would kill me, just as the more than one hundred people who have died up there honestly doubted it would kill them.

Jonathan Waterman, who climbed Denali for ten years as a mountaineering ranger, wrote, "I would be lying if I claimed never to have considered my own death on Denali. On every climb, climbers wonder if this is the time they'll 'get the chop.'"

R. Bruce Duncan wrote of Denali, "Climbers such as I are powerless before it, unable to control where it will throw down avalanches, open crevasses, spread unseen cold or buckle us to our knees in high wind and blizzards. We are completely at its mercy."

Vern Tejas, who first successfully climbed Denali solo in winter, ascended the glaciers while pulling a long aluminum ladder that he straddled in the middle. If he fell into a hidden crevasse the ladder would theoretically land on both sides and suspend him safely above the chasm. He called the ladder "Bridget."

Climbing Denali by the most popular route, the West Buttress (pioneered by photographer/cartographer Bradford Washburn in 1951), amounts to a long walk made relatively heavenly or hellish by the weather. Get a good stretch of windless sunshine and you'll likely make the summit. Hit a storm and you could be pinned down for days, tent-bound at high elevation, sleeping fitfully, drinking thin soup and melting snow for water, all followed by a quick retreat back down to base camp at 7,200 feet on the Kahiltna Glacier. From there you'll fly out as you flew in, by ski plane to the town of Talkeetna, on the Susitna River.

In 1968, forty people attempted the prized summit; ten made it. Today, more than one thousand climbers try each year, many from foreign countries. Typically forty to sixty percent are successful, if you measure success by getting on top. Lowell Thomas Jr., a high-elevation bush pilot and former lieutenant governor of Alaska, and son of the famous radio personality, dropped off and picked up hundreds of Denali climbers over the years. "I never asked them if they made it to the top," he once told me. "I asked them if they had a good climb."

◄━━►

NATIONAL PARK SERVICE rescue rangers do what they can in severe emergencies, but they don't jeopardize themselves and don't attend to minor injuries and such. Many climbers have a "big game" attitude and want a trophy. Fine, the rangers say. We expect you to take care of yourselves; exercise a high degree of self-sufficiency. The mountain comes first, the climbers second. We keep it clean. If not, Denali could quickly end up like too many of the world's prized peaks, littered by all manner of abandoned gear and paraphernalia.

After one particularly deadly season, defined by a terrible weeklong storm (winds to 110 mph, 60 inches of snow at base camp), Melanie saw two climbing rangers in the park, near Eielson Visitor Center, keeping to themselves, drinking in the solace. She told me later they had grief-stricken eyes from seeing too much tragedy. A high percentage of the fatalities and required rescues belonged to Korean climbers. That November the National Park Service (NPS) sent a team of mountaineering rangers to South Korea to give programs on climbing safety and risk aversion. Since then, fatalities have been rare.

Surrounded by snow and high granite walls, with clouds racing overhead, and avalanches never far away, conditions on Denali can be freezing one moment and hot the next, baking you in a solar array with intense sunlight bouncing off everything. At 14,000 feet, the ultraviolet index is nearly three hundred percent higher than at sea level, given the thin atmosphere. You take one step upslope and gasp for air, another, and gasp, one step after another, one day after another. You get frostbite, sunburn, headaches, and perhaps pulmonary or cerebral edema—your lungs fill with fluid, or your brain swells—or none of the above. It's a crazy, vexing game. Should you get edema, even hints of it, the only sure cure is to get down—fast. If not, you die.

Waterman wrote that Denali

> . . . has caused me every conceivable exultation and anguish: I have shamelessly wept on its slopes, crapped my pants, fallen to my knees in prayer, and wished I had been anywhere but up on that cold mountain. But every time I got off, the small beauties returned: a flock of sandhill cranes in migratory formation below our plane at seventeen thousand feet, the very tip of the summit blushing in a midnight sunset, and the memory of friends laughing through cold and storm. The miseries all vanished. And now, more than any other mountain, Denali is the fulcrum upon which my life turns.

As his climbing days matured, Waterman turned to the dubious profession of writing. In his climbing memoir, *In the Shadow of Denali*, he lamented the end of the golden age of mountaineering on Denali, how "many modern climbers are 'bagging the summit'—as if it is another bird to be checked off the list—oblivious to the surrounding wilderness and the passage of our predecessors."

———

"THIS IS how we find ourselves," Richard says as we drink our tea and watch sunrise define the range. "Some guys climb tall mountains. Other guys sit on the tundra and look at tall mountains."

"Is that what we're doing now, finding ourselves?"

Richard shrugs.

I tell him I went high into the Alaska Range a few years back. My guide, a European-born guy named Krigi, called those mountains heaven, "a place of deep peace and creation, nearer to God than you'll ever be in any church." Six of us landed by ski plane in the Don Sheldon Amphitheater, east of Denali base camp, and skied up the northwest arm of the Ruth Glacier past a fin-backed ridge of rock, Rooster's Comb, and beyond to the base of Mount Huntington, a spectacular peak brought into chilling detail in David Roberts's first (and some say his best) book, *The Mountain of My Fear*.

Up the glacier we traversed, probing for crevasses, traveling in two teams of three, each team tied to a 165-foot-long climbing rope. We tied prussic lines to the rope so we could self-rescue if we plunged into a crevasse. Every so often Krigi would cut loose with long sweeping telemark turns, a master of his own snowy ballet. At 10,000 feet elevation we set up camp and cut blocks of hard-packed snow to create a kitchen and latrine. Day and night, avalanches thundered off the high walls with great billowing plumes of snow, our own Yosemite Valley being sculpted in front of us.

One night in our large cooking tent, Krigi spread out a map of the six-hundred-mile-long Alaska Range and explained in his melodic voice that it's not an extension of the Rocky Mountains and the Continental Divide. That distinction belongs to the ancient and deeply weathered Brooks Range, the northernmost mountain range in the world. The Alaska Range—higher and more youthful and tectonic—is a crescent-shaped realm riddled with faults, folds, earthquakes, rock-ribbed gorges, snowy peaks, and huge glaciers. Denali National Park embraces the highest mountains and spills north to encompass the wildlife-rich area between the Alaska Range and the Outer Range, the core of the park, from Riley Creek to Wonder Lake, that Krigi described enigmatically as "one degree north of heaven." Meaning what? I didn't know and still don't. One degree latitude?

He showed pictures of some of his epic climbs all over the world. In one, he appeared so small and alone atop a corniced ridge, backdropped only by sky, that we stared like awestruck children. Finally somebody asked, "Where'd you climb from there?"

"Oh," Krigi said, "I turned left at that cloud."

Back to the map, I traced my finger over the northwest and southwest corners of the park, near Lake Minchumina and the Cathedral Spires, that delineated Denali National Preserve, two distinct areas established in counterpoint to the park to provide for subsistence hunting and trapping.

Many of Alaska's national parks have attendant national preserves, established during the great lands act of 1980. The NPS says this designation "allows for uses not typical in national parks or national monuments in the continental United States. Within these preserves, sport hunting and trapping are permitted subject to state fish and game laws, seasons, and bag limits; and to federal laws and regulations. Subsistence hunting, fishing and gathering by rural Alaskans continues on many park lands here. These customary and traditional uses of wild renewable resources are for direct personal or family consumption." This helps to keep alive the most ancient and fundamental skills of procuring one's own food. I understand this. So does Richard. I caught my first fish at age eight and shot my first deer at age ten. I believed my Aunt Elda when she said my family was directly descended from Daniel Boone, until every other kid in grade school had the same story—or Davy Crockett, or Kit Carson. Everybody was descended from a famous pathfinder, trailblazer, Indian fighter. Such were the fables told to us by proud mothers, fathers, uncles, and aunts.

The National Park Service patrols these national preserves to make certain nobody—especially commercial trophy hunters—operates illegally inside the adjoining national park. I once flew hunting patrols in a Piper Super Cub with pilot Ray Bane, a former schoolteacher and NPS cultural resource specialist in arctic Alaska and superintendent of Katmai National Park. "We're dropping off our Phantom Ranger," Ray would say after buzzing a hunting camp and throttling back as he flew over a small rise to give the impression we were landing nearby. "Yessirree, the Phantom Ranger is the best ranger we got. He's everywhere and he's nowhere. We should give him a raise."

Ray made a name for himself by leaning hard on lodge owners and other in-park capitalists who rationalized everything to their own financial benefit, and for telling author Joe McGinniss that while summer is nice, "All this is a lie. A beautiful lie. Winter is the truth about Alaska."

Years later, Ray retired to Hawaii. He liked to windsurf.

—~—

"AND KRIGI?" Richard asks me.

"He disappeared in the Himalaya."

"Really?"

"He turned left at the cloud . . . I never knew his last name."

"Maybe he didn't have one."

"Maybe he didn't need one."

"Like Bono and Sting."

"More like Rumi." The Persian mystic from eight hundred years ago.

We share a small laugh, Richard and me, but inside I feel something break.

My heart.

— ⁓ —

YES, we used to laugh hard and take crazy risks and consider ourselves brilliant, charming, invincible, even handsome on some days, never mind what the women said; we'd show them. Huddled in a wet tent in Glacier Bay as new rangers in Alaska (two years before I arrived in Denali), Richard and I were Don Quixote and Sancho Panza, the dreamy knight and his peasant companion out tilting at windmills and wrestling bears and sharing passages from Charles Bukowski: "We are here to laugh at the odds and live our lives so well that death will tremble to take us."

That was before we'd lived in Alaska for twenty-five years, and had friends die; friends killed by bears and big seas, in small boats and planes, swallowed by bad weather. Friends who turned left at the cloud; who were just as funny and alive as we'd been back then and paid dearly for a single mistake, a wrong choice.

We thought a lot about bears back then, in Glacier Bay, counting coup on an animal that could kill and eat us, because counting coup on anything less wasn't counting coup; it was just counting. Richard would leave the tent at absurd times, in wind and cold rain, and say, "I won't be long," and be gone either too long or not long enough, I couldn't decide, and finally return with big news, his wool hat askew on his muddy head, pulled down to his sparkling eyes. His thick blond mustache filled with droplets of rain;

his face radiant, teeth shining in a scurrilous grin. The Mad Hatter. I'd tell him to shake off before entering the tent . . . too late, as he'd throw himself through the door and land inside, sopping wet.

"I saw a bear," he'd say excitedly.

"You did? Where?"

"Out there."

"Out there where?"

"Out there everywhere. They're everywhere out there. All over the damn place. I have to tell you."

"Tell me."

"They aren't like those Jellystone bears you see on TV, the ones that eat tourists and Twinkies and picnic baskets from the backseat of a Plymouth or a Ford, or garbage from the local dump. These guys are big coastal brownies that walk the shore and turn over rocks."

"Turn over rocks? Why turn over rocks?"

"To eat stuff."

"Alaska coastal brownies eat salmon."

"They eat other stuff, too."

"Stuff under rocks?"

"Small fish maybe, and barnacles."

"Barnacles? I don't think so."

"No, it's barnacles. They're eating barnacles."

"What kind of a bear eats a barnacle?"

"A hungry bear."

"I've been hungry before and I've never eaten a barnacle."

"You've never been a bear."

IN DENALI, we face another bear: the grizzly.

When found along the coast, *Ursus arctos* is a coastal brown bear, what some Alaskans call a "brownie." When found inland, in Denali, far from the ocean, the same species is called a "grizzly." Brownies are often larger due to a higher protein diet, mostly from salmon. In the heart of Denali National Park, grizzlies tend to have striking blond coats set off handsomely by dark ears and legs, and are called "Toklat grizzlies." These are the bears Richard, Larry, Stan, and I want to see, not too close, not too far. We've already seen a few from the bus, at a distance, on the journey to Wonder Lake. But we'd like to see more, maybe have one or two give us a thrill, walk through our camp and stay awhile, tell a story.

The Kantishna Hills is not ideal bear habitat, but it's the best we can do. The park is partitioned into eighty-seven backcountry units (the most popular forty or so abutting the road), with many accommodating a limited number of backpackers per night, all to avoid crowding, to give each camper a sense of being alone. Unable to get a unit in the park's more popular hiking areas—and prime bear habitat— my friends and I have settled here, in the hinterlands. Our food is packed in smooth-sided, black plastic bear-resistant canisters, designed, as the name implies, to thwart bears, despite their long teeth and claws. We clever humans can open them easily with a coin.

"Do bears carry nickels?" Richard asks.

"Nope."

"You sure?"

"Pretty sure."

❧

LARRY AND STAN take off hiking. Richard and I stay in camp to guard the tents and chocolate, and to eat Top Ramen while sitting on the tundra watching the clouds and mountains reshape each other. Sparrows chatter up the day. I see a noodle disappear into Richard's mouth. "If Top Ramen tastes like this," I say, "what do you suppose Bottom Ramen tastes like?"

"There's no such thing."

"Suppose there was."

"It'd taste bad."

"Yeah."

"Better than barnacles, though."

"What kind of bear eats barnacles?"

"What kind of man eats Top Ramen?"

"You think it's going to rain?"

"Eventually, yeah."

"Snow?"

"Eventually."

"I gotta' tell you something."

"Tell me."

"I could get used to this."

"Top Ramen?"

"No, the birds, the tundra, the rivers, mountains and glaciers, the beauty and wildness and immensity, the bears and wolves, the way everything jives with everything else and resets our clocks back to the way the world used to be. You ever been more alive than you are right now?"

"No. Well . . . maybe once, in Paris, with a French girl."

"I'm being serious."

"So am I."

"You ever think we got it all backwards?"

"Got what backwards?"

"Progress. Happiness. Fulfillment. Where they come from. Little things like that."

"You think too much."

"I was just thinking that."

"Answer me this. How long could a guy survive out here without all this plastic-wrapped processed food and fancy equipment?"

"You mean as a hunter-gatherer Koyukon dude from long ago?"

"Yep."

"Spears or rifles?"

"One spear."

"Sharp or dull?"

"Sharp spear, dull mind."

"Not long. Better to have a dull spear and a sharp mind. The first thing you'd do is sharpen your spear."

"Oh, yeah . . . right."

"Look at our lives," Richard says with that same grin, "our lives are hell." Which means we are two lucky guys out on the tundra. He enjoys saying the opposite of what he means. Better to be here than stuck in city traffic, rats in cubicles and cars, analyzing synergies, synergizing analogies, anesthetized by indoor living and push-button friendships. Such a price we pay in the pressure cooker we call the path to success, everybody trying to be somebody. Road rage does not make kind men of mankind. And what is mankind? Break the word down: *mank* and *ind.* It makes no sense. But these are trivial matters. What matters is food.

"Listen to this." I read the ingredients on a drink packet: "malic acid, tricalcium phosphate, maltodextrin, sodium citrate, monopotassium phosphate, calcium silicate, yellow five, monoglutanamalawhatever?"

"If you can't read it," Richard says, "don't drink it."

We drink it. It's hot. It's tasty.

THAT NIGHT we four talk and laugh and wear the friendship of each other like comfortable old clothes, with everything made better in the fresh cool air. We receive no visitors. Of the three hundred or so grizzly bears that live in the central core of Denali National Park, not one drops by. That's okay. Bear or no bear, it's not the bear itself but the possibility of seeing one that makes us see everything else in greater detail.

Richard, Larry, and I know each other from our ranger days in Glacier Bay. Stan and I grew up together in Spokane, rode our bicycles like Batman and Robin, and traded base-ball cards and Beatles trivia. It nurtured us well, that lovely, inland city that was something of a younger, less worldly sister to its older sibling, Seattle. Whereas Seattle had Jimi Hendrix and "Purple Haze," Spokane had Bing Crosby and "White Christmas." Did we care? No. We'd ride our bikes everywhere unafraid, partake in mischief but never crime, and come home happy and exhausted.

We loved those carefree days being Lewis and Clark to discover America all over again. Any place without rows of homes and commercial development was a new frontier for collecting butterflies and bugs. No vacant lot escaped us; each was rich with a million little things other people might find useless but we knew as treasures. He among us who discovered a kestrel feather or a grasshopper longer than his thumb was king for a day.

"Where've you been?" Mom would ask Max and me as evening fell and we arrived home famished, me on my Red Schwinn, Max on his tired paws.

"Just around," I'd say.

Mom would smile as if we reminded her of her own unbridled youth in North Dakota where kids played in barns and hay wagons and everything ran to the horizon and you could walk forever toward it and never get there and not really care, where nights were as quiet as the outer rim of the universe. Was it still that way? Must everything change?

━━◦━━

STAN TELLS ME that Spokane developers finally got their way and built a bunch of homes on the bluff, above Hang-man Creek, by terracing one above another in the soft sand. Insane. And it's not called Hangman Creek anymore. It's Latah Creek, a more appealing name to the chamber of commerce.

We reminisce about our high school buddy, Tim Carl-berg, soused on beer on New Year's Eve 1969 when a bunch of us gathered in Steve Dunlap's basement to listen to Casey Kasem's countdown of the top one hundred songs of the 1960s. We sang along and waited all night for the number one song. Tim was so excited to hear "Hey Jude" that the minute Paul McCartney's voice lit up the room, Tim jumped, hit his head on a rafter, knocked himself out, and didn't come to until the end of the song.

All during our senior year, Tim would play "Hey Jude" at full volume as he drove around the South Hill in his dad's pink Cadillac, elbow folded out the open window, the Cadillac careening down residential streets. On garbage day when bright new plastic cans lined the streets like Christmas ornaments, Tim would wait until after the garbage truck had made its run, then drive with two wheels on the sidewalk to hit one empty can after another, sending them bouncing across people's lawns and into the street. Some were so light they flew up and over the Caddie.

Then one day he hit Big Mama, a beast filled with rotten fruit that the garbage truck had missed. It dented the bumper and lifted ponderously over the hood to spill its entire guts onto the windshield, banana peels on the grill, soup cans striking the side-view mirrors. Slime everywhere. "Shit," Tim yelled. We laughed so hard our spleens hurt, and sang "Hey Jude" like maniacs. And still none of us could hit the high notes like Paul, lifting the coda into a stunning finale that climbed a full octave. We marveled at how a seven and a half minute song could seem too short; how the end should have imparted feelings of loss yet did the opposite. Back home, we'd flip "Hey Jude" over to the B side and listen to "Revolution," the guitars screaming the opening measures as John put gravel in his voice and said we all wanted to change the world.

Yes, but how? As author/musician Jonathan Gould would one day observe, "'Hey Jude' asks us to open our hearts. 'Revolution' asks us to free our minds."

It was a rich and terrifying time to be seventeen, defiant with war, music, and a pink Cadillac that slayed plastic garbage cans.

⌐∾⌐

"YOU GUYS are still in high school," Larry says to Stan and me.

"Everybody is still in high school."

"Some more than others."

"The Beatles sang about changing the world and ended up arguing with each other and living in mansions."

"Pete Seeger doesn't live in a mansion. He lives in a cabin above the Hudson River that he built himself with hand tools."

"Pete Seeger isn't a Beatle."

"A lot of people aren't Beatles."

"Enough with the Beatles."

"And now George Harrison is dead," I say softly, "from lung cancer. He was only fifty-eight."

"John Lennon died at forty."

"People don't die anymore, they pass away."

"And the World Trade Center Towers are down, and we're at war. Again."

Nobody responds.

We watch clouds spiral off Denali and layer themselves below, how everything around us appears as a refrain, a break from the crowded, modern world. A chance to get back.

And what is the purpose of the mighty mountain? To collect the tender snowflake.

And the purpose of the snowflake? To build a glacier.

And the purpose of the glacier? To carve the mountain and melt into a river that rounds the stone that sharpens the mind of the hand that holds it.

Mountains, like revolutions and freshly baked bread and the best music, rise up from the bottom.

All things must pass, said George. All things must fade away. Nothing lasts forever. Everything ends.

"John had his bitter wit," wrote Richard Lacayo in *Time* magazine. "Ringo Starr had his affability. Paul McCartney his winking charm. What Harrison possessed was something more unexpected in a rock star: the air of a man in search of mature understandings. He may have been the youngest Beatle, but from early on he struggled toward the melancholy wisdom of later life. . . . We listen to [All Things Must Pass] differently now, cherishing it as a warning against old complacencies and a promise that the darkness of this moment too shall pass."

George was the first Beatle to say "no more live concerts," no more madness, with thousands of screaming fans throwing jelly babies (similar to jelly beans) that bounced off their faces and guitars as they tried to sing (but couldn't hear themselves above the racket). How ironic, he noted, after all their hard work, to end up like "performing fleas." He took his bandmates to India to search for other states of mind, to slow down and listen. We're not human doings, after all; we're human *beings*.

After the breakup, George fronted the 1971 "Concert for Bangladesh" to pioneer rock philanthropy, setting the model for other celebrity musicians for decades. Most remarkable, George showed no animosity—and offered best wishes— when his former wife Pattie Boyd married his good friend Eric Clapton.

People said he excelled at forgiveness; he was at peace, unafraid to die. His wife Olivia said that when it came his time, and he let go, the entire room filled with light.

~~~

ALL THOSE YEARS AGO, sitting on that rock in the middle of Hangman Creek with Super Max the Wonder Dog, sunsplashed after flying off the sand cliffs above, I thought it was my dog that gave me my greatest joy. It was not, though he came close, being one cool mutt. I know now, among friends in Denali, embraced by wild country, that love and companionship bring me my greatest joy, while open space and music make anything seem possible.

A national park this big and wild helps me to acknowledge that in the midst of this little global experiment called civilization, we still have the wisdom to restrain ourselves, to preserve things as we inherited them, to leave the apple unpicked. We can make room for others, discover our highest ideals, give the black man his freedom, the woman her vote, the gay couple a license to marry. Of course, one could go to prison for holding such things dear. Many have. "It always seems impossible until it is done," wrote Nelson Mandela from his South Africa cell. Money subverts democracy until the big guy builds his glass palace and the little guy throws a rock.

Or sings a song.

You can't buy happiness. But you can beat a drum. You can buy a guitar.

Kentucky farmer, essayist, novelist, and poet Wendell Berry observes that there are no sacred and unsacred places, only sacred and desecrated places.

Has Hangman Creek been desecrated? I leave that for others to answer.

It isn't the boy with his bicycle and his beloved dog who turns the meadow into a mall. It isn't the boy who closes the frontier. It's who he becomes—who he *chooses* to become. We all grow up to taste the bitter fruits of change. Everything ends, I know. Even the Beatles. I'll get over it one day. Maybe.

But for now, for this simple, profound moment, sitting on the tundra with good friends, embraced by the landscape of Denali—by institutions, values, and laws designed to honor and protect it—I feel something wonderful swell inside, opening to the future. Something heavenly, sacred and free, with room to run to every horizon.

My imagination.

# CHAPTER EIGHT

# The Bear Is Nowhere
# and Everywhere

"RICHARD, you awake?"

He stirs.

"Richard . . . I think I just heard something . . . outside the tent."

More stirring. It's the middle of the night, black as ink. Frosty. Cold. Hard to believe in late August, only nine weeks after summer solstice. Winter's curtain coming down. Each day six minutes shorter than the one before. Earth wild on its axis.

"Richard, you awake?"

"No."

"I heard something. Did you hear something?"

"What?"

"That noise."

"What noise?"

"The noise outside the tent."

Maybe it's *inside* the tent. Maybe it's my eyelashes brushing against the sleeping bag pulled tight around my face, or the stubble of my bearded chin like sandpaper against the bag, filling my ears with the roar of all things possible and impossible. A bear, wolf, wolverine, or fox. Maybe it's Bristles, or Son of Bristles, though porcupines are forest animals, and my friends and I are camped now atop the treeless Kantishna Hills. Tundra country. Not good habitat for porcupines. Maybe it's a dinosaur, since dinosaur fossils were recently discovered in Denali National Park, and these days technophiles talk about bio- and geoengineering the entire planet, playing God on a whole new scale. Construct honeybees. Build butterflies. Fabricate frogs. De-extinct the big boys, they say. Jazz things up. So what if species go extinct? We'll bring them back. If not dinosaurs in Jurassic Park, then mammoths and mastodons in Pleistocene Park.

And the right and wrong of it all? In the absence of the sacred, species become toys.

*Pleistocene Park.* A Russian biologist has already acquired the land and now awaits advances in manipulating stem cells, recovering ancient DNA, and reconstructing lost genomes—plus a few permits here and there—to grow the megafauna and repopulate the Siberian steppe of twenty thousand years ago. Build a road. Provide tours. See Dick and Jane take in the saber-toothed cat. See the saber-toothed cat take in Dick and Jane.

Maybe it's my imagination, itself a wild creature.

"Richard?"

He stirs.

"One of us needs to get up and see what made the noise."

"Okay."

"I volunteer you."

"Okay."

A minute later he's back asleep, the bum; he volunteers for a dangerous job only to pass the burden to me. What kind of friend is that? I hear his breathing, the rhythm of his dreams. If only I could sleep like that; I sit up. It takes a while to pull myself from the warm cocoon of my bag and get dressed. The late August air cuts with unexpected cold. I zip open the tent, jam my feet into stiff boots, and stand. The night embraces me. Ten zillion stars glimmer overhead, spiraling into the heart of the Milky Way. A thin scythe of the moon rides the Alaska Range, over paper clouds and a peak too unfamiliar to name. Frost covers the tent, dwarf birch, and willow; the ankle-high branches scratch my rain pants as I walk about. Stop, I tell myself. Stop and listen. *What's out here?*

For a moment my ears are my dominant sense. Then slowly my eyes adjust and pick up details: folds in the land, the rise and fall of open topography, nearby hills, distant mountains; patterns of bearberry, lingonberry (low-bush cranberry), crowberry, Labrador tea, all distinguished members of a low-profile, high-latitude, richly textured community that makes a fitting counterpoint to the stars above.

Looking around, I flick on a headlamp and wince at the intrusive light that knifes the night. If anything is moving near or far, I can't see it. I don't hear it. Larry and Stan's tent appears as a small black dome against the starry horizon. I'm careful to *not* shine my light on it. I find no bare ground, no exposed mud where an animal might leave a track. No hummocks or tunnels from the diggings of arctic ground squirrels. No pieces of fur caught in the dwarf birch. West of here, the land drops into a draw filled with alder and tall willow, where I might find a moose, a mammoth, a mastodon, a bear.

No, those mammoth days are gone. Let's leave them in the past.

Furthermore, the Kantishna Hills are not excellent bear habitat. The grizzlies of Denali prefer mountainous foothills and alluvial terraces and sundry slope aspects and large river bars—from Sable Pass to Thorofare Pass, ideally— where a variety of terrain offers more food, specifically roots, berries, and arctic ground squirrels, the prime rib of Denali: hard-won protein for bears, wolves, foxes, and birds of prey.

---

IN HIS groundbreaking predator-prey study of 1939–1941, Adolph Murie found the remains of ground squirrels in one-fourth to one-third of all sampled wolf scat. In those same

years, he found ground squirrel remains in eighty-six percent of all sampled golden eagle pellets. "The staff of life of
the eagle in Mount McKinley National Park is the ground
squirrel," he noted.

> *Ground squirrels are widely distributed over the sheep hills inhabited
> by the eagles, and occur from the river bars to the ridge tops. They are
> plentiful on the slopes where [golden] eagles may often be seen hunting
> for them, sailing along a contour close to the ground. In passing over
> sharp ridges one wing sometimes almost scrapes the ground as the eagle
> pivots to skim over a new slope. Its sudden appearance over a ridge
> probably is quite a surprise to many a ground squirrel.*

Surprise also serves the red fox. It runs at great speed
undetected through thick vegetation and behind hummocks
to get into striking range. Then holding still, the fox waits
for the squirrel to reappear. Murie once observed a single
fox trotting back to his den with three ground squirrels in
his mouth, stacked head to tail like cordwood. Another time
he watched a fox pounce at a ground squirrel and miss. The
fox "put so much energy into his pounce that he rolled over.
As this fox continued on his way the squirrels in the neigh-
borhood sat on their hind legs and scolded him loudly, and
sparrows darted at him."

While the eagle and fox use speed and stealth, and the
fox digs a little, the grizzly digs a lot. Upon seeing a ground
squirrel disappear into its burrow, a hungry bear sets out to
excavate him. It might take a while, and prove futile—even
humorous—as the ground squirrel pops up from the other
end of his multi-tunneled world to watch the bear, rump in
the air, digging furiously at the other end. If the bear is a
mother with cubs, and the cubs are circumspect, they can
alert their mother to the squirrel's whereabouts. Quickly
she gives chase and begins digging anew, this time from the
other end, slowly closing off the squirrel's escape routes.

Murie found that only two to sixteen percent—a "small but probably important part of the [bear's] diet"—consists of ground squirrels. Still, a single bear might eat upward of two hundred ground squirrels each summer.

Bears also get protein by bringing down young or injured moose, and caribou, and by displacing wolves from recent kills. All of which makes for more drama than watching a bear with its head down eating berries. By late August, Denali's grizzlies exhibit a behavior biologists call "hyper-phagia"—excessive eating—to build up fat for winter. One study concluded that a single grizzly, fattening up for winter, eats upward of two hundred thousand berries in a single day. Assuming the bear is eating sixteen hours each day, that's two hundred some berries per minute.

These numbers struck me as ridiculous until I watched a grizzly work a berry patch. In one swift motion he used his paw to lift a small branch loaded with berries. He then raked it with his teeth and gums and tongue, deftly taking in all the berries, together with some leaves and small, pliable stems. It took maybe ten seconds, and was repeated so often and fast as to make me think the bear actually was at times eating at least two hundred berries per minute.

All summer and into fall, the bear powers down roots and berries rich in natural sugars that metabolize into fat. Add to that an occasional ground squirrel and an injured moose or caribou, half dead, still on its feet, easy prey, and the diet is complete. Thus the omnivore survives, man and bear, each an enthusiastic consumer of plants and animals; each wary—and a mirror—of the other. We could lose the bear, but only at the cost of losing the better parts of ourselves that make us wild, keen, strong. It is a weak man, I believe, who shoots a bear and doesn't eat it. A killer, not a hunter. It is a gentle man, a poet, who regards the bear around and within, the bear out the window and in the mirror, the bear that lives just over the rise and under the skin.

—◦—

"I RECALL the first bear track I ever saw," Adolph Murie wrote. "It was my initial day afield in McKinley Park and my brother and I were crossing from Jenny Creek over a rise to Savage River, on our way to the head of the river." The year was 1922. While America picked itself up after the brutality of the Great War and the shock of the Spanish influenza and began to seduce itself with Gatsby-style wealth, Adolph, only twenty-two that summer, raised in Minnesota, would discover in Alaska a deeper path to happiness. Olaus, ten years older, already an accomplished wildlife biologist and artist who'd covered hundreds of miles in wilderness Alaska by foot, boat, and dog sled, now apprenticed young Adolph, who added:

> One lone track in a patch of mud is all we saw. But the track was a symbol, and more poetic than seeing the bear himself—a delicate and profound approach to the spirit of the Alaska Wilderness. A bear track at any time may create a stronger emotion than the old bear himself, for the imagination is brought into play. You examine the landscape sharply, expecting a bear on every slope as your quickened interest becomes eager and enterprising. The bear is somewhere, and may be anywhere. The country has come alive with a new, rich quality.

Somewhere, anywhere . . . nowhere, everywhere.

Even in England, where hundreds of years ago men extirpated bears, Shakespeare found room for them in *A Midsummer Night's Dream*:

> Such tricks hath strong imagination,
> That, if it would but apprehend some joy,
> It comprehends some bringer of that joy;
> Or in the night, imagining some fear,
> How easy is a bush supposed to be a bear!

SLOWLY, the day arrives and everything takes shape. Clouds gather in the east and soften the sunrise. I bow to the mountains, put a pot of water on the small stove, and walk about to gather blueberries. I'm not as fast as a bear; even so, in minutes I gather a quart. Some of the berries are robust, nearly half as big as marbles. My campmates rise and stretch.

"Breakfast is ready," I tell them. "Hot tea and cold cereal, with blueberries."

We eat as if we too, all four of us, will soon den up for the winter.

"Where's the bacon?" Richard asks me.

"In the Princess Hotel at the other end of the park."

Stan adds, "There's a Harley-Davidson shop there, too, in Glitter Gulch, in the Nenana River Canyon, if you want a really big motorcycle."

"What about rubber tomahawks?" Richard asks. "A national park isn't a national park until it has a tourist town with tacky gift shops that sell little rubber tomahawks."

"Remember that convenience store in Wasilla that sold little model M-16 and AK-47 barbecue lighters?"

"A pizza would be nice."

Larry says, "I heard the other day that national parks return ten dollars to the US economy for every one dollar invested by taxpayers."

"Hey, Kim, did you see what you heard last night?"

"No." But what *did* I hear?

OUR LAST DAY in the Kantishna Hills. My three friends decide to day-hike to the west while I opt to stay in camp to write something profound, maybe go crazy and commit an act of literature. They razz me about this until they are gone, laughing and talking into the distance. Soon the great silence returns. The big quiet. I sit facing Mount BeKindly. An hour goes by, two, three, four. Not a word. It's hard work writing so little. As the adage goes: My essay could have been shorter, but I ran out of time.

◆～◆

"BREVITY, BREVITY, BREVITY," Mrs. Jovanovich once said to me in high school senior English. "What's wrong with brevity, brevity, brevity?"

"Uhhh . . . I dunno," I replied.

"It needs to be said only once."

"Oh, yeah . . ."

Man was I stupid. Mrs. J. must have seen something in me that nobody else did, bless her heart: a small break in my teenaged armor where the light could get in. She had my classmates and me study that champion of nature, William Wordsworth, who influenced Henry David Thoreau who influenced John Muir and Teddy Roosevelt, and from there to another Roosevelt, FDR, and back across the big pond to Churchill and from there—who knows?

Get outside, Wordsworth would say. Find yourself. "Come forth into the light of things, let nature be your teacher."

Mrs. J. liked Simon and Garfunkel, and the Beatles, and she was *old*, in her early forties. She was also cool. She described music as a gift, writing as a craft, something achievable to anyone who worked hard. Of course math and science had their charms, especially the natural sciences for me, biology, geology, paleontology, ecology. All deserving of the best recruits, though I would not be among them. And engineering? Forget it.

"Follow your passion, not the money," Mrs. J. told us. "Live simply, do what you love, love what you do; the money will follow. Fall in love with the geometry of words, the joy of self-expression. Get out of Spokane. Go taste the world. It's one big mango."

"I've never eaten a mango."

"Exactly."

❧

AFTER THAT came Utah, the Butterfly of Love, and Cactus Ed Abbey. And finally, Alaska. I was ruined.

What then to write? What to say? Do I entertain or inform? Describe things as they are or as they ought to be? Ask the reader to celebrate or agitate? It's risky business to conjure up words, ideas, rhetoric; to dabble in Aristotle's "art of persuasive theory." Imagine no heaven, countries, or possessions, as John Lennon did. Strive to unfold the folded lie, as Edward Abbey did. Be the voice of the voiceless, the brake on the wheel. Explore those truths that are *not* self-evident. Write to illuminate, to shine a light. And with light comes heat. Therein lies the hard beauty. If you want easy, write a feel-good love story, a Hallmark card, an invitation to a wedding, a dance. Write an obituary, a sweet good-bye. If you want easy, sit on the sofa, watch the game, shout at the TV. If you want hard, question authority, the flag, the king, the coach, the priest. Embrace the poet and the poor, read novels published by small presses, written by authors you've never heard of; sleep on the ground, volunteer at an orphanage, throw away all your gadgets but one. Study Thoreau, Gandhi, and King. Gently break an unjust law. Dare to say that as a nation and a people we are not who we were told we were; that it's time to stop the control of nature for the benefit of man, and instead to control man for the benefit of nature. How? Imagine moral imperatives that make impossibilities surrender into new realities. Imagine the end of economic growth—not as something to fear, but to celebrate. As Abbey said, "Growth for the sake of growth is the ideology of the cancer cell."

I suppose we could grow our economy forever if we had six more Earths. Plunder one planet after another. Probably not a good idea. Bad manners. Take heart, I tell myself. Public libraries still outnumber McDonald's eight to one in the United States.

—◦—

IMAGINE THIS. There's a bear I think about all the time, one that intrigues me more than any other, that's always hungry and never full and insists on growing forever. It's everywhere. It's The Economy. Our national obsession. We bow before it, convinced that the larger it is, the happier we'll be. It's the big teddy bear in the corner, the care bear on the bed, soft and comforting. It's also the restless bear in the basement that threatens our long-term well-being. We feed it entire landscapes, forests, and ways of life. We dam rivers and lop off the tops of mountains and start wars to keep it going, keep it growing. We dig and drill and cut and fill; foul our water and air and change our weather and climate until no place is untouched, including national parks. All because keeping the economy alive isn't good enough. It must grow. If it isn't growing, and growing vigorously, it isn't "healthy." And if the economy isn't healthy, we tell ourselves, neither are we. Such is our mantra, our myth, our song of progress and prosperity.

How did this happen?

It began, I believe, with the reach that exceeded the grasp, the drive to survive, with human migrations and settlement patterns, and the rise of agriculture—a stable food source—some ten thousand years ago. With this stability came decreased child mortality and increased human lifespans. All good, for a while. Population growth and economic growth became a double helix, of sorts, that accelerated with the Industrial Revolution, shifting into high gear some 250 years ago. Growth begat growth, and more growth on top of that. And still it wasn't enough. To this day and beyond we need more homes, more businesses, more roads, more jobs.

Economist John Maynard Keynes once calculated that from the time of Christ until the beginning of the Industrial Revolution, the human standard of living roughly doubled. No more. In Christ's time we already had fire, farms, commerce, sail, trade, governments, wheels, and wars. Economic growth perked along modestly until we started pulling carbon from the ground and burning it to create magnificent power, efficiency, envy, and wealth. In effect, we began to burn the ancient history of the earth—millions of tons of semidecomposed plants trapped in underground strata for millions of years.

This *new burn* changed everything. It doubled our material standard of living not every two thousand years as before, but every two to three *decades*.

Modern civilization has never experienced vigorous economic growth without burning coal, oil, and natural gas. In the grand sweep of human history, this rate of consumption and growth is an exception, not a rule. We expect it to continue because it's the only thing we've ever known. We expect it to continue because we're hardworking, God-fearing, and deserving.

One barrel of oil converted to diesel and burned in a bulldozer or truck does as much work as one man with a shovel doing manual labor all day every day for ten years. Oil gives each of us in industrial societies our daily superconsumptive lives, our routines and taken-for-granted patterns of driving here, flying there, buying this, eating that. Oil gives each of us, in everything we do, the equivalent of two hundred slaves. This so-called new burn is why our world looks so different today than it did in the time of Christ, and continues to change—radically. This is how we light up the night and keep thousands of jets in the air every minute. This is how we fill our oceans with plastics and polymers, and use our military to police foreign lands for a billion dollars a week, and feed the world with industrial agriculture and genetically modified foods that produce billions of ears of Frankencorn that the farmer himself can no longer eat but that serve as raw material for high fructose corn syrup, a staple of the American obesity epidemic. This is what double-wraps all our shiny choices on the shelves at Costco, Walmart, and Piggly Wiggly, and gives us cities built on landfill. This is Hydrocarbon Man, the New Us, Mister Cheap Energy, restless like that bear in the basement, forever in pursuit of more, and more after that, a bargain that many moralists and ecologists say cannot and will not continue. The American Dream, they say, is an American Fantasy.

"Anyone who believes exponential growth can go on forever in a finite world is either a madman or an economist," says historian Kenneth Boulding.

"The human presence is now so large that all we have to do to destroy the planet's climate and ecosystems and leave a ruined world to our children and grandchildren," says Yale University's James Gustave Speth, "is to keep doing exactly what we are doing today. . . . For all the material blessings economic progress has provided, its impact on the natural world must be counted in the balance as tragic loss."

A WHILE BACK, bestselling author and historian Stephen Ambrose visited Alaska as part of the Alaska Humanities Forum. I listened on the radio as he addressed a large audience, sounding something like a bear himself with a raspy, authoritative voice. He summed things up by saying the closing twentieth century was the most brutal in recorded human history, but one that ended on a positive theme at great cost: democracy prevailed over totalitarianism.

The audience, near as I could tell, appreciated this.

"Doctor Ambrose," a young woman then asked, "if that's the theme of this closing century, what will be the theme of the coming twenty-first century?"

"No question," he said. "It'll have to be the restoration of nature. If not, the damage we do to the earth will threaten the survival of civilization as we know it."

Whoa. The audience, near as I could tell, did *not* appreciate this.

I was sitting on the sofa Melanie and I shared facing each other "feets-to-feets" to tell stories and laugh. We had no television or newspapers, only radio that we listened to a couple times a week. It was pure luck to catch Dr. Ambrose, Mister American History, bestselling author of *Citizen Soldiers*, his book about D-Day, and *Undaunted Courage*, about the Lewis and Clark Expedition.

Alaska's first lady, Susan Knowles, her husband an oil man from Oklahoma, asked for more questions, but the energy had been sucked out of the room. *Restore Nature?* You kidding? That's all we've got here in Alaska, the last frontier. Nature up the wazoo. Man, this guy really knows how to spoil a party.

How exactly we should restore nature, Ambrose didn't say. He must have meant something more than picking up litter in downtown Anchorage. He might have been aware of the high stakes but unwilling to address them, as it's not conducive to a good night's sleep. Restore Nature? It probably means a lot of sacrifice and innovation. It probably means fewer human beings on this still lovely blue-green planet—no easy thing. Some of my favorite people are human beings. I love the way they laugh and gain wisdom and hold the ones they love, and love the ones they hold, and find dignity amid misery and reach across languages, ideologies, and oceans with compassion and care. Would Ambrose advocate a drastic drop in the birth rate? Again, no easy thing. Babies are beautiful. Small children are magical. I wanted a child once. Part of me still does and always will. We can't have it all; we shouldn't even want it all.

To restore nature on a scale Ambrose suggested would require a fundamental shift in our priorities and how we live, a referendum on civilization and our definitions of progress and ownership. It would require a political system absent of two major parties both drunk on the same money. It would require a green economy built on renewable energy and constant inventiveness. And—dare I say it?—a deep respect for all living things.

As Pete Seeger said, "If it can't be reduced, reused, repaired, rebuilt, refurbished, refinished, resold, recycled, or composted, then it should be restricted, redesigned, or removed from production."

THIS IS THE BEAR that inspires me, the one that adapts and learns from its mistakes, that sharpens my imagination and gives me hope. In my dreams I hear Zed the Aborigine beating his guitar like a drum, his burlap bag filled with rocks and books, nothing more. If he could be happy with so little, why do others need so much? I see his eyes, older than the rest of him, luminous with something I cannot define. Even now.

I LOOK AROUND. No bears. Maybe I should go hiking, forget the economy. Burn my money like Chris McCandless did (it would be a small fire). Drop the writing game. Get a real job. Swing a hammer. Sweep a floor. Paint a door.

The next day, eastbound back through the park, the bus rumbles along as Larry, Stan, Richard, and I struggle to stay awake. We're tired from the night before, staying up late on the tundra, talking philosophy, drinking whiskey, smoking "SEE-gars," as Richard calls them.

Denali National Park presents us with one incredible view after another, an infinite landscape, images of resilience, hands on the clock of the universe. We leave Wonder Lake and pass the beaver ponds, fifteen miles of relatively flat depositional topography rich with ducks fattening up for their southbound journeys after a busy breeding season in the arctic. We ascend Grassy Pass and inch along the Eielson Bluffs, a stunning erosional feature flanked to the north by Thorofare Ridge, to the south by a head-over-heels talus slope that drops hundreds of feet to the braided Thorofare River.

Our driver, Alan Seegert, quietly competent, ever watchful, is one of the best. He recently coauthored a handsome, authoritative little book, *Birds of Denali*, with biologist Carol McIntyre and naturalist Nan Eagleson. In the introduction they state that while the park is best known for its "outstanding scenery and unparalleled opportunities for seeing grizzlies, moose, caribou, sheep and wolves," it's a misconception that the park "teems with wildlife." It's lean, hard country, too far north for the Africa fantasia look and feel. Sixteen percent of the park is covered year-round with ice and snow. Of the more than 165 bird species that breed and refuel here, only a few stay year-round. "Denali birding rewards not by force of numbers," they say, "but in the spare elegance of the far north and its denizens, held within the supernal light."

Back by the beaver ponds, I had watched Alan stop the bus, direct our attention to the waterfowl, and quietly slide open his side view window to listen for sparrows. Along Eielson Bluffs he suggested we close our eyes if the drop-off is too frightening. "I sometimes close my eyes too," he added with a wry grin.

Along the road the drivers signal as they pass, using their hands to alert each other about wildlife ahead, one signal for a moose (wrist against the temple, fingers splayed to mimic large antlers), another hand signal for a wolf (fingers pulling into a point off the nose), and so on. They know every bend, creek, river bar, and ridge, and practice etiquette between buses and impose passenger rules on each bus, enforcing them to whatever degree is needed. As we approach a nearby caribou, Alan reminds us to be quiet, to lower the windows with care; keep hands and cameras inside the bus. "Move around and share the view," he says. He stops for a couple minutes, then inches the bus forward slowly, keenly aware that while people up front might see the animal, those in the back cannot. He moves the bus again to give everybody a view, if possible, then departs in time to let a following bus (or two or three) see the caribou—a bull with magnificent antlers—before it walks over a rise. For many park visitors here for only one day, tied to a tight itinerary, it's a bus driver, not a ranger, who speaks on behalf of the park and its wonders, who tells stories and illuminates the already luminous. Drivers know wolf packs from one year to the next, where they travel and hunt. They recognize separate bands of Dall sheep, and where they might cross the road. They know where a family of foxes live; where birds nest.

One driver has harvested his summer garden. While stopped at a wildlife sighting, he passes fresh carrots from open window to open window to his fellow drivers. Others pass newspapers, brownies, and stories, always stories. They talk about fellow drivers who'll spend their winters in Nepal, New Mexico, Chile, and Guatemala, and still another who'll be on radiation and chemotherapy in Anchorage, fighting the dreaded "Big C."

——◆——

MANY DRIVERS are steadfast members of Denali Citizens Council, a regional conservation organization that's advo-cates for "Denali's wildlife, wilderness and way of life." DCC is forever busy rebuffing one assault after another on the pristine character and natural soundscape of the park: snowmachining (snowmobiles), mining, wolf hunting, trapping and poisoning on the park boundaries, and the incessant whine (like mosquitoes) from the tourism industry for more and better access. Many issues boil down to ideology: the State of Alaska versus the US National Park Service, a mind-set of seeing animals as "game" versus animals as "wildlife"; of regarding the park as "locked up" (from economic opportunity and the manipulative hand of man) versus it being just fine the way it is—exquisite, in fact—a holy place. While the State of Alaska manages all hunted fur-bearing species as crops (baiting bears and killing cubs in their dens; killing wolves to provide hunters with steady numbers of caribou and moose), the National Park Service sees wild animals as brethren in need of sanctuary from a world already severely damaged by the heavy hand of man. Of course many state fish and game biologists—people who know rockfish, salmon, caribou, and other species intimately—love Alaska in all its rugged wildness, but at times they have little or no power. A single wrongheaded governor can dispirit an entire agency and do great damage. As a result, many biologists leave their jobs. And who replaces them? Wrongheaded "yes" people who acquire tenure and never leave.

And so we have gardening versus guardianship; "ego" versus "eco." We have humans atop a pyramid filled with all living things below as they talk of "harvest" and "sustained yields," versus humans in a sphere with everything else, open to new ideas and ways of seeing and being, eager to learn and repair as one species among the many. To arrive at such an enlightened place has been a difficult evolution for the National Park Service, but an evolution nonetheless, while the State of Alaska remains calcified in a dogmatic past.

Thus we tame the wild.

National parks around the world suffer from what ecologists call "ecosystem decay" or the "insular effect." As pressures outside parks intensify, with more cutting, trapping, killing, fencing, building, and paving right up to the boundaries, the parks in effect become islands. The smaller the park, the greater the effect. Add to that human population pressure, environmental toxins, introduced species, additional habitat loss and the biggest threat of all—climate change—and it's over. Bryce Canyon, Lassen Volcanic, and Zion National Parks contain only about sixty percent of the large mammal species they had half a century ago. Ecologists estimate that global extinction rates are five hundred to one thousand times higher than they were at the beginning of the Industrial Revolution. By the year 2100, one-third of all species on Earth in the year 1900 could be gone.

We are in the midst of a sixth great extinction, a massive die-off. And this time we have no asteroid to blame. No supervolcano. No cosmic wobble.

This time it's us.

BACK ON THE BUS, we see a few bears at a distance, their heads down, eating berries on the crimson tundra, gold buttons on a blanket of red. Nothing near. While the tourism industry lobbies for more access, the National Park Service grapples with the slippery question of limits, the fine line between access and excess. How many vehicles are too many? Is the occurrence of near-road wildlife decreasing? Might certain animals be avoiding the traffic? The billowing clouds of dust? Might they be changing their behavior? If so, can it be measured? Proven? And if it can be, will the tourism industry agree to fewer buses?

Richard loves wordplay, and talks about the bears of *Denial* National Park. Let's shut the park down one summer out of every eight, he says. A good idea. Rotate the off-summers with the other seven national parks in Alaska. Give everybody a summer-long break: rangers, biologists, bus drivers, lodge owners, luggage handlers, dishwashers, pizza throwers, cashiers. Invite them to spend a summer doing something different, daring. Try on a new identity. Build homes in Haiti, a rock garden in Nepal, a baseball diamond in an Iowa cornfield. Or do nothing, the great nothing that invites you to think about everything. Let the animals have the park the way it used to be before it was a park, before we came along with our cameras and curiosity, our business models and spread sheets. Such are the dreams of a troublemaker.

We rumble over the Toklat River Bridge, up and over Polychrome Pass, past the spur road to the East Fork Cabin.

Anybody home?

No bears. Then, while climbing Sable Mountain, we see traffic ahead, a clot of six or seven shuttle buses and tour buses and several private vehicles. Tripods erected on the shoulder with cameras and long lenses. "It's got to be a bear," Alan says. "Everybody keep quiet and give those around you a chance to see it."

It is the most beautiful bear in the world. Head up, looking around; blueberry leaves on its lips. It's right there, thirty feet away. Now twenty feet. Now ten. Holy moly. It walks right past the bus, not there but *here*, in the bus, or so it feels, animating forty people with a spirit that says we're all made of the same stuff, the stardust in our eyes.

A roadside professional photographer (now inside his truck) signals that the bear has cubs. We wait and are soon rewarded when two little ones—so-called cubs-of-the-year—emerge from thick willow and come frisking down to the road to join their mother. When born in their winter den in January or February they weighed only one pound each. Any of us could have cradled them in the palm of one hand. Unlike newborn caribou and moose that can stand within an hour of birth, bears are born helpless (altricial versus precocial), like humans. Now, six months later, after nursing into spring and summer and learning from their mother how to feed on the tundra, the cubs have achieved considerable weight and personality. Each has a distinctive collar of lighter fur around its neck, common among Toklat grizzlies. They chase each other and play about, engaged in the important work of youth.

I watch Richard with his camera. He's taking the best photographs he can. Forget *Blurred Denali*. Forget de-extinction. We still have the bear and wolf, the caribou, moose, Dall sheep and lynx, the hawk owl, golden eagle, and common redpoll, as well as many others, all wondrous. Let's keep them.

Shut down the national park? Deny people the chance to experience the earth that shaped our hunter-gatherer forebears? Never. What was I thinking? *This* is Pleistocene Park, the ice age, the genesis of glaciers, granite, and bears, where a bus that carried forty strangers hours ago now carries a tribe.

This is how we make the world a better place.

Alan quietly shifts into gear and we roll on, different than before.

Strangers no more.

# CHAPTER NINE

# The Battle below Mount Galen

THE LAND is made of stories. They color and texture everything.

A lynx makes a brief appearance near Igloo Creek and melts back into the forest. Two wolves circle an injured caribou in the Teklanika River. A fox den is active again near Stony Dome; it's been active ten of the last twelve years. A merlin chases a belted kingfisher at Wonder Lake. Wolves howl up the moonrise over Moose Creek. Hikers see a wolverine on Thorofare Ridge. A mother grizzly crosses Stony Creek while her twin cubs hold back, protesting with barks and whines. She returns to nudge them across and finally carries each one by the nape of the neck, little paws dangling above the cold current.

Hail falls two inches deep near Reflection Pond; the icy kernels are so large they strip new leaves from the tundra plants. Arctic poppies are riotous along Highway Pass. And don't miss the moss campion—large clusters of tiny pink flowers—halfway between Polychrome Rest Stop and the Toklat River.

Up and down the park road, Denali stories have their own energy. Some are high voltage, some are even true.

Did you hear about the climbers who got disoriented in a storm on Scott Peak? A heavy snow covered their tracks and they descended by another route and ended up on the wrong side of the mountain. At lower elevation, out of food, exhausted and lost, they nearly starved eating soapberries, and tried to spear ptarmigan with ski poles. A search plane spotted them six days later and called in a helicopter that picked them up and flew them to Eielson Visitor Center where they greeted their relieved parents. Thin, weak, and weather-beaten, the climbers looked like scarecrows. Smiling scarecrows, happy to be alive.

Did you hear about Daryl Miller, the climbing rescue ranger, and his buddy Mark Stasik, a timber-framer and climber from Talkeetna? They completed the first ever winter circumnavigation of the Denali-Foraker massif: 350 miles in bitter cold and hellacious winds, crossing crevasses and icy ramparts. At one point, weathered in by a whiteout, they huddled in their tent to cook dinner and thaw out a pint of rum. Suddenly they had what Daryl called "the flash fire from hell"; fuel from their cook stove "spraying everywhere." He turned it off, but like most backcountry stoves it took a minute to burn down. Flames engulfed his head, chest, and gloved hands.

"Get out," Mark shouted.

Daryl dove for the vestibule. Mark threw out the flaming gear and followed. Both men rolled in the snow with the smell of singed hair.

"You okay?" they asked each other as smoke rolled off their parkas.

"Yeah, I'm okay. You?"

"Yeah."

"Damn," Mark said, "that was the best tent fire I've ever been in."

Minutes later they were back inside to avoid freezing.

The storm broke and they continued on. They crossed a pass that upon their return, when Brad Washburn saw a photograph of the route, said, "Daryl, that is not a pass; it's just a place where you guys crossed the Alaska Range." As the old explorer's adage goes: *Find a route or make one.* The epic forty-five-day journey ended when Daryl and Mark

crossed the frozen Chulitna River and walked into their Talkeetna homes. Daryl had lost twenty-five pounds. "Most
surprisingly," he wrote, "we'd returned as better friends
than when we left. . . . The rest of our experience—the soli-
tude and the fear, the joy and the agony, the hardships and
the pleasures—is all but impossible to explain."

<hr />

DID YOU MEET the Japanese wildlife biologist who observed
wolves in the park for three days? He said wolves have been
extinct in his homeland since 1927, due to habitat loss.
Inspired by Denali, he hopes to reintroduce them to Japan.
Somebody asked: How long will it take until your people are
ready to share their islands again with wolves? His guess:
one hundred years.

Did you meet the couple from France making a film
about the value of open space and deep quiet? They said a
single motorcycle screaming through Paris in the middle of
the night awakens more than a quarter million people. They
also said hospital patients in intensive care units around
the world aren't healing the way they should because all
the softly beeping machines prevent them from sleeping
soundly, getting deep rest. That's what Denali is all about,
they said: deep quiet, deep rest, deep time.

Did you meet Don Young, Alaska's lone representative
in the US House since the 1970s? He flew into the park
by helicopter, keeping the view to himself while sharing the
noise with everybody else. He visited Kantishna and spoke
on behalf of the mining industry, announcing that Denali,
while a beautiful place, belongs to more people than just "a
bunch of granola-eating hippies."

The next morning I ate sausage and hash browns at a
Healy roadside diner and hoped one day to be a real man
like Don Young. And riding in a helicopter? No thanks. I
prefer the road.

LOCAL Denali author, photographer, and historian Tom Walker writes in his compelling book, *Denali Journal*:

*The park road means different things to different people. It has private legends. Mine goes like this: "In that willow patch I once saw a wolf. There a fox. There a grizzly. And once, here at this milepost, a lynx crossed." Each mile holds stories and shadowed memories. Long stretches of road remain where I haven't seen animals, but the berries and fall colors in those places have been more than compensation.*

Follow that bear trail for a quarter mile and you'll find the ground patterned with feathers. Overhead will be a goshawk nest. Follow that creek and keep to the left. Climb two thousand feet. Take a sense of adventure, a good book, and rain gear. Sleep on the ground for a night or three or five. Soon Dall sheep will be all around you, grazing. Keep quiet and they'll regard you with mild indifference. Halfway up that slope you'll find a nesting Lapland longspur. Go slowly. Stop often. Be watchful. The bird survives by being motionless and discreet. Otherwise, it's fox food.

Tom laments that before the park got crowded, people felt more free to get off the shuttle buses and day-hike willy-nilly, comfortable in knowing that when they returned to the road, even as late as nine o'clock, an eastbound bus would pick them up. Today, nearly every bus is full. Few people get off and jump onto another bus. The intrepid day-hiker, plunging into rivers and over ridges, going light and pushing the night, is rare. These days, most people are easily corralled onto the same bus all day; many are point-and-shoot digital photographers. The shuttle buses stop for an animal or a nice view, and forty-some cameras snap and whirl. They're not shuttle buses anymore; Tom says they're "shutter buses." He fears the park is now viewed more than experienced; witnessed more than felt.

Tom's not the kind of guy to name wild animals, feeling it "perhaps diminishes them in some way." But a bull moose once so impressed him that he called the bull "Big Daddy." It was late September, the time of the rut, when sexually mature bull moose go girl crazy (cow crazy, in moose speak). I understand this, thinking back on my time with Foxy Felicity, the Butterfly of Love, and my Lebanese girlfriend who studied French literature and turned out to be another guy's Lebanese girlfriend who studied French literature.

On a Monday afternoon, Tom observed that Big Daddy's antlers were perfect, "the long fighting tines unmarred. He had sixteen points on the left antler, eighteen on the right. By Tuesday morning, three tines were broken off and another was fractured and loose. There were two long bloody gashes in his shoulder." All night he had defended a dozen cows in "thick timber" from intruders, primarily four young bulls that constantly challenged his claim. Tom had no doubt found these animals far from the park road and gone alone with his tripod, camera, and long lens, moving with caution and keen awareness. He wrote:

> *A loud moan from one side or another of the thicket would be a cow announcing the unwelcome advance of a bull. Big Daddy would charge off to protect that cow, when a moan in another direction would make him race the other way. Once, the next-biggest bull came racing down the middle of the thicket with Big Daddy in vigorous pursuit. No saddle horse has galloped faster, and when Big Daddy came to a three-foot-tall deadfall, he leaped it [all fourteen hundred pounds of him] with amazing agility. Both bulls disappeared into the timber, the smaller jabbed on by a violent antler thrust to the rump.*

Moose never made sense to me until I saw them in winter. Long nose, long legs, high shoulders, high knees. They shovel down to pull up succulent leaves and stems and reach high to browse an out-of-the-way willow branch, and with one swift kick can crack open the skull of a wolf, all in deep snow.

Alaska writer Sherry Simpson, author of a collection of elegant essays, *The Way Winter Comes*, describes moose as having "strange grace," adding:

> *People say moose are homely and awkward and somewhat absurd, the product of some misalliance between cow and camel that contrived that hump, that hero sandwich of a nose, that vaguely ridiculous bell dangling from the throat. In likening the parts of a moose to those of other animals, we miss the functional beauty of the whole, the biological rejoinders to an environment that produces every kind of hardship: short summers, terrible winters, not enough food, and a couple of the world's most earnest predators. Bears snooze away winters tucked in cozy dens; wolves enjoy the companionship of their own kind. But moose, they tough it out, eating bark and twigs, wading through snowdrifts, burning up their own flesh through the long dark nights.*

In 2003, when nobody is watching, two massive bulls move over the autumn tundra in upper Moose Creek, west of Mount Galen, and face off. Both are in their prime and no doubt feeling feisty, each a prisoner of his convictions. They lock antlers, pushing and jousting as the two become one, inseparable. They spend hours, probably days, trying to disengage, but cannot, perhaps because one bull's wavy, misshapen antlers lock inextricably into the other bull's antlers. A tine from the antler of one pierces the eye of the other. Still, the contest continues. Blood on the ground. Death in the air. At times they probably just stand mirroring each other, their breath like that of two steam locomotives on the same track. How long they stay on their feet we can only guess. How long they live thus entangled we can only imagine. And what of the manner of their dying?

Think of the wolves, bears, ravens, coyotes, wolverines, and others that arrive to partake of the feast: more than twenty-five hundred pounds of moose meat in one place, all consumed before winter. Some of it consumed no doubt while the moose are still alive.

Perhaps it's something in the cosmos that year, the same year we invade Iraq to rid Saddam Hussein of the weapons of mass destruction he never had, and to rid the world of Saddam himself and his fruitcake sons. We embark on an "operation" that will cost upward of two trillion dollars and more than ten thousand Iraqi lives, with thousands of American lives broken and lost and countless homes and families shattered for decades and generations.

We'll be welcomed as "liberating heroes," says Vice President Dick Cheney, another prisoner of his convictions. He adds that Saddam Hussein is an evil man. We never hear Cheney push for an invasion of North Korea, where Kim Jong-il, by all accounts, is far worse. (Never trust a man named Kim.) Invading North Korea would be a bloodbath, while our marching into Iraq is akin to Star Wars versus the Flintstones. A victory of sorts, followed by a tar pit and the fog of war.

Those who support the invasion compare it to World War II. Those who oppose it compare it to Vietnam. Over the next eight years Halliburton (where Cheney was CEO before serving as vice president) will profit more than forty billion dollars through government war contracts.

I cannot watch two moose jousting, two bears fighting, two men arguing, without thinking of war. True, this is unfair to the moose and bears. "So long as there are men," Albert Einstein lamented, "there will be wars." I grew up with Vietnam, the lies, fear, and deceit, the wall in Washington with fifty-seven thousand names etched into black granite, the flags overhead, the red roses and love poems scattered about. My brothers nearly ended up on that wall; they did not, but neither were they spared. Nor was my mother, or father. Nor was I.

Wars, like affairs, are easier to get into than out of.

In the 1983 movie *War Games*, a young computer hacker breaks into a military program and unleashes what appears to be imminent global thermonuclear war. To stop it he must find the reclusive scientist who wrote the program. He does, and together they arrive at the bunkered military facility where a nervous general believes America is under attack and so prepares to launch a counterattack. The scientist (the part was written for John Lennon) studies the computer display, the trajectories of hundreds of nuclear warheads headed our way, and sees it for what it is: an elaborate ruse, a game, the computer testing us. He calmly says, "It's acting like a machine, general. Do the world a favor and don't respond like one."

Years later at a graduation ceremony at the US Army Academy at West Point, an impressive phalanx of graduating cadets marched onto a field in perfect order, hundreds of future generals in full regalia, each wearing a large, ornate cap. A sudden gust blew the cap off one cadet. From the stands, onlookers watched as the procession stumbled over it, row after row kicking it along, the disruption rippling through the entire graduating class. Not one cadet improvised and deftly bent down to pick it up and put it under his arm so the others might march forward without stumbling into their futures.

"No," President Kennedy said to the joint chiefs during the 1962 Cuban Missile Crisis, "we're not going to bomb Cuba." Only one man in Kennedy's cabinet, his attorney general and younger brother, Bobby, supported the president. His military advisors said bombing Cuba might start a war, but so be it. Kennedy disagreed. Not only did he stand up to Khrushchev and the Soviet Union, he stood up to his own joint chiefs and cabinet. He said no. There has to be a better way.

That better way was the Peace Corps, the Berlin Airlift, and Civil Rights. Kennedy would have signed the Wilderness Act as well, but he was cut down in Dallas. President Johnson signed it ten months later.

Of course I argued with my older brother about Vietnam, and Laos and Cambodia; he always won, or had the last word. The irony: to wage war over war and to end up where we begin. The hawk eats the dove.

THE SAME YEAR of the great moose battle west of Mount Galen, other Alaska dramas unfold. A young man named Dan Bigley goes salmon fishing one bright July morning and encounters a coastal brown bear on a riverside trail on the Kenai Peninsula. Already agitated, perhaps by a more dominant bear or by other fishermen, the bear slams into Bigley, knocks him to the ground, yanks him from the brush, takes a swipe at his face, a couple bites, and moves on. All in seconds. A lover of wild places, Dan's job until then is taking troubled kids into the outdoors to help them find purpose in their lives. He has just bought a cabin in the Chugach Mountains and spent a first night with Amber, the woman of his dreams.

The bear attack leaves him blind and disfigured.

Three months later, Timothy Treadwell, a self-described brother of wild bears, camps for his thirteenth straight summer in Katmai National Park, on the Katmai Coast, across Shelikof Strait from Kodiak Island. According to author Nick Jans, Treadwell is

> . . . *the sort of guy most Alaskans loved to hate. You don't go around on Kodiak Island or Katmai crawling on all fours, singing and reading to bears, giving them names like Thumper, Mr. Chocolate, and Squiggle. You don't say things to them like, "Czar, I'm so worried! I can't find little Booble." Not unless you're from California,*

*that is, and your name is Timothy Treadwell. He looked the part—*
*boyish good looks and a shock of blond hair half-tamed by a back-*
*ward ball cap.*

A Malibu surfer, bartender, and waiter, Treadwell
headed north to find his true calling as a bear whisperer, to
defend *his* bears from poachers, tourists, even the wayward
National Park Service. He has no authority, but as Jans
writes, "that lack of authority is superseded by the badge
tattooed on his heart."

In the end, love saves Dan Bigley. It separates his blindness from the dark. He'll write in his memoir, *Beyond the*
*Bear*, coauthored with Debra McKinney, "After what happened, I tried to set Amber free. I failed."

She marries him.

And in the end, love kills Timothy Treadwell. One bear
is all it takes. It's the first bear-caused fatality in Katmai's
eighty-five-year history.

NOTHING like this has happened in Denali, or in many
other places, yet these sensational moments are the stories
that define Alaska and get passed around homes, parks,
and schools; these are the stories that attract television
and movie producers. The fights to the death and out-of-
nowhere attacks that turn a life upside down until the victim—if he lives—turns it right-side up and moves on. Each
becomes a story and a statistic. We cannot escape numbers,
nor should we want to. There's beauty in a bell curve; perfection in the laws of nature, the universal equation. But
stories inhabit the heart, not the head. They remind us of
what's sacred. This is why we need wildness: to give us stories and mystery and grace, a laugh in the night, a canvas
upon which to paint our imagination. Stories keep us alive
and more—they keep us heart strong and young.

Pity the poor child whose grandfather says, "Come sit next to me, sweetie. I'll read you some bedtime statistics."

If a child were to ask, "Tell me about the beaver," the lover of numbers might answer, "The beaver is the largest rodent in North America. It can weigh up to sixty-five pounds . . ."

The master storyteller might say, "Let me tell you about Wounded Beaver, the wisest beaver of them all. Many years ago he was captured by Wolf, but at the last minute he tricked Wolf and escaped." The story would entertain, teach, and inspire. Listeners would learn how Wounded Beaver got away and gained wisdom, and how they too, the listeners, might one day gain wisdom.

All learning was once through observation, practical trial and error, and story . . . the best stories told in the warm light of a fire, the speaker and listeners gathered under the skins and furs of the animals they hunted and admired. In the great arc of human history, this fire burned—and these listeners lived—only yesterday. Their stories, like treasured books today, were honored and passed down from generation to generation, made divine in their precision.

◆━◆

DEEP in the limestone heart of the French Pyrenees, the Niaux Cave says something about who we are. Fifteen thousand years ago a group of artists descended the dark passages and entered a massive domed room—an underground St. Peter's—and with candles in one hand, crude brushes in another, painted the walls with bison, ibex, mammoths and other animals. The paintings show no humans or vegetation, no ground reference. They are not hunting scenes. So what are they?

Was this a holy place?

Did people sing here? Pray?

The animals appear as if they're floating.

This was fifty centuries before agriculture brought us hierarchies, cities, and nations. These artists had no written language that we know of, but they had heart, they had imagination. They lived close to death and often died young.

While I ran around Europe as a young man looking for the Beatles and the Italian girl who stole my money belt, Zed the Aborigine, also a young man, visited this cave (or one similar). I can't remember what he said, exactly. What I do remember, from the nights we camped together on the Colorado Plateau and Nine Fingers played the guitar, riffing between Jimi Hendrix and Jimmy Page, is the gravity in Zed's voice when he told me about his time in the cave with friends.

England's Paul Kingsnorth would one day stand where the Paleolithic artists stood, and where Zed stood as well, and write,

> *Whoever was here, and whatever they were doing, they were forging a connection to something that transcended everyday reality. These paintings are not expressions of economics or natural history. They surely sprang from the same sense of power and smallness and wonder and awe that I feel as I stand in the place where the artists would have stood. This was a reaching out to, for, something beyond human comprehension. This was a meeting with the sacred.*

NOT UNTIL the following spring do hikers work their way up Moose Creek and discover the remains of the two bulls, antlers locked, skulls attached, large pieces of hair and bones scattered about; a few vertebrae still in order, a femur here, a scapula there; the droppings and signs of other wildlife, a vast circle of vegetation trampled flat from the encounter.

Word spreads fast. A story is born, shaped by each storyteller. Have you heard? Two bull moose fought to the death last fall up Moose Creek, below Mount Galen.

People hike out to bear witness. Many take photos. Some stand in awe, or write in journals, or speak in soft tones of reverence and disbelief.

Craig Brandt, a wildlife photographer and heavy equipment mechanic at Toklat Work Camp, visits the site with his girlfriend. They take photos and fall asleep. When a Japanese man comes upon them, he thinks they're dead from having shot each other. That's what people do in America, no? They all have guns and shoot each other.

Craig awakens and assures the man he has no gun, only a camera.

In the months ahead, a discussion arises: What to do with the interlocked antlers? Leave them to slowly rejoin the great cycle of life and death on the tundra? Or remove them and mount them outside the new Eielson Visitor Center for all to ponder and enjoy?

The final decision doesn't interest me so much as the language; the tone that implies the battle scene as hallowed ground, the antlers as sacred objects.

But what exactly is "sacred"? Like truth, the word falls easily off the lips. It's a chimera of sorts, cheapened these days by salesmen of all stripes.

I turn once again to the thoughtful scholar Paul Kingsnorth, a sleep-on-the-ground guy who writes:

> *The original Latin word sacrare meant "to make holy" or "to set apart." The "sacrum" of a temple is a holy place, which most people are not permitted to approach. Within this holy place is supposed to reside some essence of God, or of the divine. The word holy, which originates in the Old English halig, has the same derivation as whole and health; it speaks of something complete, entire, and unsullied.*

Here then is Denali, where we find the holy in wild nature. Not just in the animals themselves or the way they inhabit us—the tracks of bears, the howls of wolves, the locked antlers of two moose—but in the eternity of life and death framed in the national park idea, the wholeness of it all, the peace and drama and steady flow.

As every national park is a land of stories, every visit to a national park is a search for our place in that story, for the divine in each of us; it's a search for something that might explain who we are and ought to be.

Harvard biologist E.O. Wilson says we cannot understand history until we understand pre-history, and we cannot understand pre-history until we understand evolutionary biology. Modern man is still an animal, a dangerous animal driven by Paleolithic emotions, medieval institutions, and god-like powers. Thus arises the confidence of ignorance, the rush into war and other bad habits.

Religion has its place, of course. Though sadly, two thousand years of organized religion has largely failed to protect the wild Earth that nurtured us then and nurtures us still.

But I remain hopeful. Everything changes, in time.

The artists of Niaux Cave no doubt knew that without wild animals their lives would be impossible. They had no Top Ramen, Healthy Choice, Supersized Nacho Rancho Big Thirst Jumbo Meal. Without wild animals moving to their own rhythms, Denali National Park would be a poor imitation of itself. It takes only one bear to fill a valley, one howl to texture the night, one track to color the imagination.

JUST OUTSIDE the park, in the Great Alaska Moose Farm and Caribou Ranch known as Alaska State Game Management Unit This or That, we find many more moose and not as many wolves as now exist in Denali. We find a good crop. Many of the wolves have been shot, trapped, or poisoned.

Is this the wholeness of the holy? The sacredness required to save what remains? Is this how the Koyukon people survived for thousands of years?

"Sell your cleverness," advises the Persian mystic Rumi, "and buy bewilderment. Cleverness is mere opinion, bewilderment is intuition."

In *bewilderment* we find the roots of *wilderness* and *wildness*, the very thing Henry David Thoreau said is necessary to preserve the world.

———

VIC VAN BALLENBERGHE began studying moose in Denali in 1980, the summer before I first arrived. Even then, and especially as the decades rolled by and his reputation grew, he seemed larger than the rest of us, part moose himself, off on his own with his telemetry gear and radio receiver, tracking bulls, cows, and calves. Author Sherry Simpson once described him as "the kind of wildlife biologist with blueberry stains on the seat of his pants. . . . He is a disciple of the old school of wildlife science, which prefers to learn about an animal by following it around, watching what it does, and trying to figure out why."

While most of Denali's moose calves end up in the bellies of wolves and bears, some starve or may die alone of injury or disease. Cows reach sexual maturity at twenty-eight months, and usually give birth to twin calves in late May. Bulls reach their greatest prowess after ten years; they usually weigh up to sixteen hundred pounds and grow antlers every year that weigh eighty to ninety pounds. When a full-grown bull or cow charges, you run. Not so with bears. Should a bear appear and come close, you stand your ground and make noise. You back away at an angle, and do your best to appear unthreatening. If other people are nearby, join them to make yourself as large as possible. With bears, you never run. But with moose, especially a cow with calves, if she charges, you run.

I've had my moments with moose, all pleasant, some remarkable. I've visited secret places where every autumn

RHYTHM OF THE WILD

they gather for the rut; sat quietly among the protective trees, listening, reading a book. I've fallen asleep among moose, dreamed of moose, seen magnificent bulls joust and clash and break themselves on the stones of their own stubbornness, muscles tight over broad shoulders, velvet hanging off their mighty antlers. But never have I seen two bulls lock together and die embraced.

Tom Walker says he knows of two other occasions. "At one," he tells me in his soft manner, "the antlers remained locked long after every bone was picked clean. At the other, the predators and scavengers must have pulled so hard on the carcasses that the antlers became disentangled."

---

I COULD spend ten thousand more hours in Denali and still not know it as well as Tom. Raised in California, he moved north in his early twenties and didn't looked back. A son of Denali, he loves every river and ridge; every bear, flower, and wolf. The log house that he built on a bluff near the Nenana River is a showpiece of craftsmanship and design. He's written several authoritative books on the history and wildlife of Denali and taken thousands of photographs, many of them gems. He quietly mentors any ranger or scientist who comes calling. Most recently, he's helped bring writers into the park's artist-in-residence program. All on his own time. If James Fenimore Cooper came to Denali today looking for a Leatherstocking, a new protagonist made thoughtful and wise by time on the tundra, he'd choose Tom Walker.

And Tom's not alone. Many Park Service employees have given most if not all of their careers to this place. It's more than a job; it's a mission, a cause, a good life. They're biologists, geologists, naturalists, environmental specialists, historians, technicians, dog handlers, planners, administrators, trail builders, road-grader operators, mechanics, maintenance men, and others. They represent hundreds of years of Denali experience. Superintendents typically come and go. Chief rangers come and go; other division chiefs as well, all passionate and appreciative, but also with one hand on the career ladder. At some point in the hierarchy, however, the ladders come down. People stay. Some build their own homes. Others acquire their own teams of sled dogs. They raise their children and grow old here, and in their seventies and eighties get up in the middle of the night to step outside at twenty below to watch the northern lights.

—❧—

ONE YEAR after the epic moose battle, Melanie and I get a campsite at Wonder Lake Campground. It's September.

"Kimmy, Kimmy, Kimmy . . ." Melanie exclaims one morning. The mountain is out, luminous as always. I sit up and peer out the tent door, and hold her.

All around us are stories.

Upon hearing about the two bull moose below Mount Galen, Melanie and I decide to stay away. Let others take the pilgrimage and share their testimonials. Such as:

> *"When I was out there, two ravens showed up and waited, as if maybe it would happen all over again."*
>
> *"The sounds alone—the antlers clashing, the moose grunting and bellowing—must have been incredible."*
>
> *"We found moose hair everywhere."*
>
> *"What a struggle. Our lives today are so easy and soft."*
>
> *"Think of the bears feeding on all that meat just before denning up. It would contribute a lot to the survival of their cubs through winter, don't you think?"*
>
> *"The place gave me the creeps."*
>
> *"I didn't hear a thing. It was so quiet, like a stillness or a mourning or a moment of silence out of respect for the dead, as if the entire landscape was holding its breath."*

*"To think the entire drama was going on, and not far away, like Chris McCandless in his abandoned bus, and nobody knew about it. How life and death can be so near and tragic yet we have no awareness of it."*

*"I've heard others say it's a 'war zone.' It's not. I've been in a war zone. I've seen war. Those two bulls were just a couple guys fighting on a Saturday night, using their antlers like baseball bats."*

*"It's ironic, don't you think? They fight to perpetuate themselves, to pass on their genes, and kill each other instead. That's men."*

*"I cried."*

*"I'll bet the predators and scavengers in this park will talk about that feast for a long time."*

THAT EVENING, after a full day of hiking and picking berries, admiring the mountain and watching sandhill cranes fly across the Alaska Range, Melanie and I walk back into Wonder Lake Campground while the ranger is giving his evening program to a dozen visitors gathered on benches around the campfire circle.

I pause to listen, and smile.

He's telling a story.

# ANOTHER TEN YEARS LATER:

# EAST FORK CABIN

# CHAPTER TEN

# Wolfing Down Pizza

ALASKA AIRLINES gets me to the terminal on time. I breeze through the gate, down the concourse and past security, and descend the escalator to be greeted by a dozen teenagers waving the National Geographic Society tricolor. With them are their two instructors, Em Jackson and David Estrada. We make introductions and take a few photos. At baggage claim the kids playfully compete with each other to carry my stuff.

So begins my week with National Geographic Student Expeditions.

Tomorrow, we'll drive to Denali.

At dinner that night in a Fairbanks restaurant I pose a question: "What would you rather be, a domestic dog or a wolf?"

The students look at me with saucer eyes: six boys and six girls, all fifteen to eighteen years old, impossibly fresh-faced and young. A few are college-bound that fall, most are set to begin their junior or senior years in high school. Raised in affluence in cities and suburbs from Boston to San Diego, not one of them has been to Alaska before.

They vote. Ten of the twelve would rather be a domestic dog. They have dogs at home. Dogs they love and miss. Dogs they treat with great affection and care.

I nod. Sounds like a good choice, a great life, being a dog in a house filled with love. Only two, Joey and Max, say they'd rather be a wolf.

"It's not easy being a wolf," I say.

"I know," answers Joey Abate from New Jersey. "I'll take my chances."

Is he giving me the answer he thinks I want to hear? "Instead of the soft sofa and short leash," I add, "you'd have to hunt for all your food. You could starve to death, get kicked by a moose, run over by a snowmachine, trampled by a mastodon, shot by a redneck, robbed by a bear."

They laugh.

"There's no Purina Dog Chow or Ace Ventura Pet Detective in the wilderness of Alaska."

Joey shrugs.

The girls fiddle with their desserts.

SOUTHBOUND. The next morning we roll down the George Parks Highway through Ester, Nenana, and Anderson, half of us in one van, half in the other. Em and David discreetly keep the kids from dividing into cliques. We stop often to talk about geology, ecology, history, photography, whatever the land and light inspires.

I call the shots, being the so-called National Geographic "expert," a title that makes me uncomfortable.

I ask the students to regard me as no expert at all, but as an expatriate park ranger guitar picker in search of a new definition of the American Dream. They seem to like that. They call me "dude."

A few miles north of Healy, we stop at the turnoff to two roads: Lignite Road going east, Stampede Road going west.

"Does this spot mean anything to anybody?" I ask.

Blank stares. A few students shake their heads.

"This is the old Stampede Trail, where eighteen years ago a hitchhiker named Chris McCandless said good-bye to the last person he ever saw and walked into the wild. It was late April, cold. He called himself Alexander Supertramp."

I point west. "The abandoned bus where he died is about twenty-five miles that way."

Everybody falls silent. They know the story. They come from well-to-do families, many back East, and have a fascination with Alaska, as McCandless did at their age. A few take photos posing next to the Stampede Road sign as I walk back to the vans parked off the highway some fifty feet away. The boys join me while every girl lingers on the Stampede, some folded into each other, heavy with sadness, no doubt thinking of the idealistic young man, so handsome and full of commitment and potential, dying as he did. Recent evidence suggests he didn't starve, but that he unknowingly poisoned himself eating the seeds of a seemingly innocuous plant called wild potato. The boys tell me that while Jon Krakauer's book is good, it's the recent movie adaption by Sean Penn, starring the heartthrob Emile Hirsch as McCandless, that slammed the girls. They all fell for him.

Back in the van, a girl named Bailey tells me, "The whole thing is so sad. It hurts more when you stand where he stood and think about all the things that could have gone another way for him."

I remember Krakauer's line about "innocent mistakes" that turned out to be "pivotal and irreversible."

"How old would he be now, if he'd lived?" a student asks from the back of the van.

I do the math. "Forty-two."

"Oh gosh . . . my dad is forty-two."

———

PAST Healy and Otto Lake, we drop into the Nenana River Canyon and stop at Windy Bridge. Time for another diversion. We walk down a steep path and climb under the bridge to admire local graffiti; the art and love messages and political mutterings of local kids their age. Again, more photos. And this time, as I had hoped, laughter.

I tell a few stories. Always stories, or a parable at least, and if not a parable, then a tale with a theme, and if not a theme, a corny punchline. Back in the van, the students teach me the verses of Jason Mraz's "I'm Yours" while I teach them the melody and harmony parts to "Across the Universe." It's a fair deal.

All twelve students are keen on photography and want to know what it's like to work for the National Geographic Society. It's precious, perilous duty, I say, especially writing books, homebound, chained to a desk. Not as glamorous as working as an assignment photographer in Botswana or Bhutan for the yellow-bordered flagship magazine, but still a sweet deal. I became a writer because I like ideas. Because today's writers might not be so different from the Niaux Cave artists of fifteen thousand years ago: searching in the dark, seeking a more durable life, a better world; or at least a finer appreciation of this one, nothing more.

Back on the road, I talk to the kids about the lesson—and the burden—of history, how those who ignore it are destined to repeat it. While those who embrace it go crazy watching others ignore and repeat it. Many are worried about the cost of college tuition: fifty thousand dollars per year to attend Brown or Yale. Some parents can afford it, others cannot. The kids hope for generous scholarships. Even small state schools cost twenty times what they did thirty years ago. I tell them that total college debt today (in the United States) is higher than total credit card debt. The kids shake their heads. "How did this happen?" asks one girl.

Says another, "And we have money. Imagine the poor."

I have no simple answer. All I know is that my tuition in the 1970s was about two hundred dollars per quarter. I joined a musician's union, played in a local band three nights a week, got free beer, and graduated with money in the bank. I was lucky.

WE ARRIVE at the Denali Education Center, have a nice dinner, and that night walk along the Nenana River. The next
morning we head out the park road for the Savage River,
as far west as private vehicles can travel without a special
permit. Our objective: to hike up Mount Margaret, the east-
ernmost end of Primrose Ridge. It's time to leave behind the
burden of history.

The mountain slams us. Three-fourths of the way up,
with another five hundred vertical feet above and a ferocious wind blasting us from the south, pelting us with rain,
I call everybody together. Half the kids look strong, a few
seem shaky but able to continue on, two or three appear
ready to break down and cry. I've noticed several on wobbly
legs, their fatigue increasing with each arduous step. The
instructors, Em and David, signal me that they think we
should abandon the summit.

"How's everybody doing?" I ask.

"Good," says Joey and a couple others.

A few keep their heads down to avoid eye contact. When
we do talk, the wind is so fierce we can hardly hear each other.

"Huddle up, everybody," I say. "This is a nasty wind. If
we push for the summit it'll be an unpleasant experience.
Here's what we're going to do. We'll contour over to that
ridge and take shelter behind that rocky outcrop, get a lee
from the wind, have a nice lunch, rehydrate, rest up and
regain our strength. How does that sound?"

"What do you mean 'contour'?"

"We'll stay at the same elevation and side-hill across,
careful not to gain or lose elevation and waste valuable
energy. Does that sound good?"

They nod.

An hour later things improve greatly. The rain stops. We eat
lunch surrounded by wildflowers and recover our good spirits.

Back on our feet, we crest the ridge to find five Dall sheep rams bedded down in their own tundra flowers. The kids can't believe it. This is their reward: to have climbed all this way and receive these regal mountain animals with golden horns and keen eyes. The sheep remain casual yet watchful; they've had visitors before. I ask the kids to stay in a tight group, move slowly, give the rams ample room.

We find a small fold in the topography, a break from the wind, and sit to admire what I tell them is "the signature animal of Denali National Park." Not the mighty grizzly or the stately wolf; not the moose, caribou, or lynx. Noble though they are, they don't hold the place in Denali's history that the Dall sheep does.

"Why?" the kids ask.

They quietly take photos; some crawl around to get better compositions. As things settle down, I tell a story.

<hr />

"ONCE THERE WAS a man who by the age of thirty-five had all the money he needed . . ." After making a small fortune in a Mexican silver and lead mine, he came north to see what remained of wild America. Here was Alaska, a second chance, a magnificent gift. This man would dedicate the rest of his life to the higher ideal of saving wild animals by preserving their habitat, their world. His name was Charles Sheldon. The world he campaigned to save is today called Denali National Park and Preserve.

Not a bad legacy.

It was an exciting time. In the first decade of the twentieth century, a self-described nature lover and "Audubonist" occupied the White House. America had never before had such a president. Young and vibrant, Teddy Roosevelt would burst into a cabinet meeting thrilled or angry—nobody could tell—to announce, "Gentlemen, do you know what has happened this morning?" Everybody would brace; heads might roll. "Just now I saw a chestnut-sided warbler—and this is only February."

For Roosevelt, who'd grown up an asthmatic child made well by going outdoors on grand adventures, and later working a ranch in the Dakotas, birds and other wild animals colored the world and gave it wonder and grace. The strenuous life was a good life, he said. Don't get soft sitting in padded chairs and fancy sofas. The best medicine was fresh air, hard work, and a deep appreciation for wild nature.

Go out there.

Remember Thoreau: "I'd rather sit on a pumpkin and have it all to myself than be crowded on a velvet cushion."

And Muir: "I only went out for a walk, but finally concluded to stay out till sundown, for going out, I found, was really going in."

Sheldon, like Roosevelt, was an Ivy League man with tremendous pluck and drive and a love for open space and wild places. "The words that his [Yale] classmates used over and over again to describe him," according to historian Douglas Brinkley, "were 'rugged' and 'no nonsense.'"

To illustrate this, Brinkley tells a story:

*One afternoon a salesman came to Yale, banging on students' doors, offering boxes of Cuban cigars. Not long after the salesman's visit, Sheldon noticed that his flute had been stolen from his quarters. Immediately he turned detective. For a long day he visited all of Long Haven's and New York's pawnshops, hoping to find his flute. His determination paid off. At one of the Manhattan shops, Sheldon stumbled on the petty thief, the flute sticking out of his suit coat pocket. Without hesitation Sheldon, like a linebacker, tackled him to the ground. He then made a citizen's arrest. The salesman went to jail and Sheldon returned to Yale with his treasured instrument.*

Born in 1867, the year the United States purchased Alaska from Russia, Sheldon might have felt a kinship to this place. Now that we owned it, what should we do with it?

Here the Yale man could go back in time while the rest of America rushed openhanded into the future. How easy he found it to gun down seven Dall sheep rams one summer evening with only eight shots. Yes, the sheep could be hard to find, living at high elevation. But once found and approached with quiet determination, they made easy targets. Market hunters, combing these mountains for wild game to feed prospectors and railroad workers, would soon shoot them all. It was theft of another kind, and not so petty. It had to be stopped.

I look at the kids. They nod in agreement.

"Otherwise," I end the story, "future generations—such as students on National Geographic Student Expeditions—would never see the only species of wild white sheep in the world."

WE BEGIN hiking down to the Savage River. The wind has abated. Patches of blue sky appear. The kids practically fly, fleet-footed, bound for the vans parked far below; vans that will carry them back east to the park entrance for ice cream and pizza. Some hold back and hike stride for stride with the old man—me—and have questions.

"So he succeeded, right?" asks Joey. "I mean, the sheep are still here, and we have a national park."

"Yes."

But it was not an easy road. Thankfully, Sheldon had capable help from Belmore Browne, who beautifully articulated the park idea (in 1915) to friends back East, including the secretary of the interior. Both Sheldon and Browne had to tread lightly and win over the right allies in the right order. Judge James Wickersham, delegate of the Territory of Alaska, disliked the idea at first and sympathized with prospectors in Kantishna, where he himself had claims. He said he wanted to protect their mining and hunting rights, and moreover, their way of life. William T. Hornaday, director of the powerful New York Zoological Society, loved the park idea and strongly opposed such special mining and hunting privileges. Sheldon recruited his colleagues in the Boone and Crockett Club; Browne recruited his in the Camp Fire Club. Together they won the endorsement of Stephen T. Mather, assistant to the secretary of the interior, who would soon find himself as the first director of a new agency called the US National Park Service.

While the American Game Protective Association commanded the public hearings, Browne, always an artist, offered this memorable testimony:

> *Giant moose still stalk the timberline valleys; herds of caribou move easily across the moss-covered hills; bands of white big-horn sheep look down on the traveler from frowning mountains, while at any time the powerful form of the grizzly bear may give the crowning touch to the wilderness picture. But while the Mount McKinley region is the fountainhead from which come the herds of game that supply the huge expanse of southcentral Alaska, that fountainhead is menaced. Slowly but surely the white man's civilization is closing in, and already sled loads of dead animals from the McKinley region have reached the Fairbanks market. Unless a refuge is set aside, in which the animals that remain can breed and rear their young unmolested they will soon follow the buffalo.*

Meaning they'll disappear as the buffalo did. "The great good that has come with our national expansion," Browne concluded, "has always been followed by evils. Are we a nation able to profit by our mistakes? Can these tragedies be prevented? Yes: but our last and only chance lies in the Mount McKinley region."

Congress signed the bill, and in early 1917 Charles Sheldon hand-delivered it to President Woodrow Wilson for his signature.

History shows that only a powerful centralized government can achieve this. On a local and even regional level, most people oppose the establishment of a national park; they say it infringes upon their cherished freedoms and economic opportunities.

In fact, just the opposite is true.

National parks create new economies.

~~~

AT A LOCAL pizza parlor that night, the kids are in a spectacular mood. For many, the hike up Mount Margaret and the discovery of five Dall sheep rams is the most difficult and rewarding outdoor adventure of their young lives. I ask one shy girl how she's doing. She says, "I feel like I could conquer the world."

"You only need to love it, Emily. Love it and honor it and change it when necessary. Find the Rachel Carson and Rosa Parks within. It's there. You are more than you think you are."

She looks at me thoughtfully.

I've told the students more than once that deep, fundamental change takes time. Some Alaskans still regard their national parks as being "locked up." They're not. They're locked *open*. Come on in. Learn to share. Be young again. Climb a mountain, run a river, sleep on the ground. Why? To reset your clock, repair your heart, rediscover what's real: the earth, your home, not a bad place to be.

The students wolf down their pizza. It's open mic night, and they dare me as perhaps I've dared them. They want me to take the stage. I grab a guitar and play Jackson Browne's "For Everyman" followed by Steve Earle's "Copperhead Road," pounding away on the offbeat—Earle does it with a mandolin and bagpipes—while the kids stomp the wooden floor and clap. Later, I tell Em and David, "This is what we do at National Geographic Student Expeditions. We invite prosperous, well-educated, well-mannered kids to Alaska and teach them moonshine songs."

THE NEXT DAY it rains, and the kids hole up inside the Denali Education Center to be students and write their research papers, one of the requirements of the program. Em, David, and I call them "students" when they're quiet and indoors, and "kids" when they're rambunctious and outside. Near as I can tell, it's more fun and healthy being kids.

Later, we drive north to Healy to visit the Usibelli Coal Mine. At the mine's entrance we wait for our guide and talk about the realities of coal. I'm surprised at how much the kids already know: that more than forty percent of the electricity generated in the United States comes from coal-fired power plants, and these kids have grown up in the comfort of that electricity, as have I; that China burns much more coal today than it did thirty years ago; that because of our coal addiction here and overseas, mercury exists in rivers and oceans around the world. And in all major seafood. And in us. The kids have studied this in high school. The more vocal ones tell me that atmospheric carbon dioxide ($CO_2$)—a planet-warming greenhouse gas produced by burning coal and other fossil fuels—will soon go above four hundred parts per million (ppm), the highest it's been in at least eight hundred thousand years, perhaps three million years, and it's increasing by about two ppm per year, and there's no sign of it stopping, even abating. They know about "methane monsters." As permafrost melts, large pockets of methane, previously trapped in the icy ground, erupt into the atmosphere. And don't forget methane hydrates (cagelike lattices of ice with molecules of methane trapped inside) everywhere beneath the ocean floor. In its first twenty years after release, methane is about eighty times more powerful than $CO_2$ as a greenhouse gas. They know all this; they know what it means. This is my generation's legacy, their generation's inheritance.

"So why do we keep digging up coal and burning it?" I ask them.

They pepper me with answers and comments:

"Because it's there, and easy to get."

"It's cheap."

"I'm not so sure it's cheap. If you factor in the long-term environmental costs and health costs, maybe it's a lot more expensive than we think it is."

"Our entire political system runs on money; lobbyists and all that, and the oil and coal industries have a lot of lobbyists, and a lot of money."

"My dad says the *London Guardian* reported that the Republican Party is the only major political party in the developed world that doesn't accept climate change, or that human beings are causing it."

"Can it ever turn around?" I ask them. They look at me skeptically, as if I've asked a trick question. I say, "When Doctor Martin Luther King Jr. stood on the steps of the Lincoln Memorial in the summer of 1963, he didn't say, 'I have a nightmare.' He could have. He'd seen terrible racial injustice, even death. What he said was, 'I have a dream.' He made us believe in a greater society, a better world. The next year, the Civil Rights Act was signed. And today we have a black man in the White House."

A few kids smile.

"The future belongs to you," I tell them, "with all its challenges and exciting possibilities. Don't shy away from it. Here comes the tour guide. Please be gracious and open-minded. Take a deep breath. Enjoy yourselves but don't goof off. You are guests here. Learn as much as you can. Reserve judgment. I'll ask you for a one- or two-word assessment upon your return. Think about it during the tour. The escort vehicle has just enough room for all of you but not me. That's fine. I've been here before. I'll wait in the van and see you in an hour."

Massive coal trucks the size of buildings thunder past as the students climb into the guide's vehicle and take off.

━━

DOES EVERY GENERATION require its apocalypse? Its dark cloud on the horizon? My parents had theirs: global thermo-nuclear war. In grade school the air raid sirens would go off and I'd climb under my desk and huddle, waiting, my knees pulled to my chest like every other dutiful student. To my left, Foxy Felicity would slide over to touch me as we sat and waited for the evil Soviet Empire to nuke Fairchild Air Force Base. Ka-boom! What a way to die, in the embrace of the cutest girl in school. I might even sneak in a kiss before we melted.

Other generations had the Holocaust, the Stalin purges, the Spanish influenza, the Hundred Years' War, the Black Plague. In sixteenth-, seventeenth-, and eighteenth- century North and South America, smallpox alone killed millions. Imagine losing ninety percent of your friends and family in one winter. In some Saxon villages, people lived their entire lives in fear of the Vikings, and for good reason. When the Vikings came, it meant death to all. In some villages, they never came; in others, they did.

I often wonder if as each of us age and fill up with bad news and its accumulated bile, and face our own mortality, do we grow fearful? Resentful? Do we assume, like the grumpy old man in front of his television, that the "world is going to hell"?

And yet, here we are. Despite tyranny, ignorance, and disease, we live on. We explore. We dream. We bring forth the unlimited power of a new youth.

I cannot tell these twelve high school kids what future awaits them. Perhaps the best I can do is offer them hope; get them to improvise and sing, suggest new pathways to creative solutions. Show them the strengths they didn't know they had, strengths they discovered in their national park.

After surviving the Holocaust, Austrian neurologist Viktor Frankl said we must turn predicament into achievement. "Our greatest freedom," he wrote, "is the freedom to choose our attitude."

Canadian journalist Naomi Klein adds, "In the hot and stormy future we have already made inevitable through our past emissions, an unshakable belief in the equal rights of all people and a capacity for deep compassion will be the only things standing between civilization and barbarism."

—◦—

AN HOUR LATER, the kids are back.

"In one or two words," I ask them, "what are your impressions? Take your time."

"Nice people."

"Practiced."

"Courteous, kind."

"Propaganda."

"Ostriches."

"Reclamation."

"Helmets, smiles."

"Coalca Cola."

"Dirty Paradox."

"Coalcaine."

"Sad."

"Hardworking."

—◦—

ANOTHER DAY at the Denali Education Center. The students research and write, talk futures, tell stories. And finally, finally . . . the next day we climb aboard a shuttle bus to head deep into the park. Em, David, and I make a pact: no talking today about climate change, ocean acidification, ecosystem decay, mass extinction, the death of democracy, or Justin Bieber. The kids are burdened enough with packing their lunches and organizing gear.

The day welcomes us with sun, rain, river, cloud, wolves, and bears, the last two at a distance. We explore the new low-profile Eielson Visitor Center, artfully built into the topography where the previous visitor center used to be. With its commitment to renewable energy and sustainability, the NPS designed the center with great care. Today, it's one of only two buildings in Alaska to achieve a platinum (highest possible) level certification from the Leadership in Energy and Environmental Design (LEED).

Inside, we discover *Seasons of Denali*, a magnificent seven-by-twelve-foot quilt by Ree Nancarrow, wife of Bill Nancarrow, the park's first permanent naturalist in the 1950s, a self-effacing veteran of the 101st Army Airborne who fought in the Battle of the Bulge, was wounded twice, and awarded two bronze stars. The quilt, with its four panels and tastefully rendered mountains, braided rivers, and tundra, along with ninety-seven species of plants, birds, and mammals, is a masterpiece. It commands an entire wall and requires a long look to be fully appreciated. A few students sit before it, study it, and write poems.

Outside, near the entrance for all to see, the two moose skulls (from the battle below Mount Galen) are on display, the antlers still locked together like an Escher painting, a Mobius strip of life and death. They too command our attention, and speculation. I hear one visitor say to another, "Jesus, what a way to die."

After lunch, we head up Thorofare Ridge.

The wind is light. Rainsqualls hit us but otherwise the hiking comes easy compared to the other day on Mount Margaret. The kids breeze up, feeling feisty, laughing, talking. One thousand feet above the visitor center, they reach the top and fan out to explore. Some get down on their bellies to photograph flowers. Others climb overlooks and take landscape shots and run free, moving with fluid grace, unlike children we see everywhere today who slouch forward, walking with their heads down, slaves to their iPhones in what Em calls "the Walking Zombie Apocalypse."

In his groundbreaking book, *The Last Child in the Woods*, Richard Louv notes that kids today don't ramble and roam. They seldom go outside. When they do, they cover an area only one-ninth the size of what kids covered forty year ago. Fearful parents today, many in cities, raise clean, wrinkle-free kids, bubble-wrapped against the worst that can happen on the evening news.

That's why it's good to have these kids—any kids—set free in Alaska. Free of television, the endless drumbeat of advertising.

HOW did we become consumed by consumerism?

In the summer of 1929, President Hoover's Committee on Recent Economic Changes observed that the biggest challenge facing growth in America was the frugality of most Americans. Industrialists worried that production threatened to become so efficient it would soon turn out goods at a pace far greater than people's desire to have them. How to solve this? Create a new culture, one that shifted from fulfilling basic human needs to creating new ones. Transform America from a nation of producers into a nation of consumers. "Economically we have a boundless field before us," concluded Hoover's committee. A field of "wants which will make way endlessly for newer wants, as fast as they are satisfied." In other words, turn *wants* into *needs*. Turn *novelties* into *necessities*.

Years later, historian Steven Stoll would write in his compelling little book, *The Great Delusion*:

*We tacitly assume—simply by the way we live—that the transfer of matter from environments into the economy is not bounded by any condition of those environments and that energy for powering our cars, dehumidifiers, leaf blowers, and iPods will always exist. We think of growth as progress. Separating these long-connected ideas is like peeling apart leaves of ancient parchment stored so long in clay jars that they have petrified into one mass. But doing the separating reveals that they are, in fact, distinct, that there can be one without the other; progress does not depend on economic growth, and economic growth does not always lead to progress.*

My advice to the kids: Climb a mountain. Learn the songs of birds. Read the secret language of storms. Befriend a flower. Listen to the land.

We're on our bellies atop Thorofare Ridge, fanned out in a radial pattern, our heads together, keying out a species of saxifrage, when a caribou appears.

"Stay still," I whisper.

A full-grown female, the caribou prances directly toward us, head up, knees high. It stops only thirty feet away, and stares, unsure what we are, given that not one of us is standing. The moment stretches itself out, back to the ice age and before, when man, woman, and beast shared shamans and dreams, and men—and hopefully women and children too—painted their stories on cave walls. Then something snaps, a memory, a fear; the caribou leaps, spins in midair, and runs off in another direction.

The kids whoop and holler.

"Did you see that?"

"Whoa."

"Cool."

"Anybody get a picture?"

No. But we have it on the fine emulsion of our minds.

BACK on the bus, eastbound, I ask the driver, Mona Bale, to slow down on the downhill run off Polychrome Pass so I can point out the East Fork Cabin. Mona, one of my favorite drivers, stops. She can guess what I want to talk about.

"That's where Adolph Murie lived, while doing fieldwork on the dynamics of predator and prey," I tell the kids, "primarily on wolves and Dall sheep, but also caribou, bears, and other species. He also lived in other park cabins, mostly the Igloo Cabin. He was the real deal, a keen observer and careful chronicler of what he saw and found, and later a lyrical writer in defense of wild Alaska. He proved that wolves not only create healthy populations of prey, they bring vitality to the entire ecosystem; they enrich the whole park. He's known today as 'the conscience of Denali.'"

"What's it like inside the cabin?" one of the kids asks me.

"I don't know."

THE BUS rumbles on.

That night, my last with the students, we share a large dinner at the Denali Education Center and tell stories, always stories, and talk over many things: What does it mean to be a critical thinker? To challenge your own assumptions before you challenge those of others? To stand atop a mountain and find God in nature, time in a flower, perfection in a caribou, poetry in a river? To question answers rather than answer questions? What does it mean to be a radical, a liberal? What did it take to free the slaves and give women the vote? To get Social Security, Workman's Compensation, a Civil Rights Act, a Wilderness Act, the first Earth Day, the establishment of Mount McKinley National Park, and its enlargement and redesignation to Denali National Park and Preserve? It took vision, hard work, and courage. It took liberal values championed again and again, always opposed by conservatives. And it's conservatives today, their fists closed tightly around their money, who despite all scientific evidence say human-caused climate change is fiction. Let us knock the wheels off their clown car. Let us write and speak with brave self-reflection and go forth, inspired by all, intimidated by none, grateful for every day, to accept seemingly insurmountable problems as golden opportunities. "Your job," I tell the kids, "is to joyously confront the crises before you. Can you do that?"

A few nod. A few appear solemn.

"Sometimes it's overwhelming," says dark-eyed Erica, bound for Cornell. "All the serious problems in the world, the magnitude is so huge."

I tell her I feel the same way sometimes. Em and David, the two instructors, agree.

"Try this," I tell Erica. "Fall in love every day. Fall in love with a friend, a flower, a cloud, a novel, a poem, an idea, a song. Fall in love with words, with life. Open your heart to the beauty around you every day. Can you do that?"

"Yes."

"Have you fallen in love with Denali?"

"Yes, we all have."

"Good. So I have a final question for you, for all of you."

"Bring it on," says Joey, grinning.

"What would you rather be, a domestic dog or a wolf?"

They laugh and throw back their heads to raise a racket, a howl, so wild and free and pack-like. This time their answers add up to the opposite of what they were a week ago: ten kids say wolf, two say domestic dog.

"What's changed?" I ask.

"Everything," Joey says. "Everything changes in the wilderness."

"How so?"

He shakes his head.

There are no words.

Only tears.

# CHAPTER ELEVEN

# The Grasshopper Effect

FIRST, we walk around the cabin and slowly run our fingers over the weathered wood and rusted nail heads. Second, we remove the window shutters on the cabin's south and east walls, each with a couple dozen nails pounded through from the inside out to discourage break-ins by grizzlies. Third, we unlock the door and step inside. No building is more welcoming or fitted to its surroundings. All this time neither Melanie nor I have spoken a word.

Finally she says, "It's like opening a gift and walking into it."

"Like walking into history," I add.

For the next ten days it's ours: Denali's revered East Fork Cabin, built in 1928 next to the East Fork of the Toklat River, a favorite among park rangers, scientists, and artists. "I can't believe it," Melanie says. "I can't believe we get to be *here*."

In one corner stands a double-wide bunk bed; in another corner, a gas-burning stove and simple kitchen where a wood-burning stove used to be. At the south window, a table and chairs offer space for research, writing, poker, and popcorn. Simple pleasures. Overhead, a bookshelf contains literature both scientific and casual. Best of all, on the west wall, over the door, a large poster says:

*If we could learn to love space as deeply as we are now obsessed with time.*

—EDWARD ABBEY

The scoundrel. There's no escaping him.

We have our packs and duffel bag filled with clothing and food, and from the National Park Service a tote of pillows, clean linen, and books, including a photographic book inscribed to us by park superintendent Paul Anderson, who worked with Melanie in the Grand Canyon in the 1970s. While Paul usually occupies the cabin this time of year— in early September, a prized time with the park ablaze in autumn—he's about to retire and has much to do. So it's ours. Somehow I've been chosen as the park's writer-in-residence. A gift that comes with stipulations: Don't burn down the cabin or run it like a hostel. Always lock and shutter it up when we leave, and call into headquarters every night by satellite phone. Let them know we're still alive. "Can you remember that?" I ask Melanie. I'm still running it through my head: we live, we call; we die, we don't call. Makes sense.

Yesterday, we created a minor kerfuffle when we arrived at headquarters without a private vehicle. "I don't think we've ever had a writer-in-residence arrive here without their own truck or car," said Tim Rains, the park's media specialist. "How'd you get to the park?"

"By train from Fairbanks," I told him. "We'll travel into the park tomorrow by camper bus and get dropped off at the spur road to the cabin, if that's okay?"

"That should work."

It worked, though not without drama. We had a dolly to roll the tote and duffel down the spur road, but hadn't planned on a howling windstorm that nearly knocked Melanie off her feet; we'd learn later that countless birch and spruce trees were leveled that day in and around Anchorage.

THE CABIN embraces us.

After a nap, we take a walk. The wind has abated, but clouds like falcons race over high peaks. Clouds of prey.

The river runs feisty and rambunctious. Not a bus on the road. Pastel light. New snow on the Alaska Range. We watch a subadult grizzly opposite the river from us. He works a soapberry patch, then climbs up to the road, chews on an orange traffic cone and knocks it over. He (she?) ambles across the East Fork Bridge and looks around, as if from a Kipling story, saying, "Them guvmint boys built this just for *me*."

On the near side of the bridge, the bear drops out of view as a bus rumbles down from Polychrome Pass. Once the bus passes, the bear emerges again and continues our way, back on the road, walking as only a bear can walk, head slightly down, shoulders rolling with entitlement, forepaws flipping forward with each powerful, graceful step. We retreat back to the cabin and sleep twelve hours that night, unmolested by the modern world. We awaken to deep silence. I tell Melanie, "If this is the way life used to be, I was born too late."

IN 1929, the same year President Hoover's economic commission recommended that the United States destroy thrift among its citizens to become a consumer society, a young forester named Robert Marshall moved into a small log cabin in the northernmost mountains in the world, the central Brooks Range, in Arctic Alaska. Ostensibly there to study trees, Marshall found a more interesting subject in what he described as people "who have made for themselves the happiest civilization," namely, the prospectors, trappers, and subsistence hunters, gatherers, and gardeners of the little town of Wiseman, where everybody appeared fulfilled and content. How could this be? How could people with so little be so full?

Marshall, then twenty-eight, had grown up the privileged son of a wealthy New York lawyer/environmentalist with a

lavish home in Manhattan and a summer home on Sara-
nac Lake, in the Adirondacks. Why give that up for a life so
rudimentary and crude? Was this just an experiment, a dal-
liance, an enchantment? A chance for a spoiled New Yorker
to play pioneer for a summer; to visit the past without being
condemned to its worst realities? Or was Marshall, himself
an environmentalist who would soon cofound The Wilderness Society, onto something?

In his acclaimed essay, "Are You an Environmentalist or
Do You Work for a Living?" historian Richard White writes that
many of today's environmentalists see work as the destruction of nature rather than a way of knowing nature. Mainstream environmentalism "creates a popular imagery that
often harshly condemns all work in nature," while less strident
streams of environmentalism "sentimentalize certain kinds of
farming and argue that work on the land creates a connection
to place that will protect nature itself." White acknowledges
that those who insist "that physical labor on the land estab-
lishes an attachment that protects the earth from harm have,
however, a great deal of history against them."

As Andy Kerr of the Oregon Natural Resources Council
says, "World War III is the war against the environment. The
bad news is, the humans are winning."

"The human weapon in Kerr's war," White says, "is work
. . . hard physical labor," while environmentalists "often fail
to think very deeply about their own work and its relation
to nature."

Good point. As I look about the cabin what do I see? All
the processed city food Melanie and I have brought with us:
freeze-dried dinners from REI (just add water, what kind
of work is that?), pasta from Fred Meyer (again, add water,
very difficult), tortilla chips and mango salsa from Costco
(jumbo-sized, now on sale, three for the price of two), and
popcorn from . . . wait, where's the popcorn? Oh, no. We
forgot the popcorn.

How charming would this cabin life be if we had to build it ourselves? Maintain it? Hunt and gather our own food? Spear a caribou and eat it? And from the hide make footwear and a coat? Use an outhouse at forty below? And when a toothache becomes intolerable, what then?

~~~

ONE DAY in the Utah desert, Ed Abbey spotted a young cottontail and was, he said, "taken by the notion to experiment—on the rabbit. Suppose, I say to myself, you were out here hungry, starving, no weapon but your bare hands." What to do? How to stay alive? He picks up a rock and lets it fly straight at the rabbit's "furry head." As if guided by a Higher Power, according to Abbey, the rock sails true and strikes with precision. "The wicked rabbit is dead. For a moment I am shocked by my deed . . . I examine my soul: white as snow. Check my hands: not a trace of blood. No longer do I feel isolated from the sparse and furtive life around me, a stranger from another world." Abbey regards the experiment as a complete success, adding, "it will never be necessary to perform it again." His conclusion is mostly an assumption: if he needed to kill to survive, he could. He would.

In the late 1960s Dick Proenneke, a retired diesel mechanic from Kodiak, moved out to Upper Twin Lake, in what is today's Lake Clark National Park, and built his own log cabin, a real beauty, and filmed himself doing it. "In his more than twenty years there," Tom Walker once told me, "he killed only two mammals." He caught fish and shopped in Anchorage once or twice a year, and received supplies from strangers who came calling after his movie and a book that profiled him, *One Man's Wilderness*, captured the attention of thousands.

"Like Kerr," White continues, "most Americans celebrate nature as the world of original things. . . . We seek the purity of our absence, but everywhere we find our own fingerprints.

. . . We cannot come to terms with nature without coming to terms with our own work "

Perhaps this is why I like Brad Ebel and his Denali maintenance gang, guys out working on the road, getting it right at every culvert and curve, gradient, and slope. They use big machinery but every so often you see a guy bent over a shovel, digging.

Christine Byl, a Healy author and self-described "trail-dog," writes in her memoir, *Dirt Work*, "If you're curious, any task can offer something new. . . . In many cases, labor happens when you can't afford to pay someone else to do it. We learn a task because the timing was right and the opportunity came along. Or the work just needed to be done. One way or another, there is always work to do, and someone who has to—gets to—wants to—do it."

ROBERT (BOB) MARSHALL greatly admired the hardworking people of Wiseman, their toughness and independence, but also their spirit of community, the quiet way they looked out for each other. What concerned him from an early age was the juggernaut of our ever-expanding industrialization that destroys the natural world around us.

Richard White, the serious academic, concludes that if we fail to pursue the implications of our labor "we will return to patrolling the borders." Which is exactly what the NPS does. "We will turn public lands into public playgrounds; we will equate wild lands with rugged play; we will imagine nature as an escape, a place where we are born again. It will be a paradise where we leave work behind." Not such a bad thing. But in so doing, White cautions:

> *We will condemn ourselves to spending most of our lives outside of nature, for there can be no permanent place for us inside. . . . If, on the other hand, environmentalism could focus on our work rather than*

*on our leisure, then a whole series of fruitful new angles on the world might be possible.*

Marshall spent the summer of 1929 in Wiseman and returned for thirteen months in 1930–1931, toughing out a winter and loving it, all of which he chronicled in *Arctic Village*, his book that won praise from no less than H. L. Mencken, who wrote of the Wisemanites, "They have no politicians. Their police force is rudimentary and impotent. Above all, they are not cursed with theologians. . . . They are freer to be intelligent, and what is more, decent."

Today, the Haul Road and Trans-Alaska Pipeline run right past Wiseman, connecting Fairbanks to Prudhoe Bay and the town of Deadhorse, the end of the road and the beginning of the pipeline, where one day, if science-based predictions of climate change come true, rusting oil facilities will stand flooded by melting permafrost and a rising acidic Arctic Ocean.

AS SOME decision makers explore both sides of this vexing issue, others do not. Theirs is a one-way journey of close-mindedness. In short, a crusade. Bertrand Russell, a good thinker and one of Ed Abbey's exemplars, observed: "The trouble with the world is that the stupid are cocksure and the intelligent are full of doubts."

My friend and neighbor Hank Lentfer once suggested, "We should each lower our carbon footprint and get around on bicycles . . . and horse-drawn buggies." Hank uses an outhouse.

"Like the Amish," I replied.

"If I had just ten gallons of gas, I'd ration it in my chainsaw to cut firewood."

"You wouldn't need any gas to bring down a moose. Just a snare, a mountain bike, a wagon, and a bunch of really strong teenagers."

"Or a gun."

"And one bullet, maybe two."

"And a sharp knife."

"Do the Amish hunt?"

"Yeah, they sneak up on a deer and build a barn around it."

"Did you know that each year one hundred million trees are turned into twenty billion mail-order catalogs?"

"Where'd you hear that?"

"I read it in a mail-order catalog."

I also read in *Alaska Business Monthly* that according to University of Alaska economist Scott Goldsmith, Alaska's population and economy would be about half of its current size were it not an oil state. Alaska today would be more like Maine, Goldsmith said, "a great place to live but not the best place to make a living."

Is "a great place to live" good enough? In Alaska, apparently not. What other state—pampered and cajoled by Big Oil—pays its residents every year to live here? And once pampered, who are we? Who am I? If only oil and coal didn't have their downsides, but they do, and we cannot afford to believe otherwise. We cannot afford to be more devoted to comfort than we are to change. We cannot afford to be hoodwinked by cable TV news where one person's ignorance is as valid as another person's knowledge, and the loudest guy wins.

Tom Walker once told me, "I think Alaska would immediately lose ten to twenty percent of its population if the oil dividend checks suddenly stopped coming. For a lot of Alaskans that money is what makes it or breaks it for them." And if the oil itself stopped coming?

BOB MARSHALL's Alaska had no oil or large coal mines, no annual dividend checks. Yet by many accounts it was a wonderful place to live. Old timers today still speak wistfully about the pre-statehood and pre-pipeline days. Again and again, early explorers (and later, anthropologists, such as my friend Richard Nelson) recorded Native peoples who lived in harmony, not dominion, with a wild world made sufficiently abundant by their reverence and skills. Among the Koyukon, still today, everything has a spirit. Not only is the hunter watchful, so is the forest and the sky. To survive—even thrive—for hundreds of generations in winter's deep cold, the Koyukon, according to Nelson, "are ever conscious that they are among spirits. Each animal is far more than what can be seen; it is a personage and a personality, known from its legacy in stories of the Distant Time."

Yes, hard times could be brutally hard. People have always starved and died in the woods. They've also starved and died in cities. Among Alaskans, it's easier and more interesting to write and talk about people who die in the wilderness. Take Chris McCandless. Take John Franklin, who got so hungry in the Canadian Arctic that he ate his own shoes. Years later, in the mid-1840s, he returned with a large expedition in search of the fabled Northwest Passage and every man starved or froze to death. Or Fred Frickett, who, during a fifteen-hundred-mile expedition of the Copper, Tanana, and Koyukuk river valleys, survived by eating rotten salmon, rotten goose eggs, and boiled meat with maggots. The stories go on and on, as Sherry Simpson writes: "so many ways to die in the north, in manners grand and surprising and sad."

She adds, "even as searchers looked for a man who had disappeared in the Chugach Mountains came the news that seventy-year-old Dick Cook, an extraordinary woodsman described by John McPhee as the 'acknowledged high swami of the river people,' had drowned in the Tatonduk, a river he knew intimately."

THE Mayflower Pilgrims hardly described virgin seven-teenth-century America as a paradise; instead, they found a "hideous and desolate wilderness" surrounding them with dark and dangerous forests that must be vanquished to make America safe and strong. In the wilderness lived the dreaded wolf, the wild dog that never joined our campfire or accepted our rules; the one that waited just out of view, malicious, malevolent, always hungry, desperate to eat little children or a fat cow or a prized pig.

Two hundred years later, in 1831, Alexis de Tocqueville, a French aristocrat, arrived in America eager to see what Europe had lost long ago: the frontier, the exciting bound-ary between civilization and wilderness that tested men like nothing else. He found it in the Michigan Territory where American pioneers compulsively obliterated forests and built farms and considered the Frenchman insane for want-ing to see wild country for *pleasure*. In *Democracy in Amer-ica*, Tocqueville wrote,

> *In Europe people talk a great deal of the wilds of America, but the Americans themselves never think about them; they are insensible to the inanimate wonders of nature and they may be said not to perceive the mighty forests that surround them till they fall beneath the hatchet. Their eyes are fixed upon another sight . . . the march across these wilds, draining swamps, turning the course of rivers, peopling solitudes, and subduing nature.*

One year later, artist George Catlin traveled up the Mis-souri River into the Dakota Territories where he witnessed Mandan Indians, brilliant horsemen, slaughtering bison for whiskey money, provoked by loud-mouthed, rifle-bearing white men who could drink, talk, smoke, and shoot, but not ride. Catlin proposed that a "nation's park" be established to save some small slice of the original North America before it all disappeared.

It took forty years to get Yellowstone; another eighteen years to get Yosemite and Sequoia. Other national parks soon followed: Mount Rainier, Crater Lake, Wind Cave, Mesa Verde, Glacier, Rocky Mountain, Hawaii Volcanoes, Lassen Volcanic, and Mount McKinley. All scenic wonders, though Mount McKinley was established to protect its wildlife, particularly Dall sheep.

In 1935, a little more than a century after Tocqueville and Catlin made their prescient observations, a small cadre of visionary scientists and writers—Bob Marshall, Aldo Leopold, Robert Sterling Yard, Sigurd F. Olson, and Olaus Murie—formed The Wilderness Society.

Their objective, in Marshall's words, was to "battle uncompromisingly" to save what wild areas remained. "The average person, living in mechanized civilization," Marshall concluded in Arctic Village, "has small opportunity for genuine adventure."

> But there is not a person past infancy in the entire Koyukuk who cannot look back on repeated adventures which would put to shame the imaginative tales consumed by millions of thrill-starved citizens of the United Sates. There is an exultation in snowshoeing at mid-winter to the Arctic Divide, in meeting the hazards involved in the passage of some swollen wilderness river, in subsisting a hundred miles from the closest human being, which adds tone, vitality and color to the entire functioning of life.

HOW LONG do any of us have? Bob Marshall made it to thirty-eight before his heart failed him on a midnight train from Washington, DC. Porters found him dead in his berth when the train arrived in New York City's Penn Station. Aldo Leopold, who once said, "Of what avail are forty freedoms without a blank spot on the map?," died fighting a neighbor's grass fire only weeks after finishing his most influential book, *A Sand County Almanac*. John Dalle-Molle, Denali's legendary resource manager, died too young of cancer. Phil Brease, the park's beloved geologist, died of a heart attack while on a field trip, doing what he loved. Rob Hammel, a ski patrolman and one of Brad Ebel's most reliable grader operators, stopped on the Seward Highway to lend a helping hand at the scene of an accident when an out-of-control vehicle struck and killed him. Gordon Haber, an independent and outspoken wolf biologist who seldom failed to offer colorful public testimony in defense of the wild animals he considered his brothers, went down in a plane while doing aerial surveys.

Each was a heartbreaking loss.

And then came Sandy Kogl, who had great vitality until one day in her garden when she turned to plant carrots and felt a pain in her rib. Other pains followed. It took months to get an accurate diagnosis: ALS, Lou Gehrig's disease. Melanie and I visited her shortly before she died. Her face was thin but still luminous with the smile she'd used to charm James Watt thirty years before. "Don't wait too long to retire," she told Melanie. "Get out there. Go on great adventures."

Forget success. Be a healer, peacekeeper, storyteller. Eat homegrown carrots and potatoes. Sleep in a small cabin; let the mountains be your mansion.

Sandy and George had gone on many long trips through the Alaska and Brooks Ranges before it was over. After Sandy died, George tried to live alone in their Talkeetna home but found it saddened him, filled as it was with profound emptiness. With help from neighbors, the old wrangler quietly packed up and moved back to Montana to be with his daughter and her family.

I recalled Sandy telling me once about driving to work, near park headquarters, and seeing tourists on the Rock Creek Bridge, taking photos. "I drive over that creek every day and take it for granted, and hardly look at it," she said, "and here were these visitors charmed by something I pass by all the time but had stopped seeing in my daily routine, a simple wild creek tumbling over boulders and past little flowers. It reminded me of how lucky I am to work in a national park. How lucky we all are. How I need to slow down and look around and listen more deeply and completely."

Perhaps the most difficult work before us is to work less, and play more. Creativity is the key. Stay young. Live simply, frugally. Turn work into play. Find what you're passionate about and do it with great gratitude. The money will follow, maybe. Be a playful worker, a hardworking player, a musician, an artist, a writer, a teacher—the best teacher in town.

Not everybody finds—or looks for—the Tom Sawyer within, the Huckleberry Finn ready to challenge the system as unjust. Recall that Tom not only avoided work by getting his friends to whitewash the fence for him, he in fact got them to *pay him* for doing his work. He's our great American hero. And for good reason. He's more creative than the others.

"Any fool can destroy trees," said John Muir, another hero. What's hard is to stand before the truck, the tank, the big machine, whatever it might be, and say "no more." You've had your run. This is where the folly ends. It's time to dig deep, get creative, do something new. Ride a bicycle to Honduras; volunteer in an orphanage. Pick papayas. Eat mangos.

---

EASY FOR ME to say? And wrong? Environmentalists are expected to avoid the rant and chant, the polemic and complaint. Let us stand before our burning home and whisper "fire." Let us hold hands and sing while nature unravels and oceans rise and disparity increases and democracy dies. All while the rich go about business as usual. This, too, is a recipe for collapse.

Aristotle waited until the final school year to teach his students the power and pitfalls of rhetoric, what he called "the art of persuasive theory." First came *logos*, the logical argument. Then *ethos*, the credibility of the speaker. And finally *pathos*, the emotional connection. And if those failed, what then? Mangos? Banjos? Bludgeon them with bluegrass?

Thomas Jefferson observed that to keep our democracy healthy and alive in the hands of the common people we'd need a rebellion every twenty years. As Ben Franklin and his distinguished colleagues departed Independence Hall after drafting the Constitution, a Philadelphia woman asked, "Mr. Franklin, what kind of government have you given us?" The old statesman and scientist, confined to a wheelchair, responded, "A republic, madam, if you can keep it."

AT TIMES in the cabin, late at night while Melanie sleeps and I write by candlelight and step outside into the big quiet where the milky moon rolls over the tireless East Fork River and the mountains hold their breath, I feel the arc of the ages. Immediately to the south rises an alluvial terrace sixty feet high, while to the north, the river, previously braided over the Plains of Murie, funnels into a tight rocky chasm. What happened here? My guess: a great volume of water once filled this place. Perhaps a massive block of glacial ice dammed the chasm and impounded a lake behind it. Sediments previously suspended by running water settled to the lake bottom and accumulated for many years, perhaps decades, only to be washed away once the ice dam broke and the river ran wild again, cutting and eroding, leaving here and there a few terraces as evidence of the past. Such are the signatures of water, of erosion and deposition, stasis and change.

This is the terrain Adolph Murie knew well, the landscape of his dreams. How could he hike these storied slopes and not be touched by deep time and recent events, influenced as well by his older brother and the other visionaries who'd founded The Wilderness Society? The road to Wonder Lake, built from 1922 to 1938, had just been completed when Murie settled into the East Fork Cabin to begin his classic study on the wolves of the park. Fresh from his coyote research in Yellowstone, he embraced a new but yet-to-be-widely-accepted science-in-the-parks ethic championed by Joseph Grinnell, George Melendez Wright, Joseph S. Dixon, and others, an ethic that acknowledged scenery was marvelous, it was obvious, but scenery without its full complement of wildlife was incomplete. These biologists, according to historian Richard West Sellars, "were gaining an increasing comprehension of the role of habitat in the survival of species; and an understanding of the importance of the overall environment . . . food chains, predator-prey relationships, and other interrelationships of animal and plant life." They also recognized "a fundamental conflict in national park management: that efforts to perpetuate natural conditions would have to be 'forever reconciled' with the presence of large numbers of people."

Just as Stephen Mather, first director of the National Park Service, used his personal fortune to help champion tourism in the parks, George Melendez Wright, the son of a San Francisco ship captain and an El Salvadoran woman of the moneyed elite, used his fortune to help initiate scientific studies in the national parks. After graduating from the University of California at Berkeley (where he studied under the influential Grinnell), Wright headed to Alaska with fellow zoologist Joseph Dixon to see what America looked like before it was industrialized, citified, and smothered with farms.

In the summer of 1926, in Mount McKinley National Park, Wright discovered what he called "an outstanding assemblage of animal life," including the first ever discovery of a surfbird nest. "Recognizing the superlative natural laboratory and unique wildlife gathering offered by McKinley Park," observed historian William E. Brown, "Wright and Dixon launched their investigations. . . Their work constituted the first comprehensive ecologically based survey of the park."

Later, with his new perspective, Wright criticized the NPS, an agency dominated by engineers and landscape architects, for "game farming" in Yosemite, Yellowstone, and elsewhere.

For many years the NPS had shot predators, primarily wolves, to make charismatic prey more abundant and easy to see. Elk in Yellowstone, for instance. Park visitors loved how they grazed and stood around statuesque, the bulls in full autumn rut, bugling in the Wyoming mist. Enjoyment in Yellowstoneland. What could be better? But something was wrong. These regal elk, once alert to the slightest movement in the grass, the sharpest edge of predation, were becoming cattle with antlers that overgrazed meadows, trampled riverbanks, and became too numerous for the ecological health of everything around them.

Beginning in 1929, Wright spearheaded (and financed with his own money) a massive wildlife survey of the western parks, designed in part to reshape the NPS into a science-based decision-making agency. Tragically, he died too young in a car accident in New Mexico in 1936.

"Although not fully apparent at the time," noted Sellars, "the loss of Wright's impressive leadership skills marked the beginning of the decline of the National Park Service science programs." In the years that followed, the number of research biologists in the NPS decreased dramatically.

Into this vacuum—and exaggerated accounts of game-slaughter by wolves in Alaska—stepped Adolph Murie. His primary objective: good empirical science. His subject: the wolves of Mount McKinley National Park. The political pressure to eliminate wolves was immense as it came from the same game-protection groups that had fought for the creation of the park only two decades before. Their iconic animal, the Dall sheep, was in jeopardy with low numbers. The wolves had to go.

Over three years, 1939–1941, Murie walked seventeen hundred miles and studied more than eight hundred Dall sheep skulls to determine their age and health at death. At one point he watched a wolf family for thirty-three hours straight, and later tweezed apart 1,174 wolf droppings to identify the species of plants, hair, and bones they contained. More than once his young daughter joined him to observe wolves playing outside their den, howling and greeting each other and frisking about. Here was the magic of Denali, a world willing to share its secrets with anyone who had the patience to listen and watch, to have his heart enlarged, his wits sharpened.

Murie's conclusion: wolves have a salutary effect on prey populations by culling out the old, weak, and infirm. They improve the vitality of *everything*. Furthermore, they howl. What cranes and loons are to birds, wolves are to dogs. Uncaged, unleashed, they are freedom.

Of course Murie's conclusions were met with derision, and still are today among those incapable of conquering their contempt for the wild dog that plays by its own rules, not ours. As chair of the Alaska Board of Game, Cliff Judkins said in 2010, "I've seen pictures [that a photographer took of wolves in Denali]—looks like some mangy dogs walking down the dusty road with the bus alongside them. But it's just not appealing to me at all. I guess people in that bus think it's just great. But it's just not what Alaska is."

What then is Alaska?

The State of Alaska Intensive Management Law of 1994 reflects the state's constitution: that wildlife on state lands must be managed for the highest sustainable yield for human consumption. In other words, for maximum productivity on the Great Alaska Moose Farm and Caribou Ranch. Surrounded by three state game management units that have active predator control programs, Denali wolves run the gauntlet. In 2000, the state established buffer zones for their protection, including the so-called Wolf Townships along the Stampede Road. Trapping and hunting became illegal. But in 2010 the Alaska Department of Fish and Game let these buffers lapse. The NPS and the Denali Citizens Council requested that the Board of Game (BOG) keep and enlarge the buffers, but the BOG voted to eliminate them.

Also in 2010, the State of Alaska sided with Usibelli Coal Mine by denying a request by the Denali Citizens Council to exclude areas adjacent to the park from a license to drill for coal bed methane. Centuries' worth of coal on the existing Usibelli lands apparently wasn't enough. Steady sales overseas and handsome paychecks for all employees wasn't enough. Big Coal wanted more. The case was bound for the Alaska Supreme Court, where the Alaska State Constitution, with its "split estate" clause, allows industry to enter onto state and private land.

It's no trivial matter then.

What is Alaska? What is Denali? And who is it for?

A TEENAGE Thai girl from Bangkok once visited Alaska. The daughter of a successful businessman, she'd already seen Paris and Cairo, the Amazon and the Nile, Hawaii's Waikiki Beach and Australia's Great Barrier Reef. Her host family—my friends Richard Steele and his wife Luann McVey, and their daughters Lydia and Laura—found her quiet and reserved as they ushered her around, hoping to please her with the vast and wild beauty. They hiked up mountains and walked on glaciers and watched brown bears catch salmon.

They caught a few fish themselves, as humpback whales spouted all around. Finally Richard and Luann, fearful that the reserved Thai girl might not be enjoying herself, pressed her for an impression. "Is everything okay?"

"Oh yes, thank you."

"Do you like what you're seeing?"

"Oh yes. It's very nice."

"Are you happy?"

"Oh yes, very happy. Thank you."

"Why are you happy?"

"Oh . . . it's all so clean and pretty here. I thought the whole world was already ruined with too many people and too much pollution, but it isn't. Alaska gives me hope for the future, for the whole human race."

———

PRIOR to our ten days in the East Fork Cabin, Melanie and I stayed for a week in the Wonder Lake Campground. On the bus ride back east (to resupply for our cabin time), I met a bright-faced Navajo Indian woman, Kim Arthur, who was interning as an archivist at Denali National Park, hoping to parlay it into a full-time job. She told me that last Christmas she'd moved back in with her family in Phoenix and found minimum wage work boxing up orders at the so-called Amazon Fulfillment Center, a place *Wired* magazine would describe as "a one million square foot cavern of consumerism . . . a uniquely 21st-century creation, a vast, networked, intelligent engine for sating consumer desire . . . a realm where the machines, not the humans, are in charge." On the big, white, windowless wall above the guarded entrance where fifteen hundred employees punched in and out every day, large black letters announced: "work hard. have fun. make history."

Kim said she lasted only a few weeks before she was abruptly let go after the holiday gift-buying rush. Getting hired there was a relief in tough economic times, she said. "But the whole experience really made me sad. And to think that some people work there for years."

~~~

LATE AT NIGHT, while Melanie sleeps and stars turn on their axis and the river plays its final autumn refrain, I find myself with a candle, reading futurist Ray Kurzweil who writes with great excitement about the coming "singularity" when genetics, robotics, and nanotechnology will enable us to transcend our own biology, break the shackles of our own evolutionary legacy, write a new human destiny, achieve inconceivable heights of intelligence and material progress, and witness a revolution that will dwarf anything from before. In this new and wondrous man-machine civilization of wearable technology, we'll never be offline. Cell-sized computers injected into our bloodstream will detect the earliest signs of medical problems and fix them instantly; we'll defy death and live forever, for centuries at least.

Not so, says British physicist James Lovelock, who in the early 1970s introduced us to the Gaia theory: the idea of Earth as a single self-regulating organism. He says we've been sleepwalking into the future for far too long. The teeter has tottered. We've passed the tipping point. George W. Bush was right about one thing: Americans are addicted to oil. As addicts, we behave poorly, even destructively, not in our own long-term best interest. By the year 2100, Lovelock says, a perfect storm of climate change, overpopulation, and economic collapse will create mayhem of such epic proportions that the world's human population will be reduced to only a small fraction of what it is today.

What am I to make of this?

For centuries utopians have said we're on the verge of universal abundance, a time of no more suffering. And for centuries doomsdayers, naysayers, and endtimers have said we're in big trouble: "The end is near."

Is this time any different?

Take a deep breath.

The river has been here for ten thousand years.

IN 1981, when he was a twenty-one-year-old college student, Dave Schirokauer drove from New Jersey to Denali and joined a long-haired ranger/naturalist on a discovery hike. The ranger wore red socks and told Schiro that working for the National Park Service in Alaska was a pretty sweet deal. Three years later Schiro returned as a park intern. Today, he's a career scientist who, like many other park employees, shares a compassion for all life, now and yet to come. Specializing in inventory (what's here?) and monitoring (how's it doing?), Schiro studies vital signs and has the long view. He sees ten years of climate numbers as one data point. "We have to make the data relevant to tomorrow," he says. "Ninety-nine percent of Denali's visitors haven't been born yet. This park is for them."

Schiro's colleague, Environmental Specialist Andrea Blakesley, describes the park as "clean but not pristine." She tells me, "Contaminants from international sources, including North America, are carried all over the world on air currents, depositing and evaporating and blowing somewhere else over and over again. They get stuck at colder, higher latitudes like Alaska in a process called the 'grasshopper effect' or 'global fractionation,' simply because re-evaporation doesn't work as well in the cold. The intercontinental transport pathways that drive global fractionation bring mercury, DDT, PCBs and other persistent ecosystem contaminants to Denali in very low concentrations, which increase as the contaminants accumulate over time and work their way up the food chain." In some parts of Alaska, fish now carry mercury at toxic levels.

This is how the coal we export comes back to us, slowly, quietly, inexorably.

So while Denali is in some respects an island, and an ideal, as is all of Alaska, it's also locked into global patterns and events. It needs our wisest stewardship, perhaps a rebellion now and then.

———

MELANIE awakens. She knows I'm writing about climate change. "How's my rebel?" she asks.

"Tired."

"Blow out the candle and come to bed."

"Soon."

"Now."

"Okay."

She holds me and calms me and tells me she's taking me hiking tomorrow. Time to think from the feet up, not the head down. The manuscript will still be here when we return, she says. I'm falling asleep to something distant yet near, a deep breathing that's not my own and yet conducts me and takes me where I need to go.

I don't want a wolf to be my trophy or pet. I don't want him as a friend. I want him to be my patient teacher, my magical, mysterious cousin on the tree of life, his branch not far from mine, nourished by the same sun and sky, made strong by the same wind and rain.

I've heard others talk about how nature works; how natural systems function and operate. They say we must work *in* nature and *for* nature. Fine. For me, though, nature doesn't work. It plays and sings. Take the rivers with their rock and roll, the storms with their symphonic peaks, the flowers with their gentle refrains. And best of all, the wild animals and birds with their syncopated sevenths and ninths, all jazzed up, suspended, moving in four-five time to the greatest rhythm of all, the mystery around and within us.

This is how I dream.

# CHAPTER TWELVE

# Hiking with Melanie

ON A COLD spring morning ten years before I first arrived in Denali, I walked across London's Abbey Road. It took less than a minute, the same as I imagined it took the Beatles when photographed for their famous album cover. The sun shone bright in a blue cloudless sky. A woman passed by with a baby stroller and smiled. She'd seen guys like me before: young, lost, curious, disheveled, almost handsome, standing in the middle of their own surprise, faces filled with fascination and unspoken hunger. I caught myself listening for harmonies and guitar riffs coming from the unpretentious building behind the white wall. Abbey Road Studios. How serene it seemed, quiet for a big city.

This is where John Lennon showed up one morning and played "Strawberry Fields Forever" on his acoustic guitar.

Paul McCartney, at the piano, like a bird, sang "Hey Jude," the song he'd written for John's young son, Julian.

George Harrison, back from his meditations in India, invited his friend Eric Clapton to play electric lead on his haunting elegy, "While My Guitar Gently Weeps."

And Ringo Starr, the lucky guy, played drums.

This is where a nineteen-year-old kid from Spokane—the person I used to be—stood alone, footsore, confused.

If anybody had given me the courage to be different, to question authority, to check "other" at the bottom of my high school career questionnaire, it was these four guys from Liverpool who turned the world upside down. And right side up.

⌒

BACK HOME, my friend Kelly and I would play our guitars for hours, years, millennia, covering the Beatles and earning our calluses while continents drifted and species evolved. Music was our universe, our obsession. We fell into it like Alice into her looking glass. We couldn't explain it because obsessions cannot be explained. That's what makes them obsessions. That's what seventeen-year-old kids do: they obsess.

Music gave me a freedom and inspiration beyond what I got when throwing a baseball or shooting guns. It required no score, no opponent, no target. The more I improved the more I enjoyed it. The more I enjoyed it the more I improved.

The future was approaching head on at a thousand miles an hour, all speed with no driver or brakes, a diesel-charged, coal-fired, get-on-board or get-run-over eighteen-wheeler, rocket-launcher, locomotive, supersonic drag racer. Go to college or go to war. Go to the left or go to the right. Love your country or leave it. Be somebody or nobody, a patriot or a traitor, a Republican or a Democrat, a conservative or a liberal, a redneck or a greenie, a hawk or a dove. There's no in-between. The middle of the road had only two things: a yellow streak and dead dogs.

In movie theaters back then, *2001: A Space Odyssey* showed Dave the astronaut tethered to his spaceship, back-dropped by deep blackness as he tried to outwit the HAL 9000 computer set to Johann Strauss's "Blue Danube Waltz." And from Arctic Alaska came another deep blackness, one far below the tundra. Atlantic-Richfield had announced the discovery of oil at Prudhoe Bay. "An elephant," they called it. A bonanza.

Nobody questioned the rightness of pumping it up and burning it, least of all me. We needed oil to prosper and grow and continue to be Number One. Oil was power as power was oil, more prized than fresh water and clean air, so it seemed.

—⁓—

FORTY YEARS after my walk across Abbey Road, my knees hurt and hips ache as I struggle up a steep tundra slope in Denali, the September sun playful behind swift clouds. The ridgeline, some six hundred feet above, taunts me with its rugged beauty and unattainability. There's music here too, a concert of water, rock, and life that requires a fine ear, a lifetime of listening, a purposeful slowing down to arrive at where I belong.

Slowing down is easier these days.

Far below, Melanie climbs toward me. She stops frequently. No flower is so common or blueberry so bland as to escape her admiration. Breathing hard under a daypack filled with water, lunch, binoculars, and field guides, she bends at the waist, rests her hands on her knees, fills her lungs and moves on.

Over the past twenty years, Melanie has interviewed hundreds of prospective interpretive naturalists about working for the National Park Service in Alaska. When they grow tentative, as they sometimes do, and worry that Alaska might be too wild and far away, Melanie says, "Make your life extraordinary. If you come here, Alaska will not fail you. Everything is possible. This is Earth at its finest. Come be part of the magic."

In Alaska, anything can happen.

Even greatness.

Among the many young trick-or-treaters who came calling when we lived in Healy was Jesse Laner, the son of our good friends Arlie and Brian Swett. Jesse grew up loving basketball, hunting Dall sheep and caribou, and riding snowmachines with friends in Cantwell. As such, he spent much more time outside than inside Denali National Park. I doubt he ever heard of Robert Marshall, or Olaus and Adolph Murie.

After earning a business degree from the University of Alaska, he moved to Colorado, went into real estate, and met the love of his life, Amy. He brought her to Alaska. Not to hunt. Not to ride snowmachines. Instead, he took her into the heart of the park, near Wonder Lake. They hiked up a small hill where in full view of the highest mountain in North America, and with his heart as big as the landscape, Jesse proposed.

Amy said yes. How could she not?

———

IN JULY 1957, fifteen-year-old Paul McCartney pedaled his bike over to a Liverpool church where John Lennon's band, the Quarrymen, pounded out songs on a flatbed coal truck. John was twenty months older than Paul, a big difference at that age. Made of moxie and rough edges, John survived on boldness and wit while Paul used his good looks, musicality, and charm. To impress John, he picked up a guitar and ripped through Eddie Cochran's "Twenty Flight Rock." According to one observer, John and Paul "circled each other like cats." Still, they hit it off. Paul asked to join John's band, and John said yes. Both boys could sing and play and compose bright, original songs. While John's work tended to be "sour and weary," according to one Beatles scholar, "Paul's tended to the bright and naïve. The magic came from interaction." Also known as "creative tension." The two teens formed a musical collaboration earlier in age than brothers George and Ira Gershwin. Paul introduced John to his friend George Harrison, a quiet guitarist who would later describe his grammar school days as "the worst time of [my] life. . . . They were trying to turn everybody into little rows of toffees." With John on rhythm and George on lead, Paul (the most gifted instrumentalist of the three) moved to bass. The hard-playing, hard-singing threesome then found a skilled drummer in Richard Starkey who went by the stage name Ringo Starr.

Of course my Spokane friends and I adopted them and brought them into our homes and knew their names, stories, and songs, their lively dialogue and quirky manners as if they were four wildly creative brothers who lived down the street and charmed every girl in town, and sang original songs and made it fun and gave us the confidence to sing as well. Maybe we'd charm girls, too. They inspired us to question authority and make something of ourselves; to be more than little toffees. On the radio we heard a housewife describe the Beatles as looking "beat up and depraved in the nicest possible way."

Sounded good to us.

Late into the night we'd huddle around Kelly's record player with cold pizza. No sooner did we begin to wrap our heads around one set of songs when a new album would arrive, as stunning, daring, and original as the one before: *Rubber Soul, Yesterday . . . And Today, Revolver, Sgt. Pepper's, Magical Mystery Tour,* the *White Album, Yellow Submarine, Abbey Road, Hey Jude, Let It Be.*

Foxy Felicity's father didn't like the Beatles when they first came to America. But she did. My mom did.

So while the future came at us at full speed, it remained forever out there as well, both immediate and distant, a dimension unto itself, wise in its own way, looking back and asking me—asking us all—what side of history I wanted to be on.

It still is.

~~~

"WE WILL convince them with our conviction," said President Lyndon Johnson upon signing the Civil Rights Act in 1964, the same year he signed the Wilderness Act, the same year the Beatles came to America.

Can we have greatness without conviction?

I find myself thinking about this as I wait for Melanie. Sitting up, I pull out pen and paper to compose a letter to Adolph Murie.

*Dear Ade,*

*May I call you Ade? In historic photos I see you white-haired high atop a ridge in Mount McKinley National Park, a thousand feet or more above the Park Road, field glasses in hand, tundra underfoot, looking, always looking. You strike me as somebody who'd say, "Sure, you can call me Ade. What's your name?" Warm smile. Soft voice, almost musical. Wool shirt and pants. Ankle-top boots. I wonder how many boots you went through in your life; how many thousands of miles you walked upslope and down over tundra, river rock, and snow. It seems odd, this assumed familiarity, since we never met. You never sought the spotlight, yet here you are today: known by travelers, teachers, scientists, students, scholars, artists, and conservationists. Even a few politicians. Imagine. Living as you did, as a visionary wildlife biologist and author, you did something remarkable. You spoke the unpopular truth. While Walt Disney seduced America with cute images of three little pigs and "the big, bad wolf," you used facts and words to quietly say the opposite. You said wolves are good; they create a more robust, vibrant, and magical landscape. You took risks. You lived with great intention and reached beyond your allotted time to create an important legacy. That's how I know you.*

NEARLY sixty years after Ade's initial fieldwork, biologist David Mech observed that he did "an excellent job with the tools available to him—binoculars, sled dogs, and a notebook." And of course, two good legs and lungs, and a willingness to be out there. Ade "laid the foundation for understanding the wolf pack as a family. He described each individual in the pack and its personality, behavior, and role in the group." Mech also noted that Ade discovered that "wolves must make many attempts at catching prey for each time they succeed."

Today, with aerial radio tracking and other techniques, park biologists can monitor the number and health of all the Denali wolf packs that collectively amount to what Mech calls "the world's least disturbed mainland wolf population."

Inspired by Ade's legacy and the work of other pioneering wildlife biologists and ecologists, and prodded by a nationwide pro-wildlife campaign, the NPS reversed a distant wrongdoing in 1995 when it reintroduced thirty-one wolves into Yellowstone. For the first time in two-thirds of a century, America's most celebrated national park howled again with the music of its principle predator. The wolf population soon tripled, and the park's ecological balance and biodiversity improved in ways that seemed almost miraculous. In a phenomenon called "trophic cascade," the wolves trimmed large numbers of elk that had overgrazed meadows and stream banks, which in turn improved the health of riparian aspens and willows and many other plants, which in turn benefited rodents, coyotes, eagles, martens, foxes, owls, and others.

~

*I think you'd be fascinated, Ade, by the frontiers science continues to explore, from ecology to neurology to genetics and cosmology and all kinds of behavioral studies. We know today, for example, and this might not surprise you, that other species mourn their dead, even hold wakes. Animals once regarded as unthinking and unfeeling are in fact just the opposite. Descartes was wrong. The world is changing, albeit slowly, but changing nonetheless, developing new sensibilities and sensitivities. A recent news item from Spain tells about a matador in the bullring, the bull bleeding and half dead, about to fall. The crowd eagerly awaits the final plunge of the killing sword. And what does the matador do? In front of everybody he sits down and puts his head in his hands. Silence fills the ring. After a moment he gets up, makes*

*no gesture to the crowd, and walks out. Just like that. He walks away*
*from his profession, prestige, honor, culture, and nation. He walks*
*away from authority and tradition. He's free.*

*Perhaps it comes down to this: at least once in our modern lives*
*we should each have a profound change of heart and the courage to act*
*on it. Leave the bull standing. Walk away. Remake ourselves, and the*
*world around us.*

*You stood in that ring, Ade. In your own way, your own time, you*
*challenged the crowd, not the bull.*

*I'm not a poet; still, I ask you to accept this:*

"Tradition," said the matador as he thrust the final sword;
"Get your tickets here," said the vendor to the hoard;
"Revolution," said the bull just before he died;
"Please make it stop," said the child as she cried.
Dust and blood, the heat of the day,
staccato lines from Hemingway.
Metaphor and matador . . .
paradox, irony, conquistador.

SHEEP droppings surround me where I sit and wait for Melanie, lost in my communion. At least a couple times each year, Dall sheep must make a treacherous transit from their summer range to winter range and back, passing through low elevation forest while leaving the security of high rocky ridges and tundra. Ade once described such a crossing, how the sheep started out at two in the morning and didn't arrive at the far hills until five-thirty. "Most of the way they traveled in a compact group, stopping frequently to look ahead. Through tall willows and scattered spruce they walked in single file." Near their objective but still vulnerable, the sheep stopped to feed for forty-five minutes. Ade surmised, "They probably were hungry and came upon some choice food. When they emerged from the woods to the open hills, they were strung out considerably and galloped up the slope in high spirits, seeming relieved to have made the crossing."

*In high spirits. This intrigues me. Could we say the sheep were exuber-ant, joyous? If other species mourn their dead, might they also love and celebrate? You were a cautious man of science, Ade; I appreciate that. To accurately test for something so intangible as love in other species is no easy thing. And so science remains studiously quiet amid the din of barking dogma and ideologies.*

⌒〜⌒

WHAT would surprise Ade most about Denali today? I sus-pect the discovery of dinosaur tracks: from the first fossil track found in the park in 2005 to a total of hundreds of known sites with thousands of "trace fossils" today, and more discovered each year. The park's dedication to research would please him, together with the recruitment of young scientists, the educational outreach, and the new name and size of the park, including—and this might embarrass him, being a modest man—the Murie Science and Learn-ing Center. It might also touch him deeply. The center is in fact named for the entire Murie family and their collective accomplishments. He'd probably be astounded by the num-ber, nationalities, and age range of park visitors, and their eagerness to see Alaska. I recall the retired Iowa farmer who walked with a cane, admitting that he should have come here a long time ago, when he was young and fit, but he's here now, by God, and smiling and grateful, so never mind the calendar or clock. And the middle-aged businesswoman standing near the river and listening, her eyes wet with tears, catching her breath, feeling her heart and mind slow down for the first time in years, saying she could "feel her soul like a wing flying over the landscape."

Despite the daily countless moments of gratitude, the thousands of people finding themselves in their national park, the traffic today might dismay Ade, given the size, total number, and noise of the buses. While they once served a valuable public service, and still do, buses in Denali now have the sound and smell of industry; a necessary nuisance, always coming, going, jostling, idling. Yes, one bus is better than twenty cars. But at what point do we have too many buses?

When our finest concert halls are full, we don't stuff people in the aisles. We invite them to the next performance. If Denali National Park is Alaska's Carnegie Hall, and I believe it is, then let the land and rivers sing unfettered. Hundreds of years ago people didn't go "see" Shakespeare; they went to "hear" Shakespeare. They sought a profound listening experience, the medicine of sound, the gravity of words, the power of story to play on the imagination. So it should be in Denali: a feast for the senses.

The park road itself still has its telescoping character: from paved in the east to widely graveled midway, to narrowly graveled out west. May it so remain.

That said, let us not forget Glitter Gulch, the summer circus in the Nenana River Canyon where the big players increase guest capacity and profits by moving more of their summer employees from the canyon into Healy, busing them back and forth daily. Across the highway, somebody builds the Denali Bluffs Hotel, and cuts a road partway up a mountain and builds another hotel, the Grande Denali, visible from miles away. But why stop there? Go higher and build the Grandiose Denali. Grab a T-shirt or a trinket "on sale," though I'm still waiting for the monk at customer service who says, "Tell me if you need anything and I'll tell you how to live without it."

━━◦━━

*Forgive my sarcasm, Ade. You might recall that Robert Marshall encouraged preservationists to develop a "pixie sense of humor" to help sweeten our message. Slip it in. Make it all–American like apple pie and bluegrass. Ethos and banjos. You might also recall that John Muir wrote of wild nature's "divine harmony," and Jack London described "a mighty rhythm." I swear something's going on out there, something ancient, cosmic, musical. To call it a system of interconnectedness is too clinical, too modern. And by out there I mean in here as well; it's in each of us, and all of us.*

*National parks, forests, monuments, preserves, wildlife refuges, wild and scenic rivers, wilderness areas, and biosphere reserves: homes for the humble bear, the mournful loon, the tireless wolf and eternal flower, the little blossoms large in our hearts. We save wild places so they will one day save us. They already have.*

HERE COMES Melanie, climbing steady, wearing a big smile and blueberry stains on her fingers and pants, rising like the sun. Little darling . . .

She doesn't get any happier than she is right now.

She sits beside me and offers some berries. They explode in my mouth. We nestle into the tundra, flat on our backs, and watch clouds. Tough duty, but somebody has to do it. I remember thinking the same thing with Rick McIntyre more than thirty years ago at Eielson Visitor Center. How blessed I felt then—as I do now. The sun skims the ridgeline above and offers little warmth but great promise. Melanie and I face northeast, on the flank of Polychrome Mountain, at about 4,400 feet elevation in a glacial cirque we call Pika Bowl, given all the pikas we hear calling from lichen-encrusted talus rocks immediately above. A glacier resided here once, not long ago, a small pocket of ice in its final stages, shaded by topography on all but the longest and sunniest of summer's days. It's gone now, but still echoes in subtle features on the land.

I close my eyes and listen, and hear only my own thoughts.

Denali National Park takes seriously the new science of "soundscape ecology," more research I think would please Ade Murie—though the results may dismay him. As reported in the *New York Times Magazine* in 2012,

> [S]ince 2006, when scientists at Denali began a decade-long effort to collect a month's worth of acoustic data from more than 60 sites across the park—including a 14,000-foot-high spot on Mount McKinley—[soundscape technician Davyd] Betchkal and his colleagues have recorded only 36 complete days in which the sounds of an internal combustion engine of some sort were absent. Planes are the most common source. Once, in the course of 24 hours, a single recording station captured the buzzing of 78 low-altitude props—the kind used for flightseeing tours; other areas have logged daily averages as high as one sky- or street-traffic sound every 17 minutes.

As such, Melanie and I savor every slice of silence we can get. The park road is less than a mile away, but the shape of Pika Bowl, curving as it does and putting a high ridge between us and the traffic, makes a nice buffer.

We climb and crest the ridge and catch our breath as the whole wild world spreads out before us. To the north: the Wyoming Hills. To the south: the Alaska Range and the East Fork of the Toklat River. To the west: Divide Mountain backdropped by the distant white dome of Denali, the Big Guy. To the east: Sable Mountain and below it, the East Fork Cabin, so small yet large in our hearts, a magnificent memory place now for Melanie and me.

Little wonder artist Andy Warhol declared, "I think having land and not ruining it is the most beautiful art that anybody could ever want."

The challenge then, is obvious: to change the game and stop what author/explorer Craig Childs calls "the mad quest to cover the earth with our countless enterprises."

I sit and write.

—◆—

*This struggle between right and wrong—between reason and faith, between preserving the natural world and plundering it—will never end, Ade. You knew that. And what do we gain if we all reach Heaven and leave behind a spoiled Earth?*

*Your friend Howard Zahniser (you called him Zahnie) wrote the first draft of the Wilderness Act in 1956, the same summer a young park ranger named Edward Abbey took a job in Utah's Arches National Monument. Nine years, eighteen public hearings, and sixty-five rewrites later, President Johnson signed Zahnie's act. But Zahnie wasn't there to see it. He'd died six months earlier. Still, his conviction, together with that of your brother, Olaus, and his wife, Mardy, and many others, saved the original church. Wild Nature. The United States today has 109 million acres of designated wilderness, and it's growing.*

*I often wonder if history will one day equate environmentalists of the 1970s to abolitionists of the 1790s, if preserving and caretaking nature will one day achieve the social justice stature of civil rights. The protests have begun. People are marching on Washington. A new field of economics, ecological economics, recognizes that nature underwrites the underwriters. If natural systems begin to fail everywhere, as they now are, we're all in deep trouble, though the poor will suffer more—they always do—while the rich conduct business as usual.*

*Scientists estimate that around the world nature does $142.7 trillion worth of "work" per year ($391 billion/day) for free: rivers running, plants growing, insects pollinating, salmon returning, microbes munching . . . on and on in countless, wondrous ways. These so-called environmental services are something economists and industrialists took for granted and never thought about, until recently. And if we damage nature to where these services are severely diminished, what then? "We do not face a choice between protecting our environment or protecting our economy," says former US Treasury Secretary Robert Rubin. "We face a choice of protecting our economy by protecting our environment—or allowing economic havoc by creating environmental havoc."*

*The environment is the economy.*

*Yet many conservatives today, bunkered in (and blinded by) their rapture for American exceptionalism, choose (and it is a choice) to deny reason; to blunder through a train wreck of poor decisions guided by old-fashioned selfishness. Rather than listen to evidence-based science, they blame the scientists and journalists for our problems, and treat nature like . . . well, like a slave.*

*"Living is easy with eyes closed," said John Lennon.*

*I doubt you were a Beatles fan, Ade. Or a follower of the Stones, Doors, or Who. Maybe you wrote a little poetry, or like me, wrote rhyme and called it poetry. Forgive my obsession with music, but I have to say Denali itself is a composition, a symphony or a song as old as the rocks, part Duke Ellington and Charlie Parker, part Johan Sebastian Bach and simple ballad. Some might mistake the simplicity as being trite. It's not.*

*How to awaken people to the purity of empirical evidence? I'm not sure. Recall that after Ferdinand Magellan's expedition circumnavigated the globe, with only one ship in five (17 of 270 men) completing the journey in 1522, confirming that the world was indeed round, conservatives still insisted it was flat.*

—◆—

MELANIE reaches for me. It's time to walk.

We follow the ridgeline, hand in hand, framed by earth and sky, alive in the present but also the past. We admire colorful lichens, dried wolf scat, a golden eagle soaring off cliffs *below us*, the faint trails of Dall sheep. We point things out but say nothing; the shapes of our hearts and hands unchanged from the hunters we descended from. Intuition keen. Steps light. Bodies fluid. Who are we? Are we walking or floating? Part rock or cloud? In some dimension of landscape and love we seem to move in a way I cannot explain, a way I remember Zed the Aborigine once described as "dream walking." We see nobody. And for this one moment the park is ours and ours alone, back in the ice age and before, when people had no desire to improve upon the natural world or to tame what anthropologist Wade Davis calls the "rhythm of the wild."

The earth was whole back then in its giving and taking.

It offered everything it offers still, that same wholeness and chance for humanity to show respect and restraint, to embrace the wonder.

As Richard Nelson describes the Koyukon and their deep spirituality, so Wade Davis writes of the Aborigines who "accepted life as it was, a cosmological whole, the unchanging creation of the first dawn, when earth and sky separated, and the original Ancestor brought into being all the primordial ancestors, who, through their thoughts, dreams and journeys, sang the world into existence."

No surprise I like it here. My friends, too. The land has timbre, rhythm, harmony, and tone. And best of all, wisdom. In the city we listen to respond; in the wilderness we listen to understand. Wilderness is to civilization what improvisation is to music.

Melanie and I find a small fold in the ridgeline and hunker down out of the wind while still in the sun, bathed in heat and light, the source of all energy and life. She closes her eyes. I estimate our elevation at 5,000 feet, the equivalent of 12,000 feet in the Rockies, given our high latitude.

—~—

*I think it's only fair to tell you, Ade, that a National Park Service historian, William E. (Bill) Brown, says you "exerted a force both spiritual and scientific" in the early development of this park. You gave us much to admire and strive for. Because you gave us new sensibilities, you are now regarded as "the conscience of Denali." A heavy mantle, for sure. The American Heritage Dictionary defines "conscience" as "the faculty of recognizing the distinction between right and wrong in regards to one's own conduct."*

*The East Fork Cabin you so loved still stands. In winter, at twenty below, it's used by rangers on sled dog patrol. In summer, bathed in light, it's occupied by visiting scientists and artists-in-residence. Sometimes bears, standing full height, scratch their backs on the weathered corners. From inside, you think it's an earthquake until you hear the low, satisfied sound of groaning.*

*It's September now. Getting cold. We'll have stars tonight, and hopefully wolves howling. Thank you, Ade.*

*In gratitude,*
*Kim*

WE HIKE out the afternoon, descend a steep talus slope, hit the park road and make our way to the Toklat Work Camp that these days is larger and louder than it used to be. Big equipment everywhere.

Brad Ebel, his eyes rimmed with sadness, tells us about a recent fatality, a hiker killed by a bear just upriver from the work camp. "This sort of thing doesn't happen in Denali," he says, "at least it didn't used to." Did the hiker get too close? Or was it just bad luck? The wrong bear at the wrong place and time? Nobody knows. Nobody may ever know. Every Park Service employee works directly or indirectly to improve the visitor experience, to help make the park sing for people from all over the world. Then something like this happens. The quiet heartbreak is everywhere. For the first time in ninety-five years, the park has a fatality due to a bear attack.

I think back to my first summer, 1981, the bus accident that killed five people, and the unjust criticism that befell the Park Service. I recall September 1992 when I attempted to follow the Teklanika River north to where Chris McCandless died and stumbled backward off a bear trail, landed on my heavy pack below the steep riverbank, pinned by my possessions while a bear stared down at me with mild indifference. And the bear walked away. Now twenty years later, 2012, a fatality . . .

"Anyway," Brad says. "The rumor is that you two need popcorn."

"Oh . . . yeah, thanks. I guess we do." I need to get ahold of myself. Popcorn seems trite in the aftermath of a bear attack. Yet life goes on in ways big and small. I think about Richard Steele, who loves popcorn and ice cream and always announces, "King Corn and Cream Kong."

"And you probably need a ride back to the East Fork Cabin," Brad adds. "I know somebody headed that way."

A ranger/naturalist named Jake gives us the popcorn and asks me to critique his photography. I see room for improvement. Can he take the criticism? Can any of us? If he cannot, will he rescind the popcorn? A delicate situation. What to say? "Do you have any porcupines around here?" I ask him.

"Porcupines? In the work camp? Yes, they mostly get active in the evening, I think, down around the A-frame cabins."

"The A-frames . . . where rangers lived in the 1980s and 1990s?"

"Yes."

My heart skips. Could this be the Son of the Son of the Son of Bristles? Bristles IV, also known as Bristles the Wise? The rivers run, the mountains move, the mighty porcupine prevails.

❧

A COUPLE MILES from the East Fork Cabin we ask Brad's buddy to drop us off so we can walk the rest of the way home. Home being the East Fork Cabin for one more night. Popcorn and Corona for dinner. We might even sleep on the porch and listen for wolves. Probably not. The light is exquisite on the Alaska Range: soft pinks blushing the highest peaks and clouds, picked up in the braided river. No traffic. Only one vehicle every twenty minutes or so. Not a single bus.

From a distance we see a young man on a bicycle, resting on the East Fork Bridge, studying a map. He straddles his bike with ease, one foot on the guardrail. Every minute or so he looks up as if to take clues from the river and surrounding peaks, perhaps to confirm where he is.

He's Matt from the Midwest, fresh out of college, off adventuring and doing his best to avoid the American grind before he begins to pay off what he calls "monster student loans." He's also a guitarist who loves the music of James Taylor.

He's not studying a map, but rather a schedule that says one more camper bus should cross the East Fork Bridge in the next fifteen minutes, eastbound. A bus with room for a bike. The light is dusky, the air cool, the sky growing cloudy with the promise of rain, maybe snow. Pink pastels fading. Darkness on the rise. Matt tells us he's riding west as far as he can get, and he's a little nervous about the ride back. The bus is a big temptation, his ticket home. He'd like to see a bear or two, but not close.

Melanie tells him a story, and Matt responds by saying this ride, this adventure, is a tribute to his father who died recently of cancer. "He always wanted to come to Alaska and never made it, so this is for him. I'm riding for him."

Melanie does this. She brings out the stories in others. She brings out the heart.

"I once rode a bike all night long through this park, thirty years ago," I tell Matt.

"You did? How was it?"

"Life changing. One of the best things I ever did."

He smiles. We leave him on the bridge with a decision to make.

Fifteen minutes later, as Melanie and I open the cabin door and remove the nailed window shutters, we see the final eastbound bus come down the road from Polychrome Pass. It rolls out of view, above the cabin, but we can still hear it. Faint but unmistakable, it stops and idles, then moves on. Near as we can tell, Matt got on.

A few minutes later Melanie exclaims, "Kim, look."

There he is on the bike, climbing Polychrome Mountain, westbound into the state of the heart, the heart of the state.

# TWO YEARS LATER:

# WONDER LAKE

# EPILOGUE

# My Inner Porcupine

AT TIMES clouds appear as mountains, snowy white and anvil black; and at times mountains appear as clouds, floating and surreal. Every morning Melanie zips open our tent to inventory them: clouds with character, some surfing the wind, others hunkered down, brooding gray; some with peaks and spurs, others flat and indifferent; some of magnificent height—grand and imposing. Mount Be Cloudy.

A husband-wife couple from Detroit, newly arrived off the camper bus, wants to know where the Big Guy is. When was he last out? They just ran the Anchorage Marathon and now intend to camp at Wonder Lake, pick blueberries, and admire mountains.

Melanie points due south and says with a grin, "It was there when we last saw it."

"Oh, boy, thanks." says the Detroit woman, her voice effervescent. "That's where it probably still is. We'll set up our tent facing that direction."

Come evening, Andy Keller, a Wonder Lake ranger/naturalist, arrives and engages visitors with stories and banter, and invites them to his program on the fiftieth anniversary of the passage of the 1964 Wilderness Act. In his flat hat, gray shirt, green pants, gold badge, and standard brown socks (or are they renegade red?) he's an icon of American outdoor education: teacher, mentor, public servant. Kids gather around him. Visitors from China, Poland, Norway, and Japan ask eager questions. Melanie and I know Andy from previous visits. Raised in Chicago, he first came to Alaska in 1979 as a Youth Conservation Corps instructor. This is his sixth summer at Wonder Lake. A former Outward Bound instructor, he holds a master's degree in northern studies from the University of Alaska in Fairbanks, where he lives with his wife, Magali, an animated Frenchwoman. "Two-thirds of her body weight is enthusiasm," Andy says. He and Magali hiked deep into the backcountry last summer, crossed tricky terrain, got thrashed, and camped for several days. "She talked about that trip all winter," Andy tells me. "It really lit her up."

Dressed in mosquito nets and rain pants, two dozen of us attend Andy's program. In a lightly melodic voice he introduces himself as "Ranger Andy," and uses an ice axe as a pointer. Standing beside a large poster-board map and displays of historic artwork, he commences to sweep us across four hundred years of changing American sensibilities, from seventeenth-century wilderness described as "a damp and dreary place where all manner of wild beasts dash about uncooked," to the early nineteenth-century *Course of Empire* paintings by Thomas Cole and, most striking to me, a painting called *American Progress*, by John Gast, an 1872 depiction of an angelic woman floating over the prairie, a schoolbook in one hand, a spool of telegraph wire in the other, a gold star on her forehead as she strings wire and leads pioneers into a more prosperous life.

All this ten years after passage of the Homestead Act that bequeathed 160 acres to any man or woman (including freed slaves) willing to build a home, make improvements, and farm the land for at least five years. For Europeans condemned to rigid social hierarchies and near-feudal despair, the American frontier was deliverance, a dream. And to think of an angelic figure showing them the way, blessing their westbound journey into a better world.

"How could this be wrong?" Andy asks.

Nobody says a thing.

By the early 1900s, John Muir wrote, "Thousands of tired, nerve-shaken, over-civilized people are beginning to find out that going to the mountains is going home; that wildness is a necessity; and that mountain parks and reservations are useful not only as fountains of timber and irrigating rivers, but as fountains of life." He said all people needed "mountain nourishment."

Sixty million buffalo had been decimated to fewer than five hundred. Ninety-nine percent of the vibrant tall-grass prairie had been plowed under; entire forests were leveled, cultures obliterated, landscapes fenced. Thanks to Muir and others, the early American conservation movement began to redefine our rightful place in nature.

"Wilderness to the people of America," wrote Sigurd Olson, "is a spiritual necessity, an antidote to the high pressure of modern life, a means of regaining serenity and equilibrium."

If Denali National Park and Preserve is anything, it's a six-million-acre exercise in wisdom and restraint that invites us to slow down, to acknowledge as a gift this living treasure we safeguard for all who follow—human and otherwise.

---

"IS ANYBODY in this audience under age eighteen?" Andy asks as he holds up a copy of *A Sand County Almanac* by Aldo Leopold. Three hands go up. "Come see me after this talk and I'll sign over a copy of this book to each of you, at my own expense, not the government's expense. It's the book my father gave to me when I was fifteen, the book that introduced America to a new land ethic, the book that changed my life and might change yours. By the way, is anybody here missing his or her iPod right now?"

Heads shake.

"Cell phone?"

Heads shake.

"Facebook?"

One hand goes up, tentatively.

Laughter ripples through the audience.

Andy concludes his Wilderness Act program by touching on threats to Denali: climate change, drilling for coalbed methane, killing wolves, a proposed dam on the Susitna River, and always the growth of industrial tourism. He switches on a recording of Fairbanks singer/songwriter Susan Grace and lets music have the final word: "There are those of my kind, running fast and running blind, and the only thing they worship is their God the dollar sign."

Afterward, Andy tells me a story about when he first worked for the federal government, in the Postal Service. He was nineteen, and sometimes wore a "Save the Whales" pin on his hat. His supervisor would say, "Have you saved any whales today, Andy?"

"No," Andy would say. Then one day his supervisor asked again, needling him. Andy responded, "Isn't it important to you that we save the whales?"

His supervisor stopped and thought for a moment, and said, "I believe in progress."

CLOUDY, RAINY. Oppressive mosquitoes. No big mountain that we can see. It's been like this for days. Still, we nap on the tundra every afternoon, easy on a bed of lichen, bearberry, and moss. The musty smell of Labrador tea. Handfuls of tart blueberries. The haunting calls of loons. The final piece of chocolate. The last chunk of cheese. I tell Melanie that if this hardship doesn't end soon, we'll leave early, take a bus back east, get a room in Glitter Gulch, eat cheeseburgers and curly fries, and complain about progress. Melanie reminds me that it's not called "Glitter Gulch" anymore.

Local businesses now call it "Downtown Denali" and "City Center."

Alan Seegert laughs when we tell him this. He's driving our shuttle bus to Kantishna, where we plan to join a small music gathering at Skyline Lodge. Later, I'll give a presentation at Camp Denali. We mention that we've seen no beavers in the ponds.

"They disappeared a few years back and haven't returned," Alan says. "Other things have disappeared too. I hardly see Baird's sandpipers, rock ptarmigan, or lesser golden plovers along Highway Pass like I used to."

"Why?" I ask.

"I can't say for sure."

We talk about changes in the park: warmer winters, glaciers shrinking, ponds drying up; spruce, alder, and willow on the rise. Will Wonder Lake Campground, constructed on open tundra, be forested one hundred years from now? Will people still visit their national parks? Alan says, "Last summer was sunny, and epic for berries and bugs. This summer was wet and cold, with very few berries and bugs."

Such differences magnify themselves for climbers on Denali. In the sunny and benevolent summer of 2013, sixty-eight percent of all summit attempts succeeded. In the cold and stormy summer of 2014, fewer than forty percent reached the top. After twenty-one days of what he called "Denali Denial," Dave Hahn, one the America's most accomplished mountaineers, summed up his experience: "Humbled, sunburned, sleep-deprived, fat-depleted, muscles tired . . . life enriched."

Alan describes a "Noah's Ark" rain in June 2014 that washed down big slides and closed the road to Kantishna for ten days. When passengers begin to ask him more personal questions, he grins into the rearview mirror and says, "There are three things you don't ask people who live here: 'Where'd you get those building materials?' 'Where'd you spend the night?' And 'Where'd you get those blueberries?'"

Alan has made more than twenty-five hundred transits of the park road since he began driving in 1977. His observations have a quiet power.

—⁓—

MUSICIANS from Fairbanks, Bethel, Healy, McKinley Village, Talkeetna, and Anchorage jam through the night by firelight, indifferent to a soft rain; the next night they perform in Greg LaHaie's Skyline Lodge, in Kantishna. They sing not to change the world—the sixties are gone, the military draft is history—but to celebrate it, to give thanks for all the good things they have: loved ones, friends, community, and a great national park that fills them daily with wildness and right livelihood. It reminds me of an essay by Rebecca Solnit, "The Art of Arrival," wherein she writes that "home has to mean something more than a house; it has to mean a place, so that going out the door can be going home as much as going in." The gathering is more "Hey Jude" than "Revolution"; more Paul McCartney love song than John Lennon protest song. When three women from Camp Denali sing "Summertime" a cappella, the audience is stunned into silence, then wild applause.

Camp Denali, only a few miles away, sits atop a ridge with a grand view of Wonder Lake and the Alaska Range. Founded by Celia Hunter and Ginny Wood, and Ginny's husband, Woody, it's evolved into one of Alaska's most prized visitor destinations, operated today by Simon and Jenna Hamm.

After a hot solar shower, I stand in Camp Denali's resource room and admire a wall of black-and-white photos from the "early days." If twentieth-century Alaska heroes are my objective, I need look no further. In search of adventure, Celia and Ginny learned to fly in the 1940s, joined the Women Airforce Service Pilots during World War II, and flew everything from sleek fighters to lumbering bombers. They arrived in Fairbanks in two Stinson aircraft on New Year's Day, 1947, and became instant celebrities. In the summer of 1951 they climbed a ridge above Kantishna to fulfill a dream to create a rustic yet elegant "camp" to share the best of Alaska with the rest of the world. As Ansel Adams said after his visit to the area: "I felt Alaska might be close to the wilderness perfection that I continuously sought."

Ginny said of those first years running Camp Denali, working hard to stay ahead of guests' needs: "You had to be a doctor, carpenter, plumber, guide and accountant." Celia wrote, "What you look like, whether you had money, whether your family was Boston Society or raised on a stump ranch—it didn't matter. In Alaska you were accepted for what you were able to do and you were free to do many things."

That freedom, that respect, inspired Celia to help start the Alaska Conservation Foundation, among other notable environmental achievements. When the park was enlarged in 1980, Camp Denali and other Kantishna-area establishments, previously just beyond the park's north boundary, became private enclaves.

◆~◆

AS I MOVE from one historic photo to another, lost in my reverie, Pete Martin opens the door. "Well, I'll be doggone," he says in his folksy voice. We've known each other for twenty years. It's good to catch up. Retired from Alaska State Parks and living now in Oregon, Pete and his wife, Claudia, have a long history at Camp Denali, both as hosts and naturalists.

Pete worries about the unraveling of the natural world and the moral decline of the United States. I tell him there's a powerful thing out there called the next generation. Joey Abate, a former National Geographic student in Denali, recently wrote to tell me that Alaska had such a profound effect on him he changed his university major from engineering to wildlife ecology. And Kim Arthur got her dream job as a full-time museum curator/archivist in Denali National Park. The last time I saw her, she was holding hands with Davyd Betchkal, the park's soundscape technician. They made a cute couple.

"Kim," Pete says, "I've been to Finland. Everything there is so sensible and fair. Two-thirds of the country is above the Arctic Circle. They have excellent health care, the world's freest press, and the best education. It's the highest tech country in Europe, yet on any given summer day hundreds of teenagers gather in city parks and none are lost in electronic gadgets. They honor trust and honesty in government, and cooperation over competition. They pay high taxes and nine dollars a gallon for gasoline, and they like it that way. Nearly everybody rides a bike. Nobody lives in obscene wealth or abject poverty. They have thirty-one professional orchestras, and a secret weapon."

"A secret weapon?"

"Saunas."

"Saunas?"

"They retreat to cabins up in the woods and share sauna time. That's when they let their guard down and share ideas."

It's the second time I've heard "let your guard down" in two days.

⎯⎯

THE EVENING before, Melanie and I attended the ranger program at Wonder Lake Campground, this time by Kara Lewandowski, who introduced herself as "Ranger Kara." Her program, simply titled, "Porcupines," began when she passed around to each of us a drawing of a porcupine, and a pencil, and asked us to write on the exposed belly of our porcupine three traits we like about ourselves, and on the tips of the outer quills, three traits we don't like about ourselves.

Employing a toy stuffed porcupine she called "Quilliam," not Bristles, she asked us to think about moving through our world as a porcupine, patient yet aware, open to letting our guard down, to cultivating our own best traits, our "inner porcupine," the things we liked most about ourselves. When she mentioned the value—the necessity—of working together to solve our most vexing problems, I recalled a line Ranger Andy had shared with me, from Pete Seeger: "Participation—it's what's gonna' save the human race."

It all seemed cosmic because of something I couldn't get out of my head; a burden I'd placed on myself three months earlier when I interviewed with Tracy Sinclare on her program, Cover2Cover, on KTUU Channel 2 News in Anchorage. I told Tracy stories about John Muir's twenty years in Alaska, based on my book *John Muir and the Ice That Started a Fire*; how Muir showed America an Alaska of shimmering beauty, with its glaciers, rivers, mountains, and wildlife. And how Muir, touched by Alaska, became the point of the spear of the American preservation movement. Alaska wasn't an icebox or a folly, he said; it was the New World's new world, a huge gift, a second chance for America to get things right.

Tracy asked, "What lessons should Alaskans learn from John Muir and apply to their lives today?"

"Break the addiction," I said. "Leave the oil, coal, methane, and natural gas where they belong—in the ground. Ninety-seven percent of the world's most esteemed climate scientists say the climate change we experience today is real and human-caused. They fear that our continued burning of fossil fuels will condemn future generations to a destabilized planet and a greatly diminished quality of life. They strongly suspect that 200 years from now the human race (what remains of it) will look back and regard this relentless burning as a morally bankrupt way of life, just as we today regard slavery of 200 years ago. Must our prosperity

be so costly? It's time to wake up, time to see Earth justice – the care-taking of all species - as social justice. It's
time to change; to make a noble and enterprising sacrifice,
one to lift us from trauma to transcendence. Let it begin
on the Fourth of July, Independence Day, 2020, a year of
perfect vision. From that day on, Alaska is no longer a fossil
fuel state. It's an innovation state. The world's oceans daily
produce five times more tidal power than is needed by all
humanity. Alaska is rich with powerful tides. Add to that
solar and wind power, and an unbreakable will. Let Alaska
lead America—and America lead the world—into a brighter
future, a better legacy. Call it the 'Denali Challenge,' as big
as a mountain. Imposing, but not insurmountable."

Finland has its saunas. Alaska has its national parks.
Let's take inspiration from the ancient rhythms around us.
The river has been here for ten thousand years.

As my interview ended, and Tracy thanked me for my
stories and candor, the cameraman packed up his equipment and said, "What you propose will never happen."

When the interview aired several weeks later, the Denali
Challenge had been cut.

Part of me was disappointed. Part of me was relieved.

AS I WRITE now, camped in the rain at Wonder Lake, I read
about the death of comic genius Robin Williams. He was
sixty-three, my age. He once said each creative person is
given "only one little spark of madness . . . if you lose that,
you're nothing."

In early 1967, after hundreds of hours in the studio work-
ing on another new collection of highly innovative songs, the
Beatles should reinvent themselves, Paul said. Be a new band.
He'd written a title track, "Sgt. Pepper's Lonely Hearts Club
Band." That's who we'll be, he said, showing a flash of John's
wild influence on him. Sure, it was a marketing gimmick.

It was also a bright, shining example that risk and creativity make their own double helix, their own DNA. And to find that creativity might involve key relationships between what Beatles scholar Joshua Wolf Shenk calls "breaking and making, challenging and refining, disrupting and organizing." Start a referendum, Paul might say. A revolution, John would add. Ironically, it was their tension, their differences that created their harmonies, their genius.

I was fifteen when *Sgt. Pepper* was released that memorable summer of love. The summer that set me on the road to otherness.

I wasn't alone. Not then, not now.

As I told my National Geographic high school students: "Go. There's a journey out there beyond what any of us know, daring and illuminating once taken, for once taken it takes you. Not so much down some path or road as from one chamber of the heart to another, one way of seeing to another, where the old definitions of 'productive citizen' and 'progress' mean nothing. Take off your shoes. Sing and dance for twenty minutes each day. Unless you're really busy. Then sing and dance for an hour. Take a deep breath. Listen. Whatever cookie-cutter life you had planned for yourself, forget it. Specialization is for insects. Industry is for machines. Yes, these are troubled times, and for some, hard times. But they're not end times. Many great problems and challenges lie ahead. It's not your job to solve them all, but it is your responsibility to be aware, to come together and tackle problems as best you can, and at the same time enjoy the beauty of this world, celebrate it, restore it, share it, and make it better one day at a time. You don't have to be anything you're not; instead, be everything you are. If your future isn't on a career questionnaire, don't worry. Improvise, experiment, explore, create, love, forgive, and give. It will keep you young. And wild."

"WHY WILDERNESS?" Edward Abbey once asked. "Because we like the taste of freedom. Because we like the smell of danger."

I scribble on a note pad:

*You and I are going to have to talk one day, Ed. You left us soon after you wrote "A Writer's Credo," 25 years ago now, leaving others with some heavy lifting. It feels lonely at times, and burdensome, throwing pebbles into the big pool. Where the ripples go I'll never know. But I know this. You had a lot of love in you, a lot of passion for what is right and true. You had your own inner porcupine. You are not forgotten.*

A HARD RAIN beats on our Kelty tarp, our so-called Noah's Tarp that takes the weather and leaves our tent dry. It's been like this for days. Toward evening, the rain abates as blue-gray light settles over the campground and softens the foothills below the big mountain, if the mountain is still there.

"Maybe it got cold and moved to Hawaii," I tell Melanie. "Maybe it became a volcano."

She stuffs a dry cracker in my mouth.

We take a last walk. At one point, a mile or so south of our camp, we stretch out on the autumn tundra, buried in the dwarf birch to let the wind sail over us, marveling at every detail. The sky is our blanket, the land our pillow. Were we wrapped in caribou skins, five thousand years ago, we could easily fall asleep, and awaken to hunt again, to resume picking berries, to tell a story and make each other laugh. To love and be loved. After twelve days of camping in our national park, we feel as if we, too, like those of long ago, could sing the world into existence.

I sometimes hear musicians speak of "voicing" as a quality that imbues not just a singer's ability, but every element of a symphony or song, from the fretwork of a guitarist to the fluid notes of a saxophonist, how the many parts become one in a way that cannot be put on paper, as if we aspire to be birds. Musicians feel this voicing, this groove. It's a spirit, a freedom, a communion that originates, I believe, from the distant wildness in our blood and bones. It's in a single leaf of dwarf birch, the colors grading from green to yellow and orange and red and a thousand transitions from one cell to the next for which I have no words. As I touch the leaf and share my admiration with Melanie, I wonder: do the plants *feel* my appreciation? My love for the land? My inner porcupine?

We come upon a spruce, no more than five feet tall, alone on a gentle tundra rise. It's been stripped of nearly all its branches and greenery. A few years back a bull caribou or moose probably used the tree to rub the velvet off its antlers. Already stunted by severe conditions this far north, the tree now suffers a double trauma. Yet it lives. Through winter's darkness and cold, in ways noble and magical, it doesn't give up. I touch it and think, *and neither will we.*

"Finland sounds nice," I say to Melanie. "I hope we can learn from them. But Finland isn't home. Alaska is home."

She takes my hand and we walk.

THE NEXT MORNING brings a change. The air is different, more crisp. I hear Melanie sit up and zip open the tent.

"Kimmy, Kimmy, Kimmy . . ."

I lean up, and there it is, right where it should be, blushed pink above the clouds, always higher than expected.

Hello, old friend.

# Acknowledgments

This book took two years to write. It also took thirty-four years, from when I first arrived in Denali National Park until now. Many people have fallen under the same mountain spell, and in some way contributed to my journey. Thank you Bill Truesdale, Sandy Kogl, George Wagner, Doug Cuillard, Bob Butterfield, Will Morris, Jane Anderson, Jeff Bohman, Brad Ebel, Bruce Talbot, Jill Johnson, Donna Gates, Ken Kertell, Rick McIntyre, Chuck Lennox, Karen Laing, Steve Carwile, Cathy Rezabeck, Jim Shives, Maggie Yurick, Rollie and Mary Ostermick, Joe Van Horn, Jon Waterman, Pamela A. Miller, Tom and Kim Chisdock, Brad and Barbara Washburn, Claire Curtis, Kris Fister, Paul Anderson, Ray Bane, Bob Gerhard, Ed Zahniser, Sue Deyoe, Jane Bryant, Craig Brandt, Rob Hammel, Tim and Denise Taylor, Phil and Barbara Brease, Tom and Donna Habecker, Dave Tilford, William E. (Bill) Brown, Nancy Bale, Chuck and Mona Bale, Marissa James, Alan Seegert, Charlie Loeb, Dave Schirokauer, Keith Kehoe, Carol McIntyre, Carol Harding, David Tomeo, NJ Gates, Andy Keller, Kara Lewandowski, Celia Hunter, Ginny Wood, Wally and Jerry Cole, Simon and Jenna Hamm, Land and Laura Cole, Pete and Claudia Martin, Annie Lowery, Anne Beaulaurier, Laurie Schlueb, Liz Berry, Hannah Berry, Bill and Ree Nancarrow, Tim Rains, Jay Elhard, Kim Arthur, Davyd Betchkal, Jennifer Raffaeli, Rob and Kimber Burrows, Isabel Browne Driscoll and Peter

Driscoll, Jim Okonek, Brian and Diane Okonek, Dave Hahn, Arthur Mannix, Eberhard Jurgalski, Chris (Krigi) Leibundgut, Richard Nelson, Jim Stratton, Susan Ruddy, Nan Elliot, Bill Sherwonit, Kris Capps, Sherry Simpson, Linda Franklin, Jeff and Lori Yanuchi, Jesse Laner, Dan Henry, Lynn Schooler, Jane Freeburg, Janet Neilson, Andrew Gertge, Ford Cochran, Scott Kish, Em Jackson, David Estrada, Joey Abate, Bailey Edelstein, Joellen Mauch, Erica Taylor, Cameron Crow, Max Zagor, Dan Stuke, Emma Phippen, Hilary Yu, Zack Meredith, Emily Billin, Justin Baker, Jodi Rodwell, Eric Brown, Matt Unterberger, Joseph Whelan, Kelly Bogan, Joe Jovanovich, Blanche Jovanovich (LeBrock), Tom Bean and Susan Lamb, Jeff Gnass, Laurie Craig, Roy Corral, Tony Dawson, Kathy Bushue, Daniel Cox, Rich Kirchner, Mike Giannechini, Alissa Crandall, Ed Bovy, Robin Brandt, Lewis Kemper, Doug Pfeiffer, Terry Boyd, Fred Hirschmann, Michio and Naoko Hoshino, Ken and Jacky Graham, Keith and Barbara Walters, Ford and Karen Reeves, and Terry and Ann Miller. For their wonderful friendship, encouragement, and hospitality: Stan and Gretchen Carrick, Larry and Karla Bright, Richard Steele and Luann McVey, Brian and Arlie Swett, Harry and Phyllis Hassinger, Tom Walker, Josala and Eddie Fetherolf, Susan Kay Weber, Greg LaHaie and Elise Lockton, and Bob Shelton. I am blessed to have as my literary agent, Elizabeth Kaplan, and for editors, Jon Sternfeld and Holly Rubino, beacons of intelligence and professionalism. Thanks also to Staci Zacharski, my production editor, to Cheryl Brubaker, my copyeditor, and to Jessica Plaskett, my publicist. A special thanks to friends and/or Denali residents/scholars who proofread the manuscript and offered valuable comments and corrections: Hank Lentfer, Andrea Blakesley, Nan Eagleson, Ingrid Nixon, Carolyn Elder, and the incomparable Melanie Heacox, out there on the tundra with tears of gratitude.

# Suggested Reading

Abbey, Edward. *Desert Solitaire*. New York: Henry Holt, 1968.
———. *The Serpents of Paradise*. New York: Henry Holt, 1995.
Brinkley, Douglas. *The Quiet World*. New York: HarperCollins, 2011.
———. *The Wilderness Warrior: Theodore Roosevelt and the Crusade for America*. New York: HarperCollins, 2009.
Brown, William E. *Denali: Symbol of the Alaskan Wild*. Virginia Beach: The Donning Company, 1993.
———. *This Last Treasure*. Anchorage: Alaska Natural History Association, 1982.
Bryant, Jane. *Snapshots from the Past: A Roadside History of Denali National Park and Preserve*. Anchorage: NPS Center for Resources, Science and Learning, 2011.
Byl, Christine. *Dirt Work: An Education in the Woods*. Boston: Beacon, 2013.
Collier, Michael. *Geology of Denali National Park & Preserve*. Anchorage: Alaska Geographic, 2007.
Davis, Wade. *Light at the Edge of the World*. Madeira Park: Douglas & McIntyre, 2001.
Donnelly, Joe. "Lone Wolf." *Orion*, Sept-Oct 2013, 36–44.
Gould, Jonathan. *Can't Buy Me Love: The Beatles, Britain, and America*. New York: Three Rivers, 2007.
Haines, John. *The Stars, the Snow, the Fire*. St. Paul: Graywolf, 1977.
Heacox, Kim. *In Denali*. Santa Barbara: Companion Press, 1992.
———. *Visions of a Wild America*. Washington, DC: National Geographic, 1996.
Helmricks, Constance. *We Live in Alaska*. London: Hodder and Stoughton, 1945.
Kingsnorth, Paul. "In the Black Chamber." *Orion*, March-April 2014, 28–37.
Klein, Naomi. *This Changes Everything*. New York: Simon & Schuster, 2014.
Krakauer, Jon. *Into the Wild*. New York: Villard, 1996.

Kurzweil, Ray. *The Singularity Is Near.* New York: Penguin, 2005.

Lopez, Barry, Richard Nelson, and Terry Tempest Williams. *Patriotism and the American Land.* Great Barrington: Orion, 2002.

Louv, Richard. *The Last Child in the Woods.* Chapel Hill: Algonquin, 2008.

Mann, Charles C. "What If We Never Run Out of Oil?" *The Atlantic,* May 2013, 48–63.

Marshall, Robert. *Arctic Village.* New York: Literary Guild, 1933.

McIntyre, Carol, and Nan Eagleson and Alan Seegert. *Birds of Denali.* Anchorage: Alaska Natural History Association, 2002.

McKibben, Bill. Eaarth. New York: Times Books, 2010.

———. *The End of Nature.* New York: Anchor, 1989.

Mech, L. David, et al. *The Wolves of Denali.* Minneapolis: University of Minnesota, 1998.

Murie, Adolph. *A Naturalist in Alaska.* Old Greenwich: The Devin-Adair Co., 1961.

———. *The Wolves of Mount McKinley.* Washington, DC: US Government Printing Office, 1944.

Nash, Roderick. *Wilderness and the American Mind.* New Haven: Yale, 1967.

Nelson, Daniel. *Northern Landscapes: The Struggle for Wilderness Alaska.* Washington, DC: Resources for the Future, 2004.

Nelson, Richard. *Make Prayers to the Raven.* Chicago: University of Chicago, 1983.

Nijhuis, Michelle. "Can Coal Ever Be Clean?" *National Geographic,* April 2014, 28–61.

Norris, Frank. *Crown Jewel of the North: An Administrative History of Denali National Park and Preserve, Volume I.* Anchorage: US Dept. of the Interior, 2006.

———. *Crown Jewel of the North: An Administrative History of Denali National Park and Preserve, Volume II.* Anchorage: US Dept. of the Interior, 2008.

Pipher, Mary. *The Green Boat.* New York: Riverhead, 2013.

Pratt, Verna, and Frank Pratt. *Wildflowers of Denali National Park.* Anchorage: Alaskakrafts Inc., 1993.

Rawson, Timothy. *Changing Tracks: Predators and Politics in Mt. McKinley National Park.* Fairbanks: University of Alaska, 2001.

Runte, Alfred. *National Parks: The American Experience.* Lincoln: University of Nebraska, 1979.

Sellars, Richard West. *Preserving Nature in the National Parks: A History.* New Haven: Yale, 1997.

Shenk, Joshua Wolf. "The Power of Two." *The Atlantic,* July-August 2014, 76–86.

Sherwonit, Bill, ed. *Denali: A Literary Anthology*. Seattle: Mountaineers, 2000.

Simpson, Sherry. *The Accidental Explorer: Wayfinding in Alaska*. Seattle: Sasquatch, 2011.

———. *The Way Winter Comes: Alaska Stories*. Seattle: Sasquatch, 1998.

Solnit, Rebecca. "The Art of Arrival." *Orion*, May–July 2014, 58–63.

Stoll, Steven. *The Great Delusion*. New York: Hill and Wang, 2009.

Tingley, Kim. "Whisper of the Wild." *New York Times Magazine*, March 15, 2012.

Walker, Tom. *Denali Journal*. Harrisburg: Stackpole, 1992.

———. *Kantishna: The Pioneer Story Behind Mount McKinley National Park*. Missoula, MT: Pictorial Histories Pub. Co., 2005.

———. *McKinley Station: The People of the Pioneer Park that Became Denali*. Missoula, MT: Pictorial Histories Pub. Co., 2009.

———. *The Seventy-Mile Kid*. Seattle: Mountaineers, 2013.

———. *Shadows on the Tundra*. Harrisburg: Stackpole, 1990.

Waterman, Jonathan. *In the Shadow of Denali: Life and Death on Alaska's Mt. McKinley*. New York: Delta, 1994.

White, Richard. "Are You an Environmentalist or Do You Work for a Living?" In *Uncommon Ground*, edited by William Cronon, 171–85. New York: W.W. Norton, 1995.

Winfree, Robert, ed. *Alaska Park Science: Scientific Studies on Climate Change in Alaska's National Parks* 6, no. 1. Anchorage: NPS Alaska Regional Office, 2007.

———. *Alaska Park Science: Climate Change in Alaska's National Parks* 12, no. 2. Anchorage: NPS Alaska Regional Office, 2013.

Zimmer, Carl. "Bringing Them Back to Life." *National Geographic*, April 2013, 28–43.

# Index

# About the Author

A former park ranger in Alaska's Denali, Glacier Bay, and Katmai National Parks, Kim Heacox has written a dozen books, most of them on history, biography, and conservation. *Rhythm of the Wild* is his second memoir, something of a sister book to *The Only Kayak* (Lyons Press), a 2006 PEN USA Literary Award finalist in creative nonfiction and now in its tenth printing. A keen musician, Kim plays guitar and piano and lives with his wife, Melanie, in the little town of Gustavus, Alaska. Find him on Facebook or visit him at kimheacox.com.